PRAISE FOR

The Far Traveler

"[A] wonderful, fluently written tale about an intelligent and tough culture in an unforgiving climate . . . For the sake alone of the opportunity of a real education about the Norse and about how to think about ancient cultures and archaeology, I hope [the] book reaches many readers."
—Patrick Stevens, curator of the Fiske Icelandic Collection, Cornell University Library

"Instead of merely telling us about the remarkable Gudrid, the Viking woman who traveled the entire known world of her time, Nancy Marie Brown brings her to life. Archaeological digs and modern sea voyages shift magically into Icelandic Sagas, and exhaustive research illuminates rather than burying the story of a family woman who was also a female Marco Polo—before even Marco Polo. Who needs fantasy—*The Far Traveler* makes historical reality every bit as fascinating."
—Scott Huler, author of *No Man's Lands*

"*The Far Traveler* is a marvelous book, an intricate weave of human experience, literary interpretation, travelogue, and history. Even readers who are not fascinated by the old Norse sagas and the ancient culture of Iceland will find themselves drawn into this compelling story. Nancy Marie Brown brings alive the story of Gudrid the Far-Traveler, a remarkable, brave, and bold Viking woman who lived around 1000 A.D. and traveled from one end of the Viking world to the other. Brown offers a shimmeringly detailed vision of a time and place long gone."
—Pat Shipman, author of *Femme Fatale: Love, Lies, and the Unknown Life of Mata Hari*

"Thanks to Nancy Marie Brown's vivid imagination, detailed research, and, above all, skilful narration, the brave world of Gudrid finally gets the treatment it truly deserves. A moving and gripping account, in a language strangely reminiscent of the saga style."

—Gísli Pálsson, author of *Travelling Passions: The Hidden Life of Vilhjalmur Stefansson*

"[Brown] displays an impressive, detailed knowledge of ship-building, longhouse construction, language (words like *ransack* and *brag* come from Norse), cloth-making, farming practices and gender roles. All this rich material accumulates to create a marvelously sneaky history of the Viking mind. A nimble synthesis of the literary and the scientific that will charm even readers who didn't know they were interested." —*Kirkus Reviews*

"[An] impressively researched account." —*Publishers Weekly*

"Brown painstakingly reconstructs the extraordinary life of 'Gudrid the Far Traveler' in this historical labor of love . . . Even more compelling than the journeys themselves is the wealth of information providing illuminating details of a woman's place in both a flourishing and a declining Viking society."—*Booklist*

The Far Traveler

NANCY MARIE BROWN

The
Far Traveler

Voyages of a
Viking Woman

A HARVEST BOOK
HARCOURT, INC.
Orlando   Austin   New York   San Diego   London

For Mom and Dad

———————

Requests for permission to make copies of any part of the work should
be submitted online at www.harcourt.com/contact or mailed to the following
address: Permissions Department, Houghton Mifflin Harcourt Publishing
Company, 6277 Sea Harbor Drive, Orlando, Florida 32887-6777.

www.HarcourtBooks.com

Map on pages viii–ix by Jeffery Mathison

The Library of Congress has cataloged the hardcover edition as follows:
Brown, Nancy Marie.
The far traveler: voyages of a Viking woman/Nancy Marie Brown.—1st ed.
p.   cm.
Includes bibliographical references and index.
1. Gudrid Thorbjarnardottir—Travel.   2. North America—Discovery
and exploration—Norse.   3. Iceland—Discovery and exploration—Norse.
4. Women—Iceland—Biography.   5. Women—Greenland—Biography.
6. Vikings—Biography.   7. Sagas.   8. Viking ships.
9. Excavations (Archaeology)—Iceland.
I. Title.
DL65.B77   2007
970.01'3092—dc22 [B]   2007006081
ISBN 978-0-15-101440-8
ISBN 978-0-15-603397-8 (pbk.)

Text set in Adobe Caslon
Designed by Linda Lockowitz

Printed in the United States of America
First Harvest edition 2008
A C E G I K J H F D B

Wits must one have who wanders afar.

—Hávamál

Voyages of Gudrid the Far-Traveler

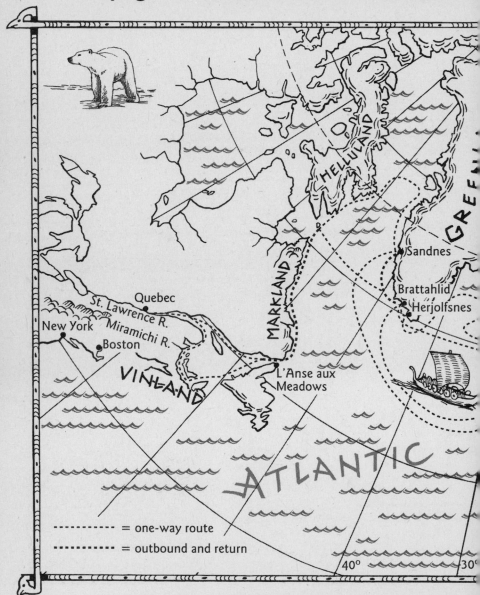

HELLULAND

GREENL

MARKLAND

Sandnes

Brattahlid

Herjolfsnes

St. Lawrence R.

Quebec

New York

Miramichi R.

Boston

VINLAND

L'Anse aux
Meadows

ATLANTIC

- - - - - - = one-way route

••••••• = outbound and return

40°   30°

circa 1000–1030

ICELAND
Glaumbaer
Arnarstapi

NORWAY
Trondheim
Oslo
Roskilde

ARCTIC CIRCLE

Isle of Lewis

OCEAN

Dublin

Rome

80°
70°
60°
50°
20°
10°

0   500 m
0   1000 km

CONTENTS

A NOTE
ON THE LANGUAGE

The Icelandic alphabet has three letters that are missing in modern English, although Old English had them. The letter "ð" (called "eth") sounds like the voiced "th" in "the"; "þ" ("thorn") is an unvoiced "th," as in "thought"; "æ" ("ash") makes the long "i" sound. A few Icelandic words appear in italics in this book but, for ease of reading, I have anglicized all the Icelandic names, changing the "ð" to "d," "þ" to "th," and "æ" to "ae," and omitting accents. (I have also omitted accents from names in other foreign languages; on the acknowledgments page and in the list of sources, the names are given their proper spellings.) I have retained the nominative endings (as in "Sigridur") for most modern Icelandic names (the exception being place-names ending in "-fjord"); for saga characters, I have dropped the endings (turning "Gudridur" into "Gudrid") to be consistent with other saga translations. For names known by several spellings—such as Eric, Erik, or Eirik the Red—I have chosen the Icelandic version. Most Icelandic last names are patronymics, made by adding "son" or "dottir" to the possessive form of the father's name. Gudrid Thorbjarnardottir is, literally, Gudrid, daughter of Thorbjorn. Leif Eiriksson is Leif, son of Eirik. For this reason, modern Icelanders always go by first names, no matter how formal the situation. I have followed their practice.

PROLOGUE

Gudrid the Far-Traveler

> Making a voyage to Vinland was all anyone talked about
> that winter. They all kept urging Karlsefni to go, Gudrid
> as much as the others.
>
> —*The Saga of the Greenlanders*

A THOUSAND YEARS AGO, AN OLD WOMAN NAMED GUDRID
stood on the threshold of her house contemplating her next
voyage. Now I stand there in her stead, looking out at a long
bank of treeless mountains. A pass to the east leads up along a
leaping stream into high pastures that, as I watch, are lit by a
shaft of sunlight and, as quickly, fade back to gray. I turn away,
get back to work. I have spent the summer with a team of archaeologists, uncovering the remains of Gudrid's house with
shovel and trowel, and today, in a misty cold rain, my Icelandic
sweater smeared with mud, I must help rebury it.

For five long weeks we traced the outline of this Viking
longhouse, finding the four rooms Gudrid lived in, the doors she
entered and left by, our only clues the colors and patterns in the
hard-packed earth. The house, built of blocks of turf or sod laid
up in a herringbone pattern, was abandoned and flattened some-
time in the half century between 1050 and 1104. The date that
sticks in my mind is 1066, the end of the Viking Age. In the years
since then, Gudrid's house was buried by windblown soil and so
preserved for the archaeologists to find, eight inches below the

plow zone in the hayfield at Glaumbaer, "Farm of Merry Noise," in northern Iceland. For the scientists, laying landscape fabric on top of the walls and piling dirt back on by the bucketful is an ordinary end-of-the-season chore; "putting the site to bed," as they say. They don't even complain about the rain.

To me, it is the untimely end of a grand adventure. True, we have photographs and drawings. The computers store a floor plan of Gudrid's house keyed to a GPS grid, so it can easily be found again. But a remote-sensing device called ground-penetrating radar had given us tantalizing images of what could be a flagstone patio outside Gudrid's front door and the central hearth in her main hall. Those floor-level features are a foot deeper than we had dug this summer, not to mention the needles, combs, spindle whorls or spoons, glass beads, brass pins, and parts of a loom that we could expect to find forgotten on a Viking woman's floor. There wouldn't be much to collect. Gudrid's family had not left in a hurry, and they hadn't moved far, just a few hundred feet up the hill to build a grander house overlooking the river plain. They would have taken all their valuables with them. But there might have been enough to let me feel I had held in my hand something Gudrid herself had dropped.

Then there was the puzzle of the horse skull, found two days ago in the middle of what should be Gudrid's weaving room. The rest of the horse might be there, too, and perhaps even a human skeleton, for in Viking Iceland a man or woman was often buried with a favorite horse. And other graves had been found just down the valley, dug into a ruined longhouse. But the archaeologists, knowing they were out of time and money, were practical. They recorded the skull's position and covered it right back up. I seem to be the only one fretting that there is no money—and no plan—to reopen the dig next year.

But the Gudrid I imagine, standing on her threshold a thousand years ago, watching the winds comb the woolly clouds across the flat-topped mountains, would not have been sad. She would have turned to look north, where the valley widens out to sea, and smiled. For her, a new adventure was beginning. Despite her age (she was soon to be a grandmother), she was on her way across the sea to Norway and then south to Rome.

This pilgrimage was not the first—or the farthest—of her voyages. Twenty years before, she had sailed west from Greenland off the edge of the known world. She was nineteen, newly wed for the second or third time and pregnant for the first. With her were her husband, Thorfinn Karlsefni, and three Viking crews in clinker-built boats. They were sailing to Vinland, a fabulous land that Leif Eiriksson, son of Greenland's founder Eirik the Red, had washed up on a few years back, when he was caught in a summer storm, sailing west across the icy North Atlantic from Norway. It was Gudrid's second attempt to get to Vinland. She meant to settle in this New World.

At summer's end, the crews beached their ships on a grassy shore and built a longhouse out of turf; there Gudrid gave birth to her son Snorri. For three years they explored their Vinland, or "Wine Land." They found salmon and halibut, tall trees and lush grasslands, wine grapes, and a grain like wheat. They saw islands full of eider ducks, bears, or foxes, mountains and marvelous beaches, fjords with fierce currents and wide tidal lagoons. And they met strangers whose language they could not understand, strangers who had never seen an axe or a bull, who were delighted by the taste of milk and traded packs full of furs for thin strips of red wool cloth; strangers who fought with stone-tipped arrows and whose numbers were overwhelming.

After three years, the Vikings abandoned their settlement. Only one of their three ships made it back to Greenland. From there, Gudrid, Karlsefni, and little Snorri sailed to Norway, where they sold their cargo of exotic goods, then turned west again, wealthy, to settle in Iceland. They spent the first winter on Karlsefni's family farm. But his mother and Gudrid did not get along, the story goes, so the couple bought a farm nearby. They named it Glaumbaer, "Farm of Merry Noise," put up a longhouse, and had a second son. When Karlsefni died a few years later, Gudrid ran the farm and raised her sons alone. She prospered and endowed a church and, as an old woman, stood on the doorstep for a moment or two, watching the wind hurry the clouds across the mountains, before setting off for Rome.

Most people know the Vikings explored North America five hundred years before Columbus. They recognize the name Leif Eiriksson and his father Eirik the Red, who discovered Greenland in 985 and set up a settlement there, for which Leif was heading when he was blown off course and spied land farther west.

Fewer have heard of the voyages of Gudrid the Far-Traveler. Yet in the 1960s, archaeologists proved part of her story true when they found a Viking settlement on the far northwestern tip of Newfoundland. After forty years of argument and analysis, the experts conclude that this small settlement, called L'Anse aux Meadows after a nearby village, was a base camp from which Vikings from Iceland and Greenland explored North America just after the year 1000. Butternuts and a burl of butternut wood worked by a metal tool prove the Vikings went well into the Gulf of St. Lawrence toward modern-day Quebec, or south to New England, where butternut trees—and the wild grapes for which Wine Land was named—naturally grow. The whorl from a spindle used for spinning yarn proves a Viking woman was with them.

Then in 2001 John Steinberg, an archaeologist from the University of California at Los Angeles, began working in Skagafjord, the valley in northern Iceland where the stories say Gudrid finally made her home. He and his crew planned to map all the Viking Age and later medieval houses in one part of the valley, to see how the settlement had changed over time. They took small soil samples to gauge the richness and depth of the soil and to look for charcoal or other signs of human activity. Where things looked interesting, they walked over the area carrying a remote-sensing device.

Surveying Glaumbaer, Steinberg and his crew found signs in the hayfield—where tradition said no houses should be—of a Viking Age longhouse. A map of the walls beneath the soil, drawn by the remote-sensing gadget, and two small test trenches suggested that the longhouse at Glaumbaer looked like no other known house of its time in Iceland. Its floor plan most resembled one found at L'Anse aux Meadows.

When I heard about the buried house at Glaumbaer in August 2002, I knew Steinberg had found the house Karlsefni had built for Gudrid when they returned from their Vinland adventure. It seemed that Gudrid really had quarreled with her mother-in-law. Plus, if the two houses were alike, Steinberg had proof that someone (Gudrid) had moved from Newfoundland to Iceland a thousand years ago. Steinberg was not ready then (and still isn't now) to make either of these claims. But he did let me help excavate the house. When I showed up at Glaumbaer in July 2005, awkwardly wielding my brand-new Marshalltown trowel, he had a few words of warning: *You're going to like archaeology,* he said. *Five weeks won't be enough.*

He was right. Archaeology used to be about finding artifacts. A bronze cloak pin and a handful of ship's rivets told us L'Anse aux Meadows was a Viking site. In Iceland, an inlaid cross and a silver Thor's hammer amulet found in the same tenth-century grave told us the Vikings hedged their bets, while a hoard of hack-silver, arm-rings, and chains proved the Vikings did bring home and bury their treasure.

But in the last ten to twenty years, modern science has made the world of the Vikings much more vivid—and complex. Studies of volcanic ash and the Greenland ice cap have allowed scientists to date layers of soil in Iceland (and thus the house walls found in them) to exact years. New ways of collecting minuscule evidence, such as pollen grains, seeds, flies, lice, and fleas, have revealed disastrous environmental changes caused by Viking farming methods. The isotopes of carbon in skeletal bone, the wear on sheep's teeth, the frequency of headless fish in garbage heaps, and the geographical distribution of seal parts have revealed what Gudrid and her peers ate, how they traded for favorite foods from farm to farm, and how they managed their sheep herds to maximize wool exports. Tree-ring studies can pinpoint when and where a Viking ship was made—or patched—while sea-trials of replicas reveal their speeds, their special handling qualities, and their weak points. DNA analyses can say where the settlers of Iceland (and thus Greenland and Vinland) came from, and show whether the tension between the new Christian religion and the ancient cults of Odin and Thor tore families apart. Metal detectors and the newer remote-sensing methods that use microwaves and other electromagnetic waves to see through the surface of the ground are locating not only buried turf houses like the one at Glaumbaer, but Viking garbage pits and hay barns and boathouses and graves; by allowing experts to map out whole Viking settlements they can reveal who was richer than whom and how power was gained or lost.

Science can now tell me what a woman like Gudrid ate and wore, what she worked at, where her place was within her society. What it can't tell me is why Gudrid was so remarkable, so utterly unlike our image of a woman of her time.

Medieval women, everyone knows, did not stray far from home. But Gudrid traveled from Canada to Rome. She crossed the North Atlantic eight times. She earned the nickname "Far-Traveler"—although no one called her that in her own day. The tag was attached to three Viking men whose travels took them through Russia and Greece and Constantinople, and on to the mysterious East.

Like theirs, the story of Gudrid the Far-Traveler comes down to us in the medieval Icelandic sagas. These forty-or-so tales of glory, love, hard times, and strife are Iceland's claim to literary fame. Scholars have called them "muscled, powerful narratives" that are surprising in their "seductiveness" and whose "artistic effects are often very finely calculated." They have inspired countless authors, from Kipling and Longfellow to Milan Kundera. J. R. R. Tolkien found much of his Middle Earth in Icelandic literature; he and C. S. Lewis started a saga-reading club at Oxford University and translated the texts from Old Norse, the Viking language. Another saga translator was the Victorian writer and designer William Morris. Asked once if he was going on a trip to Iceland, he replied, "No, I am going on a *pilgrimage* to Iceland." Quoting Morris, the Argentine poet Jorge Luis Borges said, "This is also my answer. Any specialist in Anglo-Saxon literature is sooner or later drawn to Icelandic literature. It is like admiring a sunset or falling in love." The American novelist Jane Smiley ranks the sagas beside the works of "Homer, Shakespeare, Socrates, and those few others who live at the very heart of human literary endeavor."

Written in Iceland in the 1200s, the sagas tell of the Viking Age, particularly that part of it, between 870 and 1030, in which Icelanders played a starring role. Much of what we know otherwise about the Vikings was written by their enemies, by monks and clerics who—in spite of the fact that some Vikings were Christian—cast the "terror from the north" in the role of Antichrist. The Icelandic sagas do not deny that warriors from Norway, Sweden, Denmark, and Iceland terrorized the coasts of Europe for hundreds of years, beginning with the sack of the English monastery of Lindisfarne in 793. But the sagas put that bloodshed into context from the Vikings' point of view. We learn what it was like to be one of those brash, blond-headed swordsmen embarking from a dragonship itching to steal the chalice from an English church or the chest filled with silver from a French merchant's loft. We sail on their swift ships to the white-marbled cities of the East, and farther west than West to Wine Land. In the sagas, we meet men who will recite a poem or tell a joke while succumbing to mortal wounds, men who excel at drinking bouts, wrestling, ball games, swimming, oar-walking, and horse fights, but enjoy nothing so much as sitting around a longfire listening to tales of heroes like themselves.

We also see the less sexy side of Viking life. A warrior hides in a tub full of whey when he's outnumbered. An old Viking, blind and shaky on his feet, hunches by the fire, ridiculed by his womenfolk for always being in the way. There's the strong man who's afraid of the dark and his neighbor who has bad dreams. There are years when they run out of hay, and the sheep all starve. There are shipwrecks and landslides and general bum luck, hopeless love affairs, and the tragic drowning of a beloved young son. And there are countless mothers and wives holding the farm together while their men mope and quarrel and fight and kill each other and take off overseas.

Compared to some sagas, the two short ones that tell of Gudrid, *The Saga of Eirik the Red* and *The Saga of the Greenland-*

ers, known collectively as the Vinland Sagas, are bare-bones. Their plots don't hang together. Their settings and characters are weak. Their use of folk-tale motifs—fortune-telling, belligerent ghosts, one-footed humanoids—is clumsy and repetitious. They read like sketches from a writer's notebook, not finished works. Once I mentored a college student in an independent-study project, assigning him an analysis of the women in half a dozen sagas. Gudrid did not fare well in the comparison. My student concluded in his final paper:

> Gudrid has one great shortcoming—she's rather bland. Although she gets caught in the sea on a skerry, lives in multiple places, and overall has an apparently pleasant life, there are no good characterizations of her day-to-day affairs. Many of the other sagas tell us enough about the characters that you get a good feel of how people lived their lives—and they are often interesting lives. Gudrid has none of these particularly intimate displays of her dealings with others—it's just assumed that she's smart and well-behaved. Being smart and well-behaved probably spells out being boring.

We never hear Gudrid whispering to her husband, bragging to her sister-in-law, or colluding with her son. We don't know that her hair fell to her knees, or that she liked to wear men's trousers under her skirts so she could comfortably ride a horse astride. The Vinland Sagas say very little about Gudrid directly. She was beautiful, we are told, which means she was probably fair and blond (dark hair being unattractive and red hair uncanny). She was intelligent (or wise, according to the other version of her story), and she had a lovely singing voice.

What my student construed as "well-behaved," though, becomes tantalizing when you realize it's not a cliché applied to every significant woman in the sagas. It's not that Gudrid is polite or ladylike, either. The translation we used says she *knew how to behave among strangers.* In the Old Norse original, that *behave* is a vague "be with," or "get along with," while *strangers* are "unknown" or "unfamiliar" people. Sagas have quirks that can fool the modern reader. One is that everything pertinent about a character is mentioned at once, when she first becomes an actor in the story. Later, when Gudrid is in the New World, trying to make friends with a native woman, we are expected to remember her skill. To someone immersed in saga style, the implication is clear: It was Gudrid who decided that the Vikings should abandon their Vinland colony. If she couldn't get along with the natives, those "unfamiliar people" of North America, then no one could.

The two sagas also imply that the Vinland expedition itself was her idea. She packed up and set off to sail there twice—with two different husbands. Although the two sagas disagree on the particulars, Gudrid's hand in the preparations each time is clear. And, unlike many saga women who expressed a desire to join their men a-voyaging, Gudrid was never left behind to mind the cows. Time and again, she got on that ship. Realizing this—that it was Gudrid who was the explorer, not just her husband—I knew that if I were to pick a saga role-model, Gudrid would be it.

CHAPTER I

At Sea

They set sail in good weather. But once they were at sea, the fair winds died. They were tossed this way and that and made no headway all summer. Sickness set in. . . . Half their people died. The seas rose, and they were faced with danger on all sides.

—*The Saga of Eirik the Red*

THE FIRST TIME I SAW A VIKING SHIP IN THE WATER, I was struck with the desire to stow away on it. Writers, even the normally sedate scholarly type, tend to wax effusive about Viking ships. They were "unrivaled," "the best and swiftest ships of their time," "the swift greyhounds of the oceans," "the ultimate raiding machine," "a masterpiece of beauty," "the most exquisite examples of sophisticated craftsmanship," "a poem carved in wood." "What temples were to the Greeks," wrote one expert, "ships were to the Vikings." Said another, "Plato may have denied the existence of ideal forms in this world, but Plato never saw a Viking ship."

The story of Gudrid the Far-Traveler, however, begins with a shipwreck. As *The Saga of the Greenlanders* tells it, Leif Eiriksson had just spent a year in Vinland as the first Norseman to set foot in the New World, and was heading home with a ship full of timber and wine grapes. He'd had fair winds all the way and had just sighted the great ice cap when one of his crewmen admonished the young captain.

"Going a bit close to the wind, aren't you?"

"I'm watching my steering," said Leif. "But I'm watching something else, too. Don't you see it?"

It was a ship—or a skerry. He couldn't tell which. The older man saw nothing until they came closer, then he, too, could see a wreck clinging to a bit of bare rock. Leif anchored close to the reef and sent his towboat over. He rescued fifteen people—to add to his crew of thirty-five—and as much of their baggage as he could fit into his already-laden ship. The wreck had been carrying house timber from Norway to the Greenland settlement; the men secured it as best they could on the rock, and the next spring Leif sent his boat out to fetch whatever could be salvaged. By then, most of the rescued fifteen had died. The only person known to have survived the journey is Gudrid.

If she had ever shared my delusions of peaceful, sunny, blue-sea sailing, surrounded by a crew of handsome men, she would have lost them abruptly on the first of her eight voyages. She knew the killing force of the sea, of weeks at the mercy of the winds, of fog that froze on the sails and rigging, when "hands blue with cold" was not a metaphor and no land, no shelter, was in sight. She knew how fragile a Viking ship was.

"You can easily sail her down if you are not doing it right," Gunnar Marel Eggertsson, the captain of Gaia, told me. Gaia was a Viking-ship replica with the dual mission of spreading environmental awareness and arriving in America in 1991, one year before the five-hundredth anniversary of Columbus's "discovery." From the west coast of Norway, where the boat was built and financed by the Norwegian owner of the Viking cruise-ship line, Gaia and her diesel-powered chase boat had followed the Viking route to the Orkneys, Shetlands, and the Faroe Islands, to Iceland and Greenland, then over the ice-filled seas to Labrador and Newfoundland. In Nova Scotia, Gaia met up with two other Viking-ship replicas, Oseberg and Saga Siglar (which had been crated and shipped by common carrier across the Atlantic). The convoy then headed south, stopping for speechifying at Boston, Newport, New York, and Washington, D.C.

Sailing a ship down is one way to sink it. I had seen videotapes of Viking-ship replicas under full sail going down with all hands in the Oslo Fjord—and winched back up to try it again. (The crew bobbed to the surface in their bright survival suits and were gathered into Zodiacs.) But I had assumed the untrained crew had simply goofed. Off the coast of Spain in 1992, Gaia's companion ships, Oseberg and Saga Siglar, sank on their way to the World Expo in Seville. The eleven crew members—all veteran Viking-ship sailors—were plucked out of the stormy sea by the crew of their modern chase boat. The replica ships were not recovered.

Gaia, Oseberg, Saga Siglar, and the later, American-made Snorri (named for Gudrid's son) are examples of experimental archaeology, of learning by doing. They teach us how these poems, masterpieces, swift greyhounds, and temples actually worked, what this technology meant to people like Gudrid. Gaia is copied from a ship discovered on the farm of Gokstad, beside the Oslo Fjord in southern Norway, in the 1880s. A chieftain had been buried in the ship in the year 900, a not-unusual way for a wealthy Viking to make his way to Valhalla. It's the soil in this part of Norway that's unusual. The burial pit was rich in blue clay, which preserved all the wood it covered. Whereas in many ship burials what's left are lines of iron rivets in the sand, for Gokstad we have all but the ship's high stem and stern. We have the rudder, the bailers, the gangplank, even the towboats—"rather crank" little vessels that would capsize easily if sailed, according to Arne Emil Christensen, who was curator of the Viking Ship Museum in Bygdoy, Norway, when I visited there in 1984.

Gokstad, on the other hand, "is a rather optimum compromise of speed, seaworthiness, and a fairly good capacity for men or cargo," he told me. "You could easily put a hundred people in it for a short trip when you don't have to sleep."

At 76½ feet long, Gokstad is only medium-sized, as Viking ships go. Even so, trees big enough for its keel—a single oak log almost 58 feet long—are rare in Norwegian forests today. When a replica was built in 1893, the oak for the keel had to be sent from Canada.

From the keel up to the gunwale are sixteen long oak strakes, each made up of several carefully joined boards. The strakes bow from stem to stern in an elegant curve; the boards come from trees with a slight bend, so the grain follows the curve of the boat. Although we don't have a Viking yardstick, it seems the Vikings had the concept of the inch. Twelve of the strakes are exactly an inch thick. The waterline strake is 1¾ inches, while the strake that held the thirty-two oar holes (each with a swiveling cover to close when the ship was under sail) measures 1¼ inches. The two top strakes are very thin: ¾ inch. The hefty gunwale is almost four by four.

This precision becomes more impressive when you realize that the Vikings had no saws. Those inch-thick strakes were split from tall oak logs with an axe. They were shaped and smoothed by axe, too—there's a fine cartoon of it in the Bayeux Tapestry, embroidered to celebrate the Norman Conquest of England in 1066. The shipwright has his tunic hiked up and is straddling the plank, scraping it with a long, curved axe, while his fellows chop down more trees.

In the early 1960s, Christensen had made an academic

study of Viking tools. Through images in manuscripts and the Bayeux Tapestry, and artifacts from excavated graves (craftsmen were often buried with their tools), he had a pretty good grasp of how the wrights put together the Gokstad ship. Except for the rivets. The strakes lap over each other, giving the technique its name, "lapstrake"; it's the same look as the clapboard siding on a New England farmhouse. But where the housebuilder uses nails, the shipbuilder needs to nip off the nail point and bend the end against an iron plate to keep the boards from wiggling apart. This clinching step—which gives us the word "clinker-built" to describe such ships—had Christensen perplexed. The Vikings had no nippers.

One day in 1973, he was watching shipwright Sigurd Bjorkedal working on a replica ship. Bjorkedal had a good set of nippers—farrier's tongs—but they went unused as he riveted the ship. Instead, he snapped off the nail points with the sharpened peen of his hammer, then reversed the hammer to pound the nail flat. From then on, Christensen concentrated on studying living craftsmen, as he wrote, *while there is still time.* "The tools are the same, so the process must be the same," he told me.

"You start with a keel roughly T-shaped. To shape a keel, take a wedge-shaped board, make four cuts, and axe away to make a T-shape. Use the axe to make the corners smooth," he said. Then affix the first strake. "Use a clamp looking like an enormous clothespin to keep it in place. How wide this plank is, and the angle of the next plank, governs the shape of the ship. You shape the top edge by eye from stem to stern in a proper curve. The whole time you can adjust the angles and plank widths by a pure sculptural process. Then you cut ribs."

Ribs stiffen the ship and hold its shape against the pressure of the waves. As with the keel and the strakes, the ribs were made from a tree with the right shape—in this case, a natural

V-shaped curve between the trunk and a branch. The V-shape is wide at the center of the ship, but narrows toward bow and stern, so several trees are needed.

The ribs in the Gokstad ship were lashed to the strakes with withies made of spruce roots. Other shipwrights preferred to tie them on with baleen, the fibrous stuff from a whale's jaw. But lashing went out of fashion before Gudrid sailed to Vinland. In her ship, the ribs would have been trunneled—fastened with wooden pegs or "tree-nails." "Trunnels for ribs, iron rivets for planks," Christensen said, explaining that "the trunnel is more flexible, it's less likely it will snap between rib and plank when the boat twists. Iron would snap. Juniper is the preferred wood for trunnels if you can get it. Juniper branches with pith in them form good, rot-resistant nails."

The pine mast would have stood thirty-six-feet tall, an estimate made by wrapping a string or measuring tape around the widest part of the ship's hull; the top of the buried mast had poked out of the blue clay, so it had rotted. Pine was also preferred for the decking and the oars.

To make a Viking ship that was flexible, light, and watertight thus took not only a great deal of wood, it required specific shapes and kinds of wood: oak, pine, spruce, and juniper; thick and straight, bent and V-shaped, tough-rooted and pithy. Viking shipwrights, it seemed, spent a lot of their time wandering in the forest marking trees to be felled and trimmed into the correct parts of a ship. The Viking ship could never have been invented in a land without trees—a land like Iceland, or Greenland. Nor could ships that wrecked on those far shores be replaced.

But it was due to the wrecks, the sinkings and sailing-downs, that the ships reached the stage of seaworthiness that seduced the Vikings to point them west, away from forested Norway.

Reading Gokstad, Christensen can see hundreds of years of trial and error. He pointed out the waterline strake, where the ribs meet the crossbeams; the strake that is three-quarters of an inch thicker than its neighbors. "It's a longitudinal stringer. It's at a critical point of the hull," said Christensen. "By experience, the Vikings knew how boats behaved in the water. Specially shaped planks like this one take up the stress."

Specially shaped planks didn't go out of fashion until water-powered saws were invented—well after the Viking Age—and some traditional craftsmen, like Sigurd Bjorkedal, were still shaping strakes by eye in the late twentieth century. When the order came in to the boat-building village of Bjorkedalen, on the west coast of Norway, for a Gokstad replica to be called Gaia, however, Sigurd Bjorkedal didn't insist on being a purist, his son Ottar told me.

"Oh no, we sawed the wood. It would have taken a lot more time to split it." We were chatting in the cabin of Gaia, moored by the Massachusetts Maritime Museum. "The people talked to us over the summer," Ottar continued, "and wanted the boat the next summer. We were only four people: we three brothers and my father. We built it over one winter. That's not any problem. You just have to work hard."

"How did you learn to build a Viking ship?" I asked.

He cocked his head, puzzled that I would have to ask. "I learned from my father. And he learned from his father. My family have been building boats for four or five hundred years, maybe before that."

Gokstad and its double, Gaia, have the spareness and elegance of line that seem to me the epitome of a Viking ship: slim, sleek, and predatory. I'm not alone: Close-ups of its hull, head-on, are reproduced on everything from magazine covers to Christmas ornaments as the emblem of the Vikings. But the ship Gudrid sailed on to Greenland and Vinland and home again to Iceland did not look like this. Hers was a *knarr,* a cargo ship, like the replica Saga Siglar that sailed with Gaia and Oseberg. Watching the three ships sail into New York harbor, side by side, I wrote in my notebook: "Saga Siglar is so squat and tubby compared to the others."

Saga Siglar ("Saga Sailor") was based on one of five ships recovered from the sea bottom near Skuldelev, Denmark, by Ole Crumlin-Pedersen, whom I met in 2006 at the Viking Ship Museum in Roskilde, near Copenhagen. The five Skuldelev ships—in five different styles, from a fishing boat to a dragon-ship for eighty warriors—had been scuttled at the head of the fjord to bar raiders from the Danish royal residence at Roskilde. Legend had it that they dated from the 1400s. But when parts were removed in the 1950s, to clear a deeper passage for motorboats, they appeared to be Viking work.

"Underwater archaeology was only just starting then," Crumlin-Pedersen told me as we toured the docks and warehouses and hands-on exhibits outside of the museum proper. "We had thought the site was so damaged we could do no harm. We had no experience."

Trained as a naval engineer, Crumlin-Pedersen suggested they build a coffer dam, which drained the fjord around the site. Then the problem was to lift the shattered wood out of the mud, while keeping it from drying out and disintegrating. "You keep the wood in water all the time until it can be treated with polyethylene glycol," Crumlin-Pedersen explained. A type of plastic, polyethylene glycol crystallizes within the wood cells. This plasticized wood can then be heated and gently pressed back into shape. "That brings out the lines of the boat."

Those lines are so various, just among the replica ships afloat in Roskilde harbor, that it's hard to say they're all "Viking ships." The *knarr*, 52 feet long and a buxom 16 feet wide, is docked beside the dragonship Havhingsten ("The Sea Stallion"), 98 feet long but a slender 12 feet wide. A smaller cargo ship, a *byrding* of more "elegant" proportions, carried only 4½ tons of cargo to the bigger *knarr's* 24 tons, while a smaller warship, called a *snekke*, or "snake," could handle only thirty warriors to Sea Stallion's eighty. And then there's the toy-sized fishing boat, 37 feet long by eight feet wide, on which Crumlin-Pedersen signed me up as an oarsman when a German TV personality wanted to take a Sunday-morning ride. Nicely maneuverable in the narrow harbor (even with a raw crew brand-new to the oars), it seemed precariously low to the waves once the sail was up. Yet when scientists compared the pattern of the tree rings in the original ship's pine timbers to wood samples from throughout the Viking world, they found a perfect match with the wood of a church in Sognefjord, Norway. The ship had been built there and had sailed the 500 miles to Roskilde at least once. By the time it was sunk to blockade the fjord, it had been patched in several places and refitted to be a small cargo ship, the oarlocks taken off and an extra strake added to give it a little more height.

With a childlike smile and a courtly bashfulness, Crumlin-Pedersen explained how he knew that the tubby model was what the sagas meant by a *knarr*. "It's because of the nickname for women in the Icelandic sagas: *Knarrarbringu*. '*Knarr* breast.' Look at it from the front. It comes right up like this—" He pantomimed a woman's tight waist and heavy breasts.

"The replica ships going to Vinland should not be based on Gokstad," he continued. "They should be based on this *knarr*, on Skuldelev 1. Gokstad is a combined sailing and rowing vessel, for a large crew. Skuldelev 1 is definitely a cargo ship. There's only a few oars for turning the ship in the wind or in harbor—it's a pure sailing vessel. Six men, working day and night, could handle it. On the other hand, you could have any number of people on board. You could move a farm with livestock and goods."

The *knarr,* as well as the other four Skuldelev ship types, Crumlin-Pedersen believes, developed after 900 out of the Gokstad style. "The development of cargo vessels seems to be a very late one in Scandinavia," he explained. "They didn't have proper cargo vessels until the tenth century. I think that's because it was too dangerous to go out with a load of valuable cargo without a sufficient number of people to protect your goods. The Gokstad ship was capable of carrying eight to ten tons of cargo, but also a sufficient crew to defend it. Then in the tenth to eleventh centuries, we have the development of cargo ships and the transformation of warships into ships that could no longer carry cargo. I see that as a sign of royal control of the sea. It was one of the main jobs of the king: to keep trade safe."

As the cargo ships got tubbier (and more practical), the warships got longer and sleeker and swifter, their design driven by fierce sporting competition among royal Viking crews. One of these late longships is eleven times longer than it is wide and made from enormous oak trees, each thin plank over 32 feet long. "For the really royal ships, the shipbuilder had access to trees no one else could touch," Crumlin-Pedersen told me. "Such a ship as this is an amazing machine!" Racing it would have been the sporting experience of a lifetime.

Then there was the other side of the coin. Imagine the mood of the Viking who was kicked off the king's royal team, or found himself on the losing side in one of the era's many contests for the throne. A verse in one of the Icelandic sagas describes just such a fellow who, having lost a leg in battle, is

leaving the sporting life behind. As Crumlin-Pedersen trans-
lates it, the fellow laments:

> Once Wood-Leg was one among heroes
> when he raced ahead in his swift vessel
> in a cool sword-attack.
> Now, fed up with life, a miserable One-Leg
> is chugging along towards Iceland
> in his deep-sea tramp.

"Chugging along" without any engine, at the mercy of the fickle
wind—and we know almost nothing about how the Vikings
rigged their ships and handled their sails.

Iceland was discovered when a Viking ship sailing west from
Norway to the Faroe Islands was blown off course. Greenland
was discovered when a Viking ship sailing west from Norway
to Iceland was blown off course. Vinland was discovered when a
Viking ship sailing west from Norway (or Iceland, in the other
saga) to Greenland was blown off course. When the Gokstad
replica, Gaia, tried to sail from Iceland to Greenland in 1991, it
got blown so far off course the crew gave up and chugged along
under diesel power for four days, sometimes using their own
backup engine, at other times being towed by their chase boat.
When Snorri, an unpowered replica of the Skuldelev *knarr*,
tried to sail west from Nuuk, Greenland's capital, to Vinland in
1998, adventure writer Hodding Carter and his crew waited five
days until a gale blew itself out, then another day in fog waiting
for the wind to return. Their westward run under an exhilarat-
ing breeze lasted 130 miles before they found themselves adrift
with four holes in their stern, caused by a too-heavy rudder that
pulled loose a crossbeam before it finally snapped. They patched

the holes with tomato-can lids, and Coast Guard Canada sent an icebreaker to tow them back to Nuuk.

Except for the tomato-can lids and the Coast Guard, it was a fair copy of Gudrid's second voyage. A year after Leif Eiriksson had plucked her off the wreck on the rock, she had married Leif's younger brother, Thorstein. Borrowing a ship, the two picked a sturdy crew, packed up their belongings, and set off for the New World. Thorstein, it seems, did not have as much sailing experience as Leif. He made the mistake of setting his course due west, where he knew Vinland lay. According to *The Saga of the Greenlanders,* "They were tossed about at sea all summer and couldn't tell where they were." Just before winter set in, they found themselves at the mouth of the Lysufjord near Nuuk, a distance they could have rowed in six days in the Viking fishing boat I tried out on the Roskilde Fjord.

A better sailor would have known that in these high, cold oceans, the westerly winds are strongest and stormiest to the south; they diminish the farther north you sail. By sailing west, Thorstein was hazarding a gale—frequent and violent off these coasts. Crumlin-Pedersen's colleague Max Vinner, from the Viking Ship Museum in Roskilde, found himself in the same situation in 1984, sailing Saga Siglar. The winds were hurricane force, the waves 30 to 40 feet high. The *knarr* could not "heave to," reducing sail and turning into the wind like a decked sailing ship: She would take on too much water. But running before the storm was also chancy. If she went too fast, the ship would surf, rising out of the water until the keel and rudder lost their grip on the waves. "Then the very worst can happen," writes Vinner. The ship can sail down. "The ship can plunge sideways from a wave-top down into the valley in front, and then be filled with water by the wave from which it has fallen." To slow their speed, Vinner and the Saga Siglar crew first tried to "goosewing" the sail, tying up the center of the broad square of wool so that only two small triangles could catch the wind. That failing, they took the sail down altogether. Under a bare pole, Saga Siglar scudded before the wind for ten hours at an average speed of 8.4 knots—as opposed to the 7.5-knot average (and 10.7 maximum) that Gunnar Marel Eggertsson held Gaia to during what he thought was a fast two-and-a-half-day sail between the Faroe Islands and Iceland. Saga Siglar, writes Vinner, "was a beautifully safe ship. . . . She carried her sail well, rose well to the waves, and her movements were easy. Above all, however, she was dry." Even running from the hurricane, she took on no more water "than the crew could manage to pump out again." In case anyone objected that Vikings didn't *have* pumps, he added, "A frightened man with a bailer is quicker than even the best pump." Yet in 1992, off the coast of Spain, this beautifully safe ship sank.

Gudrid's ship did not sink. But when the wind let them go, the saga says, no one on board knew where they were. They had been blown off course.

To Viking poets, the wind was the neigher, the wailer, the whistler, the coldly dressed, the roaring traveler, the squally one, the wolf of the sail, the waverer, the never silent. The sky was the weaver of winds. The sea was the ring of the island, the house of sands and seaweeds and skerries, land of fish, land of ice, and land of sailing wind. The best ship imaginable, owned by the god Odin, caught a fair wind whenever its sail was hoisted. (It could also be folded up and kept in the god's pocket for convenience.) Being blown off course was so common that the Vikings had a word for it: *hafvilla,* literally "bewildered by the sea," or as we might say today, "at sea." But being blown off course presupposes the Vikings could *set* a course. How, without a compass or a clock, did Thorstein and Gudrid ever expect to know where they were?

To sail safely down the coast of Norway, according to Arne Emil Christensen, you needed only to recall your fairy tales. "The landmarks, mainly characteristic mountains," he writes, "are featured in fairy tales that explain them as petrified trolls and giants, who in the old days had their quarrels and friendships. The stories told on board not only passed the time but instructed young crewmen in the art of navigation: Such tales helped the sailors remember the landmarks."

Between Norway and Greenland, landmarks are scant. A manuscript written by an Icelander who traveled frequently to Norway in the 1300s describes the voyage from Hennoya, on the coast north of Bergen, to Hvarf, the southernmost tip of Greenland (the name means "Turning Point"), in this way: "Hvarf is reached by sailing due west from Hennoya in Norway, and then one will have sailed to the north of Shetland so that it can only be seen if there is good visibility at sea, and to the south of the Faroes, so that the sea is halfway up the slopes, and to the south of Iceland so that they can see its birds and whales."

Islands, mountains, birds, and whales. As Christensen writes, "No mention of tools used for navigation can be found in the text; apparently the sailor had to learn how to use nature as a guide." Islands are often topped by banks of cumulus clouds. Mountains are magnified by mirages, common in the far north where the sea is coldest. Auks and gannets fly up to a hundred miles out to sea each morning; if they have fish in their beaks, you can follow them back to land, for they are returning to feed their nestlings. Whales of some kinds, like humpbacks, haunt the shallower water close to land; others stay in the deeps.

The sun and the stars were also a sailor's guides. The North Star, Polaris, was named by the Vikings *Leiðarstjarna,* "the leading star." The low northern sun was the Vikings' only clock. At home on the farms, they would mark time by the sun's position above certain mountain peaks. At sea, the height of the sun at noon and the length of the day compared to home told them their latitude, how far north or south they had drifted. When Bjarni Herjolfsson got blown off course on his way from Iceland to Greenland—the voyage on which, according to *The Saga of the Greenlanders,* he spotted Vinland before Leif Eiriksson did—he rejoiced when the sun finally came out so he could "get his bearings."

How precise these bearings were is a mystery. Based on the boyhood recollections of a modern Icelandic sailor, one expert suggests that the Vikings simply used a clenched fist at arm's length to measure the sun's height. "According to my own observations," he writes, "a clenched fist with raised thumb is equivalent to about 15 degrees of elevation. The thumb thus represents 7 degrees, and each of the other fingers 2 degrees." Comparing this reading to the sun's elevation at home at noon gives "a fair indication" of the latitude.

Numerous scholars have championed navigational devices that improve on the precision of the fist. Half of a wooden disk with notches along its rounded edge, found on a Viking farm in Greenland, has been identified as half of a bearing-dial. With a vertical pin in its center, it works something like a sundial, the pin's shadow telling the time of day or, depending on the dial's markings, the sun's direction. Other archaeological scraps have been tentatively identified as bits of an astrolabe or a quadrant, instruments that measure the altitude of the sun and stars. Arab astronomers in Spain were familiar with both well before the year 1000. Gerbert of Aurillac, who reigned as Pope Sylvester II from 999 to 1003, studied mathematics in Spain and wrote a treatise on the astrolabe; a few years later, the German monk Hermann of Reichenau wrote up detailed instructions on how to make one. The quadrant is described in an Icelandic manuscript written late in the thirteenth century, although no saga sea-tale mentions one being used. A "solar stone" that is mentioned in the sagas has been identified as a mineral, Icelandic feldspar, that polarizes light, showing the direction of the sun even if it is hidden by the horizon or clouds. But modern experiments show it works only if the sky is clear at an angle of 90 degrees away from the sun. "When this is the case," writes another expert, "it is easy enough to find the direction to the sun, for example by setting a knife-blade on a fingernail."

This, essentially, is the problem with all of these tools: They work only when the sun or stars are out. In the Land of the Midnight Sun, Polaris is not often seen during the summer sailing season. In the Ocean Called Dark, neither is the sun.

The Ocean Called Dark is the name Adam of Bremen, writing in 1070, gave the seas around Greenland. That "numbing ocean's dark mist, which could hardly be penetrated with the eye," marked "the darksome bounds of a failing world," he wrote, based on tales he had heard in the court of the king of Denmark. Modern writers describe the frequent Greenlandic fogs in much the same way. American anthropologist Frederica DeLaguna, sailing the Greenland coast in the summer of 1929, writes, "We journeyed that day surrounded by mist and snow and rain. I could not believe that there was land near us." Newspaperman J. R. L. Anderson, who traced the Vikings' voyage in a modern sailing yacht in 1967, was lost in fog west of Greenland from June 14 to June 20. "We lived mostly by our ears in a sightless cold world," he writes.

> Psychologically, those days of fog were the most trying of the whole voyage. A gale is a fine, dramatic thing; you may be battered and hard pressed, even in real danger, but the force and fury of the wind and sea at least lift the spirit—you are fighting something you can see to fight. Ice

had been perilous and often frightening, but it had been beautiful and interesting, too. Fog has the vindictiveness of the secret poisoner—the strongest man cannnot fight fog, because he does not know what he has to fight. After twenty-four hours of fog you feel that you have sailed somehow beyond the rim of the human world, to a lightless Hades from which there is no escape.

The arctic explorer Vilhjalmur Stefansson called the fog off Greenland "preternaturally dense," explaining that such fog is common "where warm and cold waters sort of brush against each other, particularly if the cold waters contain fragments of ice," which is the case year-round along Greenland's east coast, thanks to the East Greenland Polar Current. During the summer sailing season, the current carries masses of ice—"monstrous great islands of ice," as the English explorer Martin Frobisher described them in 1576—down the east coast, flips them around Hvarf, and sends them north, up the west coast almost as far as Nuuk, where a "relatively warm" current keeps the coast ice-free by shunting the bergs west, toward Vinland. According to a modern-day "field guide to icebergs," 40,000 icebergs the size of a 15-story building break off from Greenland's glaciers each year. Of these, 1 to 2 percent—400 to 800 bergs—reach Vinland. Uncountable numbers of "bergy bits" (as big as a house) and "growlers" (a grand piano or a small car) travel with them. The combination of fog and ice can be deadly to a thin-hulled wooden ship.

The story of sailing in Greenland waters, writes Jens Rosing, former director of Greenland's National Museum, "is the story of long cold watches, fogs, shining days when everything shimmers in the light, terrifying storms, and undercurrents so strong that the ice, against all reason, moves up against even the most powerful storm winds. . . . The Icelandic sagas and annals speak time and time again of the wrecks of Greenland ships, of ships that vanished with man and mouse." The sagas tell much the same story, missing only the ice, of all the seas Gudrid sailed.

To protect themselves from such catastrophes, the Vikings had no Coast Guard. They had no chase boats, no winches, no diesel backup engines. They didn't even have a friendly Eskimo in a kayak, as the artist Rockwell Kent did when his yacht wrecked off the coast of Greenland in 1929, to paddle home and radio for backup. All they had was magic. In *The Saga of the Volsungs* is a sailor's verse:

> Wave runes shall you make
> If you desire to ward
> Your sail-steeds on the sound.
> On the stem shall they be cut
> And on the steering blade
> And burn them on the oar.
> No broad breaker will fall
> Nor waves of blue,
> And you will come safe from the sea.

In a Viking longhouse in Greenland, dating from the days of Gudrid, archaeologists in the 1950s found a wooden rod covered with runes. On one side is the *futhark*, or complete runic alphabet—what one rune specialist called "the most powerful magic factor to defend and protect one." On the other side is a verse, carved in precise runes that are easily read—yet remain mysterious. *On the sea, sea, sea, where the gods sit*—or watch, or lie in wait—it begins, and then its meaning grows unclear. One specialist thinks it's a riddle about a mirage. Another thinks it's a joke. The most persuasive reading makes it a prayer, or an epitaph: *Bibrau is the maiden who sits in the blue.* "Bibrau," similar to the Icelandic word for mirage, is otherwise unknown as a name. "The maiden" could be a goddess, the Virgin Mary, or an ordinary girl. "The blue" could mean the sea, or the sky (the giant from whose skull the gods fashioned the heavens was called "The Blue One"). Yet *On the sea, sea, sea, where the gods sit* sounds so melancholy that this rune stick brings to my mind a similar stick, found in an otherwise-empty coffin in a Viking cemetery: *This woman, whose name was Gudveig, was laid overboard in the Greenland Sea.* Perhaps the same was the fate of Bibrau, whose lover was so poetic.

But it was not the fate of Gudrid the Far-Traveler. In spite of being shipwrecked and blown off course, she did not die at sea. Instead she was twice saved to sail again, as soon as she could, west, away from Greenland, away from Iceland, away from Norway and her trees, west off the edge of the known world, into the blue.

CHAPTER 2

Ransacking the Past

As they were looking through Einar's wares, a woman passed by the open doorway. "Who is that beautiful woman?" asked Einar. "I have never seen her here before."

"That is my foster-daughter, Gudrid," replied Orm. "Her father is Thorbjorn of Laugarbrekka."

"She'd make me an excellent wife," said Einar. "Has she had any offers?"

"Indeed she has, my friend," replied Orm. "She's not to be had just for the asking."

—*The Saga of Eirik the Red*

THE OTHER VERSION OF GUDRID'S STORY BEGINS NOT with a shipwreck but with this glimpse of Gudrid through a young man's eyes. Here is the scene: On the tip of a mountainous peninsula jutting from the west coast of Iceland sat a small Viking longhouse. Turf-clad, except for one wooden door, the house looked like a low hill in the jewel-green field. A turf wall encircled it, keeping the horses from grazing in the manured homefield. Toward the sea, the land dropped off into ragged cliffs alive with nesting seabirds. Seals sunned on the seaside rocks. A *knarr* and a six-oared fishing boat, both clinker-built and tarred black, lay beached in a tiny harbor of black sand. Behind the turf house rose a pyramidal black hill, then the clean white flank of the glacier called Snaefellsjokull, "Snow Mountain's Glacier."

Beneath the glacier hid a volcano, known to the inhabitants of the house only from a pleasant side effect: Water hot enough for washing bubbled up from the ground not far away.

The *knarr* belonged to Einar, a young and ambitious Icelander with a fondness for fancy clothes. He had spent the winter in Norway, whose king was fostering a new plan—towns—and a new merchant class. Einar, though his father had been a Viking's slave, aspired to this class. His ship came home loaded with luxuries impossible to find in Iceland. Stacked in Orm's shed, where Einar was setting up shop, were bales of linen and silk and fine wool dyed bright blue and red. He brought lumber, both oak and ash. Pine tar for preserving ships' timbers. Barley and hops for brewing beer. Honey to make into mead. Perhaps even beeswax, for many of the Viking folk along this coast were Christians, and had been taught they must worship by candlelight.

Orm owned the longhouse. He kept cows and sheep and was loyal to the chieftain who had granted him land. Gudrid was the chieftain's daughter. Since her mother died, she had been raised by Orm's wife. She was about fourteen when she passed the open doorway of Einar's shop. Something about her—her looks, her dress, the way she walked or smiled—impressed the young man. Despite Orm's warning, he decided to ask for her hand.

His suit was denied. Gudrid's father wouldn't marry his daughter to the son of a slave. Orm's hint that the young merchant's wealth could be of use offended the chieftain. Ashamed that his money troubles were talked about, Gudrid's father swapped his farm for a ship and took his daughter to Greenland to start a new life. Orm shrugged his shoulders and, loyally, went with him.

The saga does not describe Orm's farm, where young Einar unloaded his ship, it names it: Arnarstapi, "Eagle Peak." I can imagine the green field and the cliffs and the harbor and paint the scene because I have driven down that long peninsula, under the eye of Snow Mountain's Glacier. I have sat where Gudrid as a girl might have sat, watching the white birds circle and waiting for a ship to come in.

Yet, daydreaming in the low summer sun, imagining what the place must have looked like when Einar unloaded his wares a thousand years ago, I bump up against the barrier faced by every reader of the sagas: Is it true?

There are werewolves in the sagas, and trolls. Soothsayers, and warlocks who rule the weather. Ghosts who walk and strangle their foes—or give their widows charitable advice. Like Homer's *Iliad*, the sagas were based on old tales told around the fire to enliven the long winter nights. Generations of storytellers can be counted on to elaborate—and to overlook.

Who was there to write down what rich Einar said when he first saw Gudrid? Einar and his fancy clothes are never mentioned again, in this saga or in any other Icelandic source. Nor is Gudrid's father reckoned among the chieftains in the other tales that take place on this peninsula. If Einar did not ask for Gudrid's hand, if Gudrid's father was not ashamed his money troubles were so well known, if he did not, therefore, up and move to Greenland—if this whole scene is fictitious—is the rest of *The Saga of Eirik the Red* fiction, too? Did Leif Eiriksson discover America? Did Gudrid live there and give birth to her son? Did she see Norway and Rome? Was she as plucky and capable, as adventurous and adaptable, as the stories imply? Are the sagas a true witness to the Viking world?

Historians have debated this point since at least 1772, when the British explorer Sir Joseph Banks brought the literature of Iceland to the attention of the English-speaking world. There's just so little to go on. No one in Gudrid's society could read or write. Literacy did not come to Iceland until the Christian

Church, made the official religion in the year 1000, set up schools in the 1030s. The first book in Icelandic was *The Book of the Icelanders,* a brief and sober history written by Ari the Learned in the early 1100s, based, he says, on the recollections of wise old women and men.

The peak of saga writing came a century later. Thousands of fireside tales about kings and mythological heroes, about Iceland's first settlers, and about men and women who had made names for themselves in one way or another were collected and gathered into manuscripts, some by masters of the literary art, others by beginners. Gudrid's story is not found in the great sagas, the ones Jane Smiley places at the heart of human literary endeavor. It fills most of *The Saga of Eirik the Red,* which can be read aloud in less than an hour. Gudrid also appears in *The Saga of the Greenlanders,* which is even shorter and contradicts *The Saga of Eirik the Red* on several important points, especially concerning Gudrid's early life.

I think of the two girls as Red Gudrid (the one in *The Saga of Eirik the Red*) and Green Gudrid (from *The Saga of the Greenlanders*). Red Gudrid left for Greenland as a pampered, protected daughter, too good for young Einar's offer of marriage. She sailed in her father's ship, surrounded by his belongings and connections. Then her fairy tale ended. The ship wandered at sea all summer. The food and fresh water ran out. Sickness set in. Gudrid watched many of the people she knew and loved, including Orm and his wife, die miserable deaths. She undoubtedly grew up. Yet her social status was relatively unaffected. The ship made a safe landfall in southern Greenland just before winter, and Gudrid and her father were welcomed as guests by Eirik the Red's cousin, who farmed there.

At this point in the story comes an example of the antiquarianism in the sagas that so attracted Victorian writers like

Sir Walter Scott. That winter, we read, the hunting was poor and meals were scanty. To learn how to alleviate the household's hunger (or perhaps to take their minds off it), the farmer decided to hold a séance. Though the saga was written at least two hundred years after the event, the seer is described in wonderful detail. She wore a long blue gown and a black lambskin hood lined with white cat's fur. She had catskin gloves, too, with the fur inside, and carried a brassbound staff. Both her gown and her staff were adorned with jewels. She could eat only the hearts of animals, one of each kind, cutting them up with her ivory-handled knife and picking them up with her brass spoon. She could sit only on a cushion stuffed with hens' feathers. To invoke the spirits, she needed a helper to sing certain magic songs. Only Gudrid knew them, and she sang them expertly. Charmed by her singing, the spirits gathered and revealed many things, among them Gudrid's future: "Your path leads to Iceland, and from you will come a large and worthy family, for shining over your descendants I see bright rays of light"—a reference, scholars believe, to her two great-grandsons and one great-great-grandson who served as bishops in Iceland in the 1100s.

The next summer Red Gudrid and her father sailed farther north to Eirik's settlement at Brattahlid ("Steep Slope"). Fifteen years earlier, before Eirik had been banished from Iceland and went off to settle Greenland, he and Gudrid's father, Thorbjorn, had been best friends. Their reunion was joyful. Gudrid and her father joined Eirik's household until their own house could be built, on a piece of land Eirik gave them, right across the fjord. They ended up with a farm as good as or better than the one they had left in Iceland, all the goods they had brought on their ship plus whatever had belonged to the people who had died, and the ship itself. By the standards of the day, they were quite well off.

Green Gudrid, on the other hand, was alone and destitute after having been shipwrecked and plucked off the icy rock by Leif Eiriksson on his way home from discovering Vinland. She was said to be the wife of the captain of the ship, a Norwegian merchant named Thorir. In return for the rescue, Leif took for himself everything that could be salvaged from the wreck. He invited Gudrid and her husband to stay with him, but that winter sickness set in. Gudrid's husband and most of the other people Leif rescued died—as did Leif's father, Eirik the Red. Leif became the leader of the Greenland colony. Gudrid, with no one else to turn to, became his ward. She owned nothing. There is no mention of her singing or her bright future (though that will come).

Strangely, for both the Red Gudrid and the Green, the rich and the poor, the result was the same: She soon married Leif's younger brother Thorstein.

A little book written in the 1970s, called in English *The Saga Mind*, explains how to accommodate such additions and contradictions. The saga writers, says the Russian literary historian M. I. Steblin-Kamenskij, "strove simultaneously for accuracy and for reproduction of reality in all its living fullness." Or, as Icelandic saga scholar Vesteinn Olason wrote more recently, in *Dialogues with the Viking Age,* when a saga writer added something from his imagination, he was not "inventing" something new, but "finding" something that had always been part of the story.

This concept of truth mingles our ideas of history and of art—the record of what actually happened with the truth a good novel can tell you about yourself and the world around you. The Old Icelandic word *saga* mingles them, too: It was applied indiscriminately to tales that sound like sober history and to ones we can easily peg as fiction. Saga-truth assumes that both Vinland tales are at bottom "accurate," based on stories passed down from generation to generation from Gudrid's day to the 1200s.

Memories are not myths, points out Gisli Sigurdsson, who teaches folklore at the University of Iceland. In 1988 Gisli published the controversial *Gaelic Influence in Iceland;* the Gaelic "gift of gab" led him to explore other storytelling cultures for his 2004 book, *The Medieval Icelandic Saga and Oral Tradition.* Though tales change with their tellers—bits left out, others embellished (as the description of the seer obviously was)—they still must ring true to their audience. "They're still within limits," he told me, regarding the two young Gudrids. "You must fill in the gap somehow. The basic idea is that she comes to Greenland, and soon enough there's a problem. She has to make a fresh start. She has to get involved with Eirik the Red's family, since in order to become somebody there, you had to make friends with Eirik.

"The only way we can explain these written texts," he continued, "is that you first had stories about separate events and characters. I think people were telling these stories in a mish-mash, without the beginning and end that we know. They were very regional. They were stories about disputes, about the qualities of the land, about someone's misbehavior. They had a very clear ethical message, both about how you as a farmer should behave, and about how a chieftain should react. These stories were being told to reinforce that ideology."

The written sagas were a way of systematizing the oral stories. "When people in Iceland in the thirteenth century saw the long written narratives they were getting in books from abroad, they realized they could use these old stories in that new form. They learned to write them down chronologically. That's not what you would do with oral literature. When you told these stories, you just told them from event to event and key word to key word. The

Icelanders in the thirteenth century were fascinated with chronology, with this new way of systematizing knowledge, just like we're fascinated by computers. They weren't saying anything new, they were just putting it into a different form."

To work chronologically, to follow a set of characters through time, a writer needed to build bridges, to fill in gaps, to connect one oral tale to another. These bridges could be drawn from another tale, or come from the writer's general knowledge about the area in which the story took place. The differences between the two Vinland sagas, then, can be set down to their writers' interests, intentions, and abilities, but also to which tales they had heard, what memories they shared, what bridges they needed to build, what audience they were addressing. *The Saga of Eirik the Red* has been traced to a nunnery in northern Iceland, whose abbess was Gudrid's seven-greats granddaughter: Gudrid was presumably an exemplar, a role model for young Christian women. *The Saga of the Greenlanders* comes down to us as disjointed chapters in a long saga of the kings of Norway. The discovery of Vinland, rather than Gudrid, lies at its heart.

When it comes to Gudrid, the memory both sagas seem to be based on is this: Gudrid had a suitor who was a merchant, plying the sea routes from Norway. She may or may not have married him, but he soon passed out of her life. She went to Greenland. She had a bad voyage. Her first winter there was hard, with hunger and sickness. By spring she had lost most of the people she loved. But she was remarkable in some way that was not dependent on her being wealthy, and she married Eirik the Red's son, Thorstein, becoming Leif Eiriksson's sister-in-law. Thorstein attempted to sail to Vinland, but failed. He and Gudrid lived for a time in Lysufjord, a lonely spot remote from their fathers' farms, and there, after a terrible illness, Thorstein died.

In the Red version, Thorstein borrowed Gudrid's father's ship and set off for the New World with no mention of Gudrid accompanying him. Foul winds drove his ship east instead of west, until Thorstein thought he could see birds off the coast of Ireland. He limped home to Greenland with tattered sails at summer's end. That autumn, he and Gudrid married and moved north to Lysufjord, where Thorstein owned a half-share in a farm.

Green Gudrid—the poor Gudrid—sailed with Thorstein. They took Leif's ship, but they had the same bad luck. They made landfall back in Greenland just before winter and slept in a tent on the ship until they were taken in by the farmer at Lysufjord.

Thorstein's death scene at Lysufjord is gloriously spooky— and remarkably consistent from one saga to the other. It is dark, and the dead are all around them. The farmhands (in the Red version) or the crew of the ship (in the Green) had died one by one as winter came on, and their bodies were piled up in the snow until they could be buried in the spring. Then Thorstein and the farmer's wife fell ill. Red Gudrid became their nurse. One night, the sick woman was stumbling back from the privy on Gudrid's arm when she let out a shriek. Gudrid tried to calm her. "This isn't wise. You mustn't get chilled. We have to go back in right now."

The farmwife would not budge. She could see the dead lined up at her door. "Your husband is there. And I am with him!"

The vision passed, and Red Gudrid hurried her charge to bed. By morning, the woman was dead—though before she could be carried out, her corpse rose up and tried to get into bed with Thorstein. (In the Green version, we see the ghost through Thorstein's eyes, as he called out in panic to Gudrid: "She is pushing herself up on her elbows and poking her feet out of the bed and groping for her shoes!") As soon as the old wife was safely coffined, Thorstein died. He, too, did not lie quiet. Red Gudrid was asleep from exhaustion when her dead husband called for her; Green Gudrid was sitting on the old farmer's lap while he "tried to comfort her in every way he knew." In the Red version, the corpse begged for a proper Christian funeral, with a priest, and told her to give his money to the church or to the poor—appropriate fare for young nuns. He mentioned only in passing that Gudrid was "fated for great things." To Green Gudrid, he spoke exclusively about her future—this Gudrid had not taken part in the séance. She hasn't heard yet that she will marry an Icelander and that her progeny will be "promising, bright, and praiseworthy, sweet and fine-smelling."

Both the Red Gudrid and the Green—these seventeen-year-old widows—convinced the farmer not to keep her to replace his dead wife, but to ferry her back to the main settlement in the spring, to her father (who died soon afterward, in the Red version) or to her brother-in-law and guardian, Leif. Both Red Gudrid and Green Gudrid knew she was destined for greatness—the idea that her future had been foretold was so fixed in the collective memory that both saga authors mentioned it, and the author of the Red version clumsily did so twice.

When the promised Icelander arrived the next autumn, captaining a merchant ship, Red Gudrid was fabulously wealthy. She had inherited Thorstein Eiriksson's share of the farm at Lysufjord, as well as her father's farm and her father's ship. As a widow, she had the right to decide where she would live and whom, if anyone, she would marry. She chose to live at Brattahlid with Eirik the Red. Green Gudrid was marginally better off than she had been when she arrived in Greenland, the survivor of a shipwreck. She had inherited Thorstein's share of Eirik the Red's estate, but Leif was in control of it. She lived at Brattahlid as Leif's ward. But rich or poor, Gudrid married the Icelandic merchant, Thorfinn Karlsefni, whose nickname means "the stuff a man is made of" or "the makings of a man." Once again, the two sagas hold a memory in common.

Then a curious thing happens in *The Saga of Eirik the Red:* Karlsefni sails for Vinland and Gudrid disappears from the story. This is Red Gudrid, the rich Gudrid, the one who caught the young merchant's eye, who took part in the séance, whose fate we have followed in such detail. From the words on the page, you would think she had stayed behind in Greenland—just as it seems she had when Thorstein Eiriksson set off on his Vinland expedition. We learn how far Karlsefni sailed, about the wind and the weather, the bears and whales, the wide beaches, the wine grapes, the wild wheat, the pasturelands, and the trees. We read about arguments that sent one ship back north and one (or two) farther south. We meet the Skraelings, the saga term for the native people, and watch the Vikings trade with them, then fight them, then flee from them. We discover that Karlsefni's ship is the only one of the three to return to Greenland. But about Gudrid there is only an afterthought. We read: "Snorri, Karlsefni's son, was born the first autumn; he was three when they left."

Green Gudrid is given a slightly bigger role. Not only did she give birth to Snorri in Vinland, she tried to make friends with a native woman. There is no echo of this event in the other saga. The only overlap between the two versions—the only shared memory of Vinland—concerns Snorri's birth and the Vikings' decision to abandon their settlement after three years. They returned to Greenland. From there Red Gudrid and her family sailed directly to Iceland, while Green Gudrid first detoured to Norway. In both sagas, the family settled in the Skagafjord valley in the north of Iceland, where Gudrid had a second son.

Exactly where in Skagafjord they lived is still under dispute, particularly by the farmers who currently inhabit the two places in question.

The Saga of Eirik the Red notes that Karlsefni's mother thought he had married beneath him. She did not care to share her house with Gudrid. Karlsefni's family farm was a large estate called Reynines, "Rowan Ness." Gudrid apparently spent at least the first winter somewhere else.

The Saga of the Greenlanders only hints at in-law trouble, but identifies the "somewhere else." Rather than taking over Reynines, the saga says, Karlsefni bought a nearby farm called Glaumbaer. After Karlsefni's death, Gudrid farmed at Glaumbaer until her son Snorri married. Then she went on a pilgrimage to Rome.

We have no corroborating record of her pilgrimage, although guestbooks in monasteries along the recommended route list other women travelers with Viking names: Vigdis, Vilborg, Kolthera, and Thurid, for instance, visited Reichenau monastery in Switzerland during the eleventh century (at about the same time as the monk Hermann was writing his treatise on the astrolabe there). That Gudrid might have gone to Rome is therefore plausible, but not certain.

Asking not *Are the sagas true?* but *Are they plausible?* will never tell me if Gudrid had a lovely singing voice or if, in Greenland, she was rich or poor. But historians and literary scholars collating the sagas with other scattered documents from the twelfth and thirteenth centuries, such as church records, annals, and books of law, have revealed many other plausible details about her life and times. I can guess what luxuries Einar brought to Iceland, and even what some of these goods cost: Twenty pounds of beeswax was worth as much as a cow. I also know that Gudrid—rich or poor—spent her days milking cows and making cheese, spinning wool and weaving cloth. While milk was the foundation of the Viking diet, homespun was the culture's chief export. When Einar left Iceland to go trading in Norway, each of his crewmen most likely took along a length of homespun two miles long and weighing two tons as "spending money"—all of it woven by women.

But to let me imagine more of Gudrid's life—to truly see that turf house sitting like a low hill in the jewel-green field—the medieval sagas must give way to modern science. The sagas hold memories; archaeology can provide me with facts and physical objects. But archaeology, in Iceland especially, is a political sport. Fashions come and go. Whereas a hundred years ago every archaeologist in Iceland was bent on proving the sagas literally true, down to the last cask of whey in which a hero hid, today's archaeologists tend to set the sagas to one side. They are not necessarily fictitious, they are simply irrelevant.

Still, as historians routinely remind their scientific colleagues, the sagas made Iceland a nation. They were penned, the story goes, to prove to the Norwegian overlords that Icelanders were not the sons of slaves and should be treated as equals. It took a while for that message to be heard. From the 1200s until well into the 1800s, Iceland was of little interest to its rulers (first Norway, then Denmark). The Renaissance did not find Iceland. The Reformation tore it apart: Before he was beheaded in 1550, Bishop Jon Arason unilaterally declared Iceland free of Danish control. The Icelandic church's rents and properties were then seized by the Danish crown, which established a monopoly over all trade with the island. That trade did not prove profitable. By the late 1700s, after a prolonged and poisonous volcanic eruption had killed off one-fifth of the human population and half their cattle, the Danish king suggested the island be abandoned and the remaining forty thousand Icelanders resettled in Jutland. Throughout centuries of want and despair, the sagas and the Golden Age of independence and valor they painted kept the Icelandic nation alive. The sagas were the tool patriots used to bring the island to the world's attention in the 1800s, and the cause of its ultimate independence in 1944. Iceland had a language and a story: Therefore, it was a nation.

Poking holes in recognized saga sites is, for these reasons, not something people are encouraged to try. Especially not outsiders like John Steinberg of UCLA, who desperately wanted to dig up the hayfield at Glaumbaer to see if the floor plan his remote-sensing device had mapped out—of Gudrid's last house—was accurate.

With no brick or timber or building stone, houses of turf, like the sod homes of prairie pioneers, are all the medieval Icelanders ever had. Once abandoned, a turf house disappears quite quickly, beaten by wind and rain back into the landscape. Those that were abandoned in the last century (poured concrete became the favorite Icelandic building material after World War II) have sunk and settled, leaving distinctive mounds on thousands of Icelandic farms—except where they've been bulldozed to neaten up the place. Archaeologists in Iceland approach these mounds like a rescue squad: When a road or a river (or the foundation of a new summerhouse) cuts into an ancient farm mound, the state sends in an archaeologist to map the ruins and salvage whatever bones or artifacts are uncovered. Several hundred pagan graves and eighteen Viking longhouses were discovered this way over the last hundred years. But as for digging on purpose in historical spots, the official opinion is that Iceland's history is far safer left in the ground.

The Icelandic verb "to research" or "to investigate" is *rann-saka,* the same as our English word "ransack." Ransacking is what Vikings did to fat English monasteries: torched the roofs, broke down the doors, destroyed the walls, and carted off the treasure. In the language of the Vikings, *rannsaka* merely meant "to search a house"; the idea of total destruction is purely English. Yet both senses apply to archaeological research. According to Orri Vesteinsson of Iceland's Institute of Archaeology, "One way of looking at the development of excavation techniques in Iceland in the last century is to see it in terms of increasingly comprehensive destruction." Or as John Steinberg had explained to me the first time I met him, *Archaeology murders its informants.*

"Is archaeology a science?" he asked me. For a scientific experiment to be valid, any scientist, following the published methods of the original experimenter, should be able to reproduce the original results. In archaeology, that's not physically possible.

"Archaeology *uses* scientific methods," John said, "but it's inherently not reproducible." By digging into a historic site like the one that hides Gudrid's longhouse, John and his crew will destroy it. They will chop up the ground, sift it, sort it, save certain things, and dump what's left in a heap.

What John will leave for posterity is not Gudrid's longhouse, but his notes and maps and reports: his *story* of Gudrid's longhouse. The local historical society, which coincidentally operates a museum on the Glaumbaer farm, will most probably build a reconstruction near the site and call it "Gudrid's longhouse"—but it won't be. It will be an architect's interpretation of John's story. It's no wonder, then, that the Icelanders from whom John must get permission to dig want him to ransack Gudrid's house as slowly and carefully as possible.

His 2004 field season was canceled. The National Science Foundation rejected his grant proposal, following the advice of an anonymous reviewer who'd said that ground-penetrating radar—the latest remote-sensing device John wanted to bring in—had already been tried in Iceland. The reviewer had apparently misread an Icelandic newspaper story, which convinced John the reviewer was Icelandic. John revised the grant proposal, including proof that ground-penetrating radar had not been used in Iceland in the way he planned to use it. The project was a go for July 2005.

As soon as I heard, I flew to Los Angeles.

In his cubicle in the basement of UCLA's Fowler Museum, John pulled the just-funded grant proposal from a file, pushed aside a cow skull on a cafeteria tray, and regaled me with the methods he'd used to find Gudrid's house in 2001. "We had an experimental grant that year," he began. "We tried *everything*."

The two surveying techniques he had used to find ancient houses in Denmark, as a graduate student in the early 1990s, were defeated by Iceland's unusual soil. The first depended on potsherds. To an archaeologist, bits of pottery are road signs marking where you are in an ancient culture and when things changed. Iceland had no Viking potsherds because its clay was not conducive to making pots.

"The clay won't stick together," John explained. "The earth in Iceland has a very weird feeling to it. It almost feels *wrong*. It coats you. It gets everywhere. It rusts your trowel. It also makes it so that phosphate is not available to grasses. All the phosphate ions attach to the clay." Phosphate testing was the second way he had mapped early settlements in Denmark; high phosphate, from manure, marks pastures and fertilized fields. But in Iceland the test didn't work the way it had in Denmark.

Iceland's odd earth does hold one advantage over Denmark's: Whatever you do find can be easily dated. Dig a trench in an Icelandic hayfield, and the trench walls will be conveniently stratified, striped like a layer cake with volcanic tephra—a term for anything that spews out of a volcano and is light enough to travel through the air some distance. Tephra has a different color and texture from soil or sand. When you run the edge of your trowel over it, it rings out, as if you had tapped a glass bottle. It feels grittier, almost spiky on your fingertips or, if you're not certain, on your tongue. (Archaeologists taste a lot of things they pick out of the dirt: Putting a sample on your tongue is also the best way to tell pottery from bone.) In northern Iceland, the tephra layer from an eruption of Mount Hekla in 1104 is particularly thick: It looks like a line of white icing between the dark cakes of soil. Equally obvious are two honey-brown lines from eruptions two thousand and four thousand years ago, well before the first people came to the island. An eruption from about the year 1000 left a greenish-gray layer that can be traced in most spots. A darker line, often swirled with charcoal or organic matter, marks the settlement of Iceland in the year 870. Archaeologists call this tephra the *Landnám* or Settlement Layer; they have found no signs of human culture beneath it. The historical dates—870, 1000, 1104, plus or minus a year or two—are quite secure. Not only is the 1104 catastrophe mentioned in church records (it wiped out several farms in the south of Iceland), signs of all three eruptions can be seen in the cores drilled from the Greenland ice sheets to study climate change. It's a lucky accident that the eruptions in 870 and 1104 frame the Viking Age in Iceland.

To make use of this tephrochronology, John's colleague Douglas Bolender, a doctoral student at Northwestern University, devised a soil-sampling protocol. He and his assistants walked back and forth across each modern farm-field on the Langholt ridge in Skagafjord, an area that encompasses both farms named in Gudrid's saga: Reynines (now called Reynistadur, or "Rowan Stead") and Glaumbaer. They logged their coordinates with GPS, reading off two satellites and a transmitter on a lighthouse offshore. They flagged each site, creating a grid of colored plastic flags 50 meters (a little more than 50 yards) apart. At each flag, they punched in their steel soil-coring tube and recorded the depth and quality (including tephra layers) of the soil. If the soil was shallow, they passed it by—only deep soil will preserve a turf house. Shallow soil means the wind has already eroded everything of interest. They examined pockets of deep soil (20 inches is as deep as the corer goes; poking it in twice, you can sometimes reach 40) for marks of a kitchen or garbage midden: flecks of charcoal, peat ash, or burned bone. If they found these below the white 1104 tephra layer, the spot was worth testing further. (Logical on paper, this protocol broke down somewhat in reality: A farmer making hay mowed down the plastic flags before the soil samples could be taken; a bull chased the soil corers through two fences and into a muddy drainage ditch, fouling all their equipment, though they preserved the precious data sheets.)

To places with interesting soil cores, John and Brian Damiata, a UCLA geophysicist, brought a variety of machines that can see beneath the earth. Adapting these remote-sensing devices to Iceland's wet soils was tricky, as was adjusting any magnetic effects for the nearness of the North Pole. The gadget that finally did work was originally designed for plumbers to detect problems in buried pipes. Called the EM-31, it measures how well the soil conducts electricity. It is unwieldy (a 12-foot-long tube carried by a strap over the shoulder), heavy (30 pounds), and temperamental.

"You have to get all the neighbors within half a mile to turn off their electric fences," John said. "Sometimes they gave me a pretty short window." At one farm, a band of young stallions seemed to know exactly when the current to their electric fence was off and would break through the wire to rumpus with the mares.

The results were disappointing. "We're making these maps," John said, "and we couldn't see anything on them." But then Tim Earle, John's mentor, now teaching at Northwestern in Chicago, suggested John "rough up the data." John wrote a computer program to look at the *differences* among readings and discovered a series of anomalies. On the new map, each showed up as a colored cluster of squiggles that stuck out from its surroundings. Choosing one, they dug a test trench. The hole came up empty: no sign of a turf house.

"Later," said John, "we found out that this machine's coordinates were one meter off"—about a yard. (John, like all scientists, thinks in meters; I still see things in inches, feet, and yards.) Once they corrected for that yard-long error, they started finding things in their trenches. "We got a lot of landslides. Then one of these anomalies wasn't a landslide, it was a wall. Once we identified that signal—that it was a turf house—we were flying high!"

The buried turf wall was in the hayfield behind the Skaga-fjord Folk Museum at Glaumbaer, a collection of historic houses on a busy road that runs the length of the valley to the town of Saudarkrokur, population 2,600. Beside the road is a stone statue of a stout-armed woman balancing a tiny boy on her shoulder—Gudrid and Snorri, the first residents—but the museum was not established to honor them alone. On a low mound, beside a trim white church that is still active, is a rambling turf farmhouse, its walls and roofs of sod forming a jumble of lumps much like a collection of hobbit holes connected by tunnels. Its wooden gables and doors are painted mustard yellow. A house has been on this site, the history books say, since saga times, a thousand years ago. The current structure, begun in 1750, was lived in continuously until it passed to the museum in 1948.

Two other historical buildings were moved onto the museum grounds in the 1990s. One houses a coffee shop and galleries. It had been built in 1886 to be a girls' school (though "this never came to pass," a museum brochure relates). The other building, a little white wood-framed house with a green grass roof, provides office space for the museum staff. Its claim to fame is its track record: The house had been dismantled and moved six times since it was built in 1862, logging over 120 miles by ice, sea, and road. Arriving at Glaumbaer in 1996, it was very nearly placed on top of the turf wall yet to be discovered beneath the hayfield.

That wall, John found, was topped by the shiny white tephra from the eruption of Mount Hekla in 1104. Curious, John angled a soil corer into the mound on which the 1750s turf house sits, right in front of the mustard-yellow kitchen door, where the family would have thrown their fireplace ash and scraps. "That ash sits exactly on the 1104 tephra layer, and under that is sterile soil," he said. "For the house we found down below in the hayfield, everything is *under* the 1104. So the main house at Glaumbaer moved about 1104."

John's Icelandic colleagues, including museum curator Sigridur Sigurdardottir and archaeologists Gudny Zoega and her supervisor at the time, Ragnheidur Traustadottir, were skeptical. They asked Gudmundur Olafsson to come up from the Icelandic National Museum in Reykjavik to take a look. Gudmundur, who has excavated more Viking Age longhouses than anyone else, spent several days on the site, dug a long trench, and was also not convinced.

No one doubted that John had found something made of turf and older than 1104. But was it a longhouse? None of the histories, censuses, or tax records showed a house there. And even if a longhouse *did* exist in the Glaumbaer hayfield, another line of reasoning went, it was just an oddity. In general, both history and archaeology agreed, turf houses didn't move. When fashions changed, the new house was simply built on top of the remains of the old. John argued, on the other hand, that if there was one invisible Viking house in the valley, there might be many.

The Icelanders suggested they take another farm—one not mentioned in the sagas—and survey it using both methods. John chose the farm of Stora Seyla ("Big Marsh"), about three miles south of Glaumbaer. Its turf house had stood until the 1920s atop a complicated mound cut through by a stream, and the nearby fields had not been bulldozed flat or plowed. With the historical records in hand, the Icelandic archaeologists marked every feature on the landscape that looked man-made. John's team tested each by taking soil cores: According to the tephra lines, none of the features was older than 1104. "So then we cored the whole place on a 50-meter grid," John told me, "past the modern boundaries of the farm Stora Seyla until we hit the fjord. One core came up with charcoal, and an adjacent one had some very deep soil." They tested that area with the EM-31.

John paged through the 2005 grant proposal to the EM-31's output: a map of Stora Seyla from the surface to six feet down, color-coded by how well the soil conducted electricity. "If you fuzz your eyes," he told me, "you see a tract of light blue and dark blue. We imagine this is the limits of a structure." It was 115 feet long. Based on this map, John's team dug test trenches. They found a turf wall, a floor, hay, and a burned birch-bark roof, perfectly preserved—and older than 1104. The main house at Stora Seyla had also moved.

John was, he admitted, a little too pleased with their results. "I was pretty arrogant," he said with a rueful smile. "I essentially attacked the Icelanders for being incompetent."

But if this technique—soil coring on a grid combined with the EM-31—worked so well, I asked, why was he bringing a new remote-sensing device—the untested ground-penetrating radar or GPR—to Skagafjord in 2005?

"Because I'm *not* an Icelandic archaeologist," he said. "I don't want to spend years excavating these sites. I have a few basic questions. How big is the farm? How much hay did they store? I want a shortcut to digging. GPR is the best remote-sensing technique available to archaeologists. What we need it for is to *not have to excavate.*

"Now we can *find* sites with the other technique, but we can't tell what we're looking at without digging into them. And we keep chewing into the wrong places. This pisses off the Icelanders no end. It's hard to convince them I'm even sort of competent. I don't know which wall is which. I can't answer all this ambiguity in the remote-sensing data. We've learned that the biggest anomaly is usually a corner, but we've learned that only by chewing into it—and we just about destroyed that corner of the house."

"You mean Gudrid's house?"

"The house at Glaumbaer. But it had to be done. There was no other way. We had to calibrate our readings."

"You destroyed the corner of *Gudrid's house*?"

He looked uncomfortable. "I think the case for saying the longhouse at Glaumbaer is the referent for the story in the sagas is true," he said. "Whether the *story* is true is another question."

On a warm winter day in March 2005, we were in Iceland, on the site of the storied house, and John was looking even more uncomfortable.

"Why do you think you can use a backhoe here?" Sigridur Sigurdardottir, known as "Sirri," rolled a heavy glass paperweight between her broad hands. She had served us tea and coffee when we arrived at her office at the Skagafjord Folk Museum, and had even unwrapped a box of chocolates; but now she was installed behind her desk, taking on the full authority of the book-lined office with its unsettling touches of practicality: refrigerator, microwave, spinning wheel. Her gaze was firm and unapologetic.

"He has already hired one," Gudny Zoega told Sirri in Icelandic.

John backtracked in his ninety-second introduction to his archaeological protocol, vainly trying to rephrase his argument. With the backhoe he intended to quickly strip the top layer of turf off the hayfield. Using trowels and shovels, his archaeologists (and unskilled volunteers, like me) would then expose the tops of the buried longhouse walls to check if the remote-sensing devices had drawn the floor plan accurately. That would be it for the 2005 field season. John was in northern Iceland now to work out where his crew of fifteen would eat and sleep, where they could have lab space, whether he could get a free car for five weeks in July and August. He had been in the country only one day and had spent much of that time searching out a certain kind of Danish backhoe that he thought was excellent for archaeology. The previous afternoon, he had found just what he wanted. Though the owner spoke no English, and John no Icelandic, they hit it off right away. "He keeps his backhoe inside, he likes it so much," John had crowed to Gudny, when we met her in her laboratory in Saudarkrokur later that evening. "It will be *perfect*." He had already gotten permission, he confided to her, to use a backhoe at Glaumbaer. The director of the national Archaeological Heritage Agency, from whom he got his official permits, had said it would be okay.

Those permits, I could see now, were useless.

Sirri's eyes narrowed. "I see," she said in English, and John fell silent.

I wrote in my notebook: *No backhoe.*

"Isn't it easily cut with a spade?" Sirri said, putting on her phone headset. She smiled at us and nodded toward the chocolate box, as if to say *enjoy!* Hospitality is a prominent cultural value in Iceland, as important now as it was in the saga days, so I leaned past Gudny and took a couple. Gudny took some, too.

After a rapid conversation in Icelandic, Sirri reported that two or three men could remove the turf in twenty-five hours. Her brother Helgi would arrange it.

"That's as fast as a backhoe!" John said.

"Yes, I know." Sirri's smile was simultaneously smug and patient. "People who know how to do it are as fast as a backhoe. The people are a little bit expensiver, but not much. I like it better not to have a machine on the field. When do you want to start?"

That settled, Sirri went to the refrigerator and brought out a plate of cheese, crackers, and grapes. Gudny and I helped ourselves; John suggested a bit of show-and-tell. He had a movie about his latest remote-sensing device to show them, to explain the new procedure he'd be using that summer. He slipped his laptop out of its case and opened the lid. Nothing. He closed it, opened it, wiggled it. Still nothing.

Sirri took some cheese and crackers. "*Tækni* is good, if it works," she said, and winked at Gudny and me.

"If I could hook it up to your monitor . . . ," John said, and Sirri directed him to the computer in the outer office.

I'd seen this movie before. It showed how ground-penetrating radar had located and mapped in colorful 3-D a first-century Roman marketplace and the Emperor Trajan's eel pond. I excused myself and went to find a window facing east. The weather was astonishingly mild for Iceland in March, and Pastor Gisli, who preached in the Glaumbaer church and worked the farm, had turned out his sheep. They were grazing on top of Gudrid's house and had cropped the brown grass quite short, but I saw no vague, humped shape of a tumbled longhouse rising from the field. The ground looked quite flat. The sheep milled around the metal hay feeders and the red hay wagon parked in the center of the field, just where Gudrid's hearth should be.

Sirri came up behind me—the *tækni* was still not working. "There are a lot of elves here," she said, looking over my shoulder, "and trolls, too." She was testing me. Coming out of the blue, that comment would have sounded strange to someone unfamiliar with the Icelanders' love of old stories.

"People always are asking, Do we believe in them?" She laughed. "I give them the benefit of the doubt. The stories are good. A good saga will never die."

CHAPTER 3

A Very Stirring Woman

Karlsefni and Gudrid sailed to Iceland the next summer,
home to his farm at Reynines. But his mother would not
have Gudrid in her house that first winter. In her opinion,
Karlsefni had not married well. Though later on she would
learn how remarkable a woman Gudrid was ...
                              —*The Saga of Eirik the Red*

JOHN STEINBERG'S ARCHAEOLOGICAL CREW DESCENDED
on the Glaumbaer hayfield in early July 2005 and spent most
of a week trying to make the new *tækni*—ground-penetrating
radar—work.

The gadget, when it had arrived, looked like a baby-jogger.
A sealed plastic box, 18 inches square and fluorescent orange,
protected the electronics, which send pulses of microwaves into
the ground and pick up their echoes. The box was fixed between two bicycle wheels. A sturdy frame provided a handle and
supported the data recorder, its computer screen shielded from
the sun (or more likely, here, the rain) by a blue canopy. Dean
Goodman, a California-based computer scientist who had written GPR-Slice, the best software to interpret ground-penetrating
radar data, had come to Iceland to show off its capabilities. His
was the movie of Emperor Trajan's eel pond. He had mapped
tombs and castles in Japan, and Native American ruins from
Louisiana to Martha's Vineyard. He looked jaunty in a Greek

fisherman's cap, pushing the gizmo up and down the hayfield as if he were mowing the lawn. Problem was, haymaking hadn't started yet in northern Iceland. The GPR jogger could hardly roll through the knee-high grass. John duct-taped a two-by-four to the front, and yoked himself up like an ox to assist. The grass was wet, and in short order he and Dean looked as though they had waded a stream.

Worse, the data was lousy. The wheels made too much noise, each bump across the lumpy ground registering as an electronic burp. So they shucked the wheels, set the orange box into a white plastic tub, duct-taped on the two-by-four, and let John play ox while Brian Damiata walked behind, working the data recorder. Until the data recorder was in his hands Brian—who is as quietly critical as John is exuberant—had been invisible. Suddenly he was in control. Although Dean objected that doing things Brian's way would mean tons more work for only a tiny improvement in data quality, Brian could not be dissuaded. He was here to get good data, and he would get it if he had to walk this field day and night. And since darkness never really falls in high summer in Iceland, he could—and did.

Over the next two weeks, Brian and John made several dis-coveries—each at the cost of a five- to ten-mile hike back and forth across a hayfield. For instance, water off the tall grass, pool-ing in the white tub, caused the microwaves to "float," scatter-ing sideways instead of penetrating the ground. John discarded the tub and gave the orange box a more aerodynamic profile by duct-taping on two rounded "fenders" he had carved from a green plastic watering can with his utility knife. Even with-out the wheels, the box bumped and bounced too much. John duct-taped a soccer-ball–sized rock to its top to add weight. The antenna wasn't shielded. If Brian's knee hit the cable that teth-ered him to the orange box, as he walked behind John carrying the data recorder, the microwave receiver saw it as data. When the battery was changed the data recorder was prone to reprogramming itself to its standard settings—which were completely wrong for Iceland's wet soils. To enter the data manually, Brian had to click "Enter" at every meter mark. But the buttons on the recorder were close together, and instead of "Enter," his finger might hit "Stop." Then they had to start the line over.

And how do you walk in a straight line for a hundred meters, the length of a football field? First we marked opposite sides of the field with colored plastic survey flags spaced a meter apart. Then we advanced a hundred-meter measuring tape from flag to flag, meter by meter across the field, as a guideline. On calm days, after the hay was cut, two of us—one on each end of the tape—could handle it and have ample time to count the horses grazing along the river or the round bales accumulating in the neighbors' hayfields, to admire the dramatic sky over the glacier-carved mountains, or to watch a pair of swans drive two interlopers away from their nest by the brook. On the day the wind hit gale force, it took six of us, staggered along the guideline, to pull the tape out taut and keep it more-or-less straight, holding it down with our toes.

By the end of the first week, John decided the crew needed an excursion. After supper we would go to Grettir's Bath, a hot spring beside the ocean a half-hour's drive north, walled up for bathing since saga times. The name honored Grettir the Strong, a saga character renowned for his superhuman strength and his fear of the dark, a killer and a troublemaker who lived as an outlaw for nearly twenty years, hunted from place to place until he came to Drangey, a grass-topped rock in the middle of the inlet that gave the valley of Skagafjord ("Bay of the Headlands") its name. Tall, lone, and visible for hundreds of miles, this island had been a crucial resource for the local farmers in

Viking days. They trapped seabirds and gathered eggs on its sheer cliffs, and hoisted sheep to its top to graze the rich grass there. When Grettir hauled up the rope ladder and declared the island his own, he was in essence raiding their pantry. All the farmers along the fjord could see the smoke of his cooking fire and know Grettir was feasting on *their* meat.

The story of Grettir's Bath begins on a night when the outlaw's fire went out. Grettir, who was built like a bull seal, determined to swim to the mainland to fetch live coals. The distance is four miles. The temperature of the sea is a few degrees above freezing. (Lately it's become fashionable for extreme swimmers, in wet suits and Vaseline, to try to match Grettir's feat; Sirri at Glaumbaer has lost track of how many have tried it, but she assured me that none had drowned.)

John Steinberg, who wanted his crew to get the full Icelandic experience from their visit to the hot spring, opened a translation of *Grettir's Saga* and began reading:

> He swam strongly, and made Reykjanes by sunset. He walked up to the farm at Reykir and took a bath, for he was feeling very cold. He basked in the warm pool for a good part of the night, and then he went into the hall. It was very hot there, for a fire had been burning earlier, and the room had not cooled off. Grettir was exhausted and fell fast asleep; he lay there until the following day.
>
> Late in the morning the household got up, and the first people to go into the room were two women, a maidservant and the farmer's daughter. Grettir was asleep, and his cover had rolled off down to the floor. The women saw and recognized who he was. The maidservant said, "What do you know, dear, here is Grettir Asmundarson, and lying there stark naked. He is certainly big enough in the

chest, but it seems to me very odd how small he is farther down. That part of him isn't up to the rest of him."

The farmer's daughter said, "Why do you keep running off at the mouth like that, you silly little fool? Keep quiet!"

"I can't keep quiet about this, dear," said the maid, "since I never would have believed it, even if someone had told me."

She kept going over and peeping at him, and then running back to the farmer's daughter and bursting out laughing. Grettir heard what she was saying, and when she ran across the room again he seized her. . . .

The saga proceeds with a pair of dirty poems that Grettir composed on the spur of the moment—puns on swords being prominent—and a cheerful rape scene that had the male scientists howling with laughter while the women snickered and looked at each other askance. When things quieted down, someone asked, Was this scene typical of the sagas?

Love scenes there are in plenty—enough that historian Jenny Jochens needed a dozen pages of her book, *Women in Old Norse Society,* to explain how a woman became pregnant. First the man "placed her on his lap . . . and talked with her so all could see it," talk that was visible as kisses and caresses. Then he might stretch out with his head in her lap and let her pick lice out of his hair. (Another sure sign of love is a woman offering to sew a man's wide shirtsleeves tight around his wrists, a daily task before buttons became common.) After a bit he might take her by the hand and lead her to a more private spot; an illegitimate baby was variously called a "forest child," a "corner child," and a "cowbarn child." There, says Jochens, the Vikings assumed the missionary position, the man "romping on" the woman's belly.

For married couples such scenes take place in the crowded *skáli*, the main room of the longhouse, where the whole household slept on the wide benches that lined the walls on either side of the longfire and could listen in while spouses who were at odds "settled the matter between them as though nothing has happened." High-class couples like Gudrid and Karlsefni might have plank walls and a door separating their sleeping space from that of their farmhands and family, but for most couples, the only privacy in a longhouse was provided by the dark.

What is striking about the love scenes in the sagas is how often sex is proposed by the woman—and not exclusively to her husband. Grettir's rape scene—the only one I can remember in the forty major sagas—is so out of the norm that a later poem lampoons him by claiming, in some four hundred lines, that he had sex not only with girls, widows, and "everyone's wives," but with farmers' sons, deacons, courtiers, abbots, abbesses, cows, and calves. In fact, the "maiden in distress" is notably missing in the Icelandic sagas. Instead we meet, as scholar Carol Clover of the University of California, Berkeley, puts it, "women who prosecute their lives in general, and their sex lives in particular, with a kind of aggressive authority unexpected in a woman and unparalleled in any other European literature."

Four or five years before Gudrid was born, says one saga, there lived on the north side of Snow Mountain's Glacier two middle-aged widows who were competing for the favors of the same young man. This fellow, Gunnlaug, had "a lust for learning." From his father's farm under the glacier, he would ride to visit Geirrid at Mavahlid, the seaside estate she shared with her grown son and his wife. Halfway, he would stop at the hut of the second widow, Katla, to pick up his friend, her son Odd. On the way home, Katla always invited Gunnlaug to stay the night, but he always declined.

"So," said Katla one day, "you're off to Mavahlid again to pat the old hag on the belly."

Gunnlaug laughed. "Are you so young that you can make fun of Geirrid's age?"

"That may be so, but she's not the only woman around here who knows a thing or two."

That night, as Gunnlaug was getting ready to leave Mavahlid, Geirrid said, "There are too many sea spirits on the loose tonight, and you have an unlucky look about you. You should stay the night with me."

Gunnlaug said no thanks, and he and Odd rode off.

Katla had already gone to bed when they reached her hut. "Ask Gunnlaug to stay tonight," she said, as her son Odd came inside.

"He insists on going home, Mother," said Odd.

"Then let him get what's coming to him."

Late that night, Gunnlaug's father found him lying outside the family house, unconscious. He was scratched all over, the flesh ripped to the bone. People said he had been "witch-ridden."

In the same saga, we meet Gunnlaug's stepmother, Thurid, who was just as lusty as the two old witches. Gunnlaug disappears from the story after this night (although we're told his wounds did heal), and his father was killed quarreling with the people of Mavahlid, leaving behind a very young widow. Thurid quickly got married again, at the insistence of her brother Snorri, the chieftain of Helgafell. But her fat merchant husband soon had complaints. A young buck named Bjorn, who lived on the south side of the glacier, had begun coming by unusually often, and "people said he and Thurid were fooling around." Anyone who has read Jenny Jochens's description of sex in the Viking Age would agree. Thurid and Bjorn sat close together and "talked," while Thurid's husband made it a practice to interrupt his farmwork frequently to come inside and check on them.

Once, though, he left them alone all day.

"Take care on your way home, Bjorn," Thurid warned. "I think my husband means to put a stop to your visits. He's probably lying in wait for you on the path, and I don't think he intends to fight fair."

Bjorn was indeed ambushed on his way through the mountains. Outnumbered five to one, he managed to kill two of his attackers, and the others fled. He limped home, badly wounded, and his father patched him up. At the next assembly, Bjorn was banished from Iceland for three years for killing the two men. He joined the most famous band of Vikings, the Jomsvikings, and made a name for himself plundering the rim of the Baltic Sea.

Meanwhile, Thurid gave birth to a son.

When Bjorn returned from his Viking voyage, he saw mother and son at a fair and remarked to a friend of his, "The boy looks exactly like me. Too bad he doesn't know who his father is."

"Stay away from her," said his friend. "It's too dangerous."

"I know it is. But my heart says otherwise."

Thurid apparently agreed, for she and Bjorn picked up where they'd left off. And although her husband didn't like it a bit, the saga says, he couldn't do much about it, since Bjorn had such a reputation now as a fighter.

Another woman who found herself married to the wrong man is Oddny Eykindill (her nickname means "Island-Candle," as in "Light of the Land"). Oddny's childhood sweetheart is also named Bjorn. He and Oddny were betrothed, but like most Icelandic boys in the Viking Age, Bjorn wanted to go off to Norway first to make a name for himself. She agreed to wait three years for him—four if he sent word.

At eighteen, Bjorn took Norway by storm. Another Icelander at the king's court, a thirty-three-year-old poet named Thord, became jealous. He buddied up to Bjorn, got him drunk, and heard all about Oddny Island-Candle. That summer Thord sailed home and rode to see Oddny. He delivered a message and a gold ring from Bjorn, then added—falsely—that Bjorn thought she should marry Thord if Bjorn didn't come home. The next year, word came that Bjorn was wounded in a duel; Thord put it about that Bjorn was dead. Oddny insisted on waiting the full four years, but Bjorn didn't come home. By the time he had recovered enough to travel, the last ship of the year had sailed. When he heard, later, that Oddny had married Thord, he decided not to go home at all.

Oddny and Thord had eight children and seemed to be happily married until one day Bjorn *did* come home. "Have you heard any news today, Thord?" Oddny said.

"No, but I'm supposing you have."

"Yes, I've heard something I'd call news. I've heard that a ship has come in, and the owner is Bjorn, who you said was dead."

"Well, you might call that news."

"It certainly is news!" said Oddny. "And now I know the kind of man I married. I thought you were a good man, but you are full of lies and deceit."

Thord invited Bjorn to spend the winter with them. "That will fix things up between us," he told Oddny.

"You're lying again if you think that."

The visit did not go well. Oddny and Bjorn spent as much time together as they could, talking and laughing, and, in Thord's opinion, "adding one insult to another." He flew into a rage and slapped Oddny, kissed and fondled her in front of Bjorn, refused to let her into his bed, snooped around trying to catch the lovers in the act, and generally made everyone miserable. Soon the two men stopped speaking to each other, except to trade insulting verses, into which Bjorn always managed to slip a mention of his love for Oddny.

"Quit making verses about me, you two," said Oddny. "None of this was my idea."

Bjorn left when the winter was up, but the feud went on for years and years, escalating from nasty verses to the killing of servants and followers. Finally Thord ambushed Bjorn in his horse pasture. Dying, Bjorn spotted Oddny's young son Kolli in the mob. "You shouldn't be fighting me," Bjorn said.

"Why should I show you mercy?" said Kolli.

"Ask your mother."

Girls like Thurid and Oddny Island-Candle were often married off at fourteen, presumably to keep them from choosing someone grossly unsuitable (such as a Romeo on the wrong side of a family feud). Yet, even so young, some had definite ideas of what they wanted in a man and took steps toward getting it. A girl named Thorgunna, for instance, thought she'd made a good catch when the young Leif Eiriksson, on his first voyage to Norway, was driven off course and forced to shelter from a storm in the Hebrides off Scotland. They fell in love, and she became pregnant. When the winds changed and Leif got ready to sail, Thorgunna said she wanted to go home with him to Greenland. But Leif had neither the pluck to elope ("there are so few of us," he said of his crew, anticipating a sea chase) or the maturity to make a formal offer to her noble father. He gave her presents instead: a gold ring, a wool cloak, and a belt of walrus ivory. Like many of the Gaelic women in the sagas, Thorgunna is a little uncanny. Fixing him with a cold stare, she warned, "You'll wonder later on if you've made the right choice."

"I'll take my chances," he said brightly, but Thorgunna had more to say: "Your child will be a boy. I'll send him to you in Greenland as soon as he can travel. And I expect you'll be as happy to see him come as I am to see you go."

Unfortunately, the saga never tells us if the boy came or not.

About the time these stories were being written down in Iceland, the most popular tales in France and Britain were those of King Arthur and his Knights of the Round Table. Chretien de Troyes wrote the romance *Lancelot, The Knight of the Cart* in the late 1100s. In it, the beautiful Queen Guenevere is kidnapped and Sir Lancelot must ride to her rescue. Once at the castle, he convinces the kidnapper to behave honorably by returning the queen unsullied to King Arthur, and they all have supper and go to bed. Then, Sir Lancelot sneaks into the queen's room and they have sex (not for the first time). They are found out, and the rest of the tale involves the tangle of lies and trials and duels needed to clear the queen's name. It remains for a later writer to suggest that Guenevere be burned at the stake for adultery.

Robert de Boron, writing in the early 1200s, however, has just such a scene in his three-part romance about the quest for the Holy Grail. A young and pious maiden abandons herself to despair after her father loses his fortune, and a demon corrupts her. When her subsequent pregnancy reveals itself, she is jailed for refusing to identify her lover, and is to be burned at the stake when her child reaches eighteen months (and presumably no longer needs a mother). Fortunately, that child is the precocious Merlin, who goes to court as his mother's lawyer and proves that the judge himself is illegitimate and therefore unfit to sit the bench. Case dismissed.

Characters akin to the two lusty Icelandic witches, Geirrid and Katla, might appear in the Arthurian romances, but the honorable saga women—like Thurid, Thorgunna of the Hebrides, and Oddny Island-Candle—are in a different class altogether from Queen Guenevere and Merlin's mother. For one thing, they couldn't care a whit if everyone knew who they were sleeping with, before or after marriage. For another, in all cases, it's the man and not the woman or her child who is punished for "fooling around." If she had lived in the Iceland of the sagas, Queen Guenevere could have enjoyed her love affair with Lancelot as openly as Thurid did hers with Bjorn, leaving it to her husband to challenge the hero to a fight if he didn't like it. Or she could have sued for divorce. One saga wife left her husband because he was impotent and didn't "satisfy" her. Another didn't give her reasons. She just walked out, dumping her husband's clothes in the urine barrel so he couldn't chase after her. Both women got back their dowries, which was a substantial sum, often the value of a farm.

Virginity and illegitimacy were also nonissues (as they remain in present-day Iceland). Olaf the Peacock, one of the richest and most powerful men in the sagas, was illegitimate, but no one would dare tell him he was unfit to be a judge because of it. In general, bastards were treated the same as the rest of a man's brood. When Njal's illegitimate son was killed one night, his mother rode to Njal's house and woke him up, shouting, "Get out of my rival's bed and bring that woman and her sons, too." She led them to where the boy lay dead. While the men were muttering about who might have done the deed, Njal's wife remarked, "You men are ridiculous. You run off and kill someone over next to nothing, yet when something happens that cries out for vengeance, you stand around talking it over." Duly chastened, her sons ride off to avenge the death of their half-brother.

In a romance like the King Arthur tales, a young woman is "occupied" throughout most of the plot with protecting her virginity, "her principal claim to an identity," saga scholar Robert Kellogg noted at a conference in Reykjavik in 1999. A young saga woman, by contrast, "is far more straightforward and grown up than this, with a sure sense of who she is that is quite independent of any subtleties of anatomy." Thorgunna of the Hebrides was in no danger of being burned at the stake, only of being burned in love.

Why do saga women have more sexual freedom than their counterparts in Arthurian romance? Scholars muse that women were more highly prized in Viking Iceland because they were rare. If Iceland was settled by Viking bands disgruntled with the king of Norway, there might not have been enough young women to go around. Yet a wife was essential to running a farm. There were certain things no self-respecting Viking man would do, such as weaving or sewing. No man would milk a ewe or make cheese. No Viking would cook, unless aboard ship, and even then it was considered demeaning. Without a woman (wife, mother, sister, or daughter), a man could not be king of his own hill. The wife taught the children their duties and obligations, which required an exact knowledge of family ties and degrees of kinship—this is what the dying Bjorn suggested young Kolli ask his mother about. (Kolli immediately put down his sword and walked away. There is no shame worse than being a father-killer.) The wife, in many sagas, determined when blood-money would be accepted for a man's death, and when the killing demanded revenge instead. She hired and fired servants and was in charge of the food—preserving it, preparing it, and sharing it out. In those years when winter lingered and supplies dwindled, the wife decided who starved. The wife made the farm's only marketable product—cloth—and she may also have done the selling, which, in a land with no towns, meant bargaining one-on-one with the captain or crew of a trading ship from Norway. In the grave of a wealthy wife in Kornsa, Iceland, dated to Viking times, was found a set of copper scales to weigh money, alongside the more usual womanly goods: kettle, shears, and cooking spit of iron; a comb; some brooches and beads; tweezers, a knife, and a bronze bell; her dog and her horse.

In Iceland, as elsewhere in the Middle Ages, love was not a prerequisite for marriage. Marriage was a social arrangement, a merger of two families, a matter of economics. Most marriages were arranged, and the girl had little or no say in it. Yet most marriages turned out like Oddny Island-Candle's: She was content; she had eight children and a fine, rich farm. "People thought things had turned out even better for her than if she'd married Bjorn," the saga says. Then Bjorn came home, and she learned that she had been deceived. The moral of the story, for this and many other sagas, is that a marriage founded on trickery or coercion can lead to chaos, and whole families—a whole society—can come crashing down because of one unhappy wife.

This pattern is most clearly seen in *Njal's Saga,* the one saga almost everyone in Iceland knows, it having been required reading in grammar school for generations. It was popular in the Middle Ages, too: There are more manuscript copies of *Njal's Saga* in existence than of any of the other sagas. From a historian's point of view, it is the best. Unfortunately, *Njal's Saga* is also the most misogynistic of the major sagas. Whereas the sexy aggressiveness of other saga women is simply magnificent, that of Hallgerd Long-Legs, the central female figure in *Njal's Saga,* has an evil sheen to it. She is petty. She is also hungry, literally and metaphorically. She is a woman of power who doesn't quite know what to do with herself.

As a girl she was outraged at being married without her consent. As a young wife, she was wasteful and extravagant. Once she went so far as to call her husband stingy. He slapped her face—and was killed for it by her foster-father, whom Hallgerd then sent to hide out with a wizard known for brewing up wild storms. Her beloved second husband was also killed for slapping her, but this time she avenged him, sending her foster-father to his own death.

Following those two marriages, Hallgerd lived as a widow for fourteen years, running her own farm and raising her daughter. Then she met Gunnar of Hlidarendi. Gunnar was the best catch in Iceland—handsome, tall, accomplished, rich. He asked for her hand. Her uncle tried to talk him out of it. "It's not an even match," he said. "You're a fine, capable man, but she's rather a mixed bag, to be honest."

When Gunnar defended Hallgerd, her uncle said, "I can see you're madly in love. You'll just have to face what comes."

Most people think *Njal's Saga* is about the close friendship between Gunnar, the man of action, and Njal, the wise negotiator. Or about the conversion of Iceland to Christianity and the changes it brought. Or about the conflict between law and justice in a land with no king. All of these themes are important. But there would be no saga, no tragedy, without Hallgerd's unhappiness. Gunnar treats her as a pretty toy: His mother wields the power, running the household while Hallgerd gossips and flirts with the farmhands (who prove their devotion by killing people for her). Every decision Hallgerd makes, her husband undercuts.

At an autumn feast, Hallgerd and Njal's wife, Bergthora, had a spat over who should sit in the seat of honor. Bergthora placed her young daughter-in-law there, instead of Hallgerd. "What do you take me for, a *hornkerling*?" said Hallgerd, meaning an old hag shoved off into a corner. Stung, she insulted Bergthora by making fun of Njal's lack of a beard.

Said Bergthora, referring to Hallgerd's first marriage, "Your own husband had a beard, I'm told, when you had him killed."

Hallgerd roared for revenge, and Gunnar jumped up from the table. "You're not making a fool out of me," he told his wife. "I'm going home."

Hallgerd soon had one of Bergthora's slaves killed. Bergthora retaliated. When Gunnar told Hallgerd to stop antagonizing his friends, she answered, "Trolls take your friends." Njal and Gunnar settled the six killings with blood-money, but their friendship was strained. One tight year, Gunnar tried to buy food from another neighbor—not Njal—and was rebuffed. Hallgerd sent a man to steal some cheese and burn down the neighbor's storehouse. When the theft came to light, Gunnar slapped Hallgerd in the face.

"I'll remember that," she said.

The cheese feud led to Gunnar being outlawed from Iceland for three years. When his horse stumbled on the way to the ship, Gunnar leaped off and, looking back at his farm, spoke the most influential lines in all the Icelandic sagas—lines that awakened the independence movement in the nineteenth century and resulted in the country's break with Denmark: "Fair are the hillsides, so fair as I have never seen them before, the pale meadows and just-mown hayfields. I am going home and I will never leave again."

Gunnar's enemies surrounded his house. He held them off until his bowstring broke. "Give me two locks of your hair, Hallgerd, and make me a bowstring."

"Have you forgotten that time you slapped me?"

"Everyone has his own claim to fame. I won't ask again."

The saga is only half over when Gunnar dies. Hallgerd is seen once more, trading insults with Njal's sons. The Njalssons are eventually trapped by their enemies in their burning house. Given permission to flee the flames, Njal chose to die with his sons, and Bergthora to stand by her man.

If *The Saga of Eirik the Red* took up three hundred pages in a modern paperback translation, as does *Njal's Saga*, instead of only thirty, we might have an image of Gudrid the Far-Traveler to match that of Hallgerd Long-Legs. Instead we can only see Gudrid mirrored in other saga women. For instance, like Hallgerd, Gudrid is described as a *skörungur,* a word translators have serious trouble with—although the saga-writer clearly thinks it's a compliment. In modern Icelandic, the word means a fireplace poker. Concentrating on what a fireplace poker does, William Morris in the 1890s came up with "a very stirring woman." And Hallgerd *does* stir things up, mostly trouble. Yet a man labeled a *skörungur* Morris called "a shaper" or "a leader." Other early translators turned a female "poker" into "brave-hearted," "high-spirited," "noble," "of high mettle," "fine," "superior," "of great magnificence," and "a paragon of a woman." They might have done better to think what a poker looks like. For *skörungur* does, in the end, have to do with manhood. The root *skör* means an edge, like the edge of a sword.

Examine, for instance, a more likable *skörungur:* Gudrun the Fair, heroine of *Laxdaela Saga*. Many of the male characters from *Njal's Saga*—such as Hallgerd's father and uncle—appear in *Laxdaela Saga*, recognizably themselves. Yet the female characters in this second saga are so strong and admirable that some readers suspect the story was written by a woman in response to *Njal's Saga*. We read of Unn the Deep-Minded, who emigrated from Scotland with all her kin, claimed a chunk of land "as big as a man's," parceled it out to her followers, and lived out her life as a chieftain in all but name, marrying off her grandchildren to make alliances. There is Melkorka, sold as a slave to Hallgerd Long-Legs's father, Hoskuld: Melkorka pretended to be a deaf-mute, revealing nothing. Not until she was caught speaking Irish to her son, Olaf the Peacock, did she admit she was the daughter of an Irish king. After her status as a princess came out, Hoskuld bought her a farm and set her up as an independent woman. Olaf married well and had five sons and three daughters. He offered to raise his half-brother's son, Bolli, to mend fences in the family, and with that we come to the crux of the saga.

Bolli was handsome and talented—second only to Olaf's own son, Kjartan. The two boys were best friends. Both fell in love with Gudrun the Fair, who had already been widowed twice when she met them. Gudrun loved Kjartan. Like every Icelandic boy his age, he decided to go to Norway to make a name for himself, and asked her to wait the usual three years for him. She suggested he take her abroad instead. He refused. She refused to promise to wait. Three years passed, and he didn't come home. But Bolli did, full of tales of the impression Kjartan had made on the king's beautiful sister.

Bolli was not "full of lies and deceit," like the man who tricked Oddny Island-Candle; his crime was more on the order of wishful thinking. Still, while Kjartan was "talking" with the king of Norway's sister, Bolli wooed and wed Gudrun. Then Kjartan returned home. His sister counseled him to "do the right thing" and make peace with his friend and cousin Bolli. She introduced Kjartan to a fine woman of good family, and Kjartan was soon happily married.

Gudrun became insanely jealous. Sometimes she thought Bolli had tricked her into marrying him. Other times she believed Kjartan had spurned her and, when he had come home and made light of her marriage, had insulted her. And indeed, he did insult her after a golden headdress he had given his wife (a gift from the princess intended for Gudrun) was stolen. Kjartan gathered his men and surrounded Gudrun's house, forcing everyone to go to the bathroom inside for several days with no indoor privy. Gudrun arranged his death and then deeply regretted it. As she told her son many years later, "I was worst to the one I loved best." This is where she surpasses Hallgerd and becomes a heroine.

But for none of these deeds is Gudrun called a *skörungur*. That comes on the occasion of her fourth marriage. At the urging of her staunch supporter, the chieftain Snorri of Helgafell, and with the agreement of her young sons, Gudrun betrothed herself to Thorkel Eyjolfsson, a wealthy trader and friend of the king of Norway. Gudrun had extensive landholdings and the backing of many men who had been loyal to her recently deceased father. Since her brothers were all exiled after killing Kjartan, Gudrun's husband would wield the influence of a chieftain.

As a mark of her power in the relationship, Gudrun insisted on holding the wedding at her own farm, bearing the cost herself. Among the 160 wedding guests, however, her bridegroom Thorkel recognized a man who had killed one of his friends. Thorkel grabbed the criminal and was about to put him to death when Gudrun stood up from her place at the women's table, brushed her fancy linen headdress out of her eyes, and called to her men, "Rescue my friend Gunnar and let nothing stand in your way!"

As the saga so nicely understates it, "Gudrun had a much bigger force. Things turned out differently than expected."

Before anyone could draw a sword, Snorri of Helgafell

turned to Thorkel and laughed. "Now you can see what a *skörun-gur* Gudrun is, when she gets the better of both of us."

What quality is Chieftain Snorri admiring? Transla-tors from 1960 to 2002 have called Gudrun and her saga sis-ters "exceptional," "outstanding," "remarkable," "determined," "forceful," "capable," "brave," "of strong character," "one to be reckoned with," and a woman "with a will very much her own." These are better than the nineteenth century's "high-mettled" and "very stirring," but they're still not quite right.

Jenny Jochens turns *skörungur* into "manly," and the best equivalent is indeed *man.* Imagine if the situation were reversed. Gudrun spotted the killer of her friend on Thorkel's side of the hall. Thorkel had the bigger fighting force. Chieftain Snorri, eager to make peace and see the wedding proceed (and it does), stepped in, laughed, and said to Gudrun, *Now you can see what a man you're marrying, when he gets the better of both of us.*

A Viking's character was not either male or female, but lay on a spectrum ranging from strong to weak, aggressive to passive, powerful to powerless, winner to loser or, in the Old Norse terms, *hvatur* to *blauður. Hvatur,* always a compliment, means "bold, active, vigorous." It appears to be related to the verb *hvetja,* a cognomen for our verb "to whet"—to sharpen (a sword), to put a good, sharp *skör* (or edge) on it. Its opposite, *blauður,* always an insult, means "soft, weak." It is, says the stan-dard dictionary, "no doubt a variant of *blautur,*" which means "moist." Hard, sharp, and vigorous versus soft, yielding, and moist. Think dirty and you've got it.

When Hallgerd Long-Legs called Njal "Old Beardless," she was not saying he was funny-looking: She was saying he was *blauður*—weak, womanish, effeminate, cowardly, powerless, and craven. A loser.

And when Chieftain Snorri praised Gudrun the Fair as a *skörungur,* and a better one than both himself and Thorkel Eyjolfsson, he was locating her far out on the male end of the power spectrum. He was calling her a winner.

"This is a world," says Carol Clover, "in which 'masculinity' always has a plus value, even (or perhaps especially) when it is enacted by a woman." There was only one standard, only one way to judge a person adequate or inadequate. "The frantic machismo" of the men in the Icelandic sagas, Clover concludes, suggests "a society in which being born male precisely did *not* confer automatic superiority, a society in which distinction had to be acquired, and constantly reacquired, by wresting it away from others."

The women who are mentioned in the sagas, the ones who are admired as *skörungur,* are the ones who have acquired that distinction. And Gudrid the Far-Traveler is one of them.

One of the delights in reading the sagas comes from untangling the connections among them. Gudrid the Far-Traveler would have known Gudrun the Fair—they were born about five years apart, and Gudrid's cousin Yngvild was married to a son of Chieftain Snorri of Helgafell, Gudrun the Fair's adviser.

At about the time of Gudrid's birth on the south side of Snow Mountain's Glacier, Thurid was "talking" with Bjorn (to the dismay of her fat merchant husband) on the north side. Next door, the two witches were competing for the same young man. In the south of Iceland, Hallgerd Long-Legs had just refused Gunnar two locks of her hair to twist into a bowstring, consigning him to his death. Eirik the Red had been outlawed for killing a neighbor (although Gudrid's father and Chieftain Snorri's foster-brothers had tried to negotiate a settlement for him), and had set off to find Greenland. And the parents of Grettir the Strong had just wed.

Gudrid's adventures—moving to Greenland, marrying twice, exploring the New World, and settling down to raise her sons at Glaumbaer in northern Iceland—took ten or twelve years, from the year 1000 to about 1012. Just before Gudrid arrived in Greenland, Leif Eiriksson was in the Hebrides, acting like a cad with pregnant Thorgunna. While Gudrid was in Vinland, Grettir the Strong was outlawed for the first time. The year Gudrid settled at Glaumbaer, Njal and Bergthora and all their sons were burned to death in their house.

The sagas are silent about Gudrid's years at Glaumbaer. We don't know when her husband Karlsefni died, only that Snorri, their son born in Vinland, was still young. But during the last few years of Snorri's minority, Grettir the Strong found a haven in a cave on the lands of Bjorn, lover of Oddny Island-Candle. (Bjorn encouraged him to eat Oddny's husband's sheep.) And Gudrun the Fair married for the fourth time, proving herself a *skörungur* at her wedding.

What had Gudrid done to earn that title? The harrowing voyage to Greenland proved her spirit, and both Vinland sagas illustrate she had a mind of her own. The séance in *The Saga of Eirik the Red* is one example. Gudrid's father denounced it as pagan nonsense, we're told, and refused to stay in the house while the ritual was going on. Fifteen-year-old Gudrid did not leave with him. When she alone of the women in the house was found to know the ritual songs, learned as nursery rhymes from her foster-mother, she had second thoughts about playing so prominent a role. She was Christian, and it would be against her religion to sing them in this context. The wise woman in charge gave her another way of looking at her dilemma: It would be un-Christian of her to refuse. She said, "You could be some help to the people here. You'd be no worse a woman for that." Gudrid thought about it and made up her mind, without consulting her father.

She is similarly strong-minded following the death of her husband Thorstein, Eirik the Red's son, when, after a winter alone with an older, unmarried man, she emerged with her independence intact. For she was a good catch when Karlsefni came to Greenland the next autumn. The wealthy Icelandic trader was taken with her immediately and married her, with her consent, at Christmas. There's no hint that Karlsefni had an eye for exploration before he met Gudrid, but he fell for her and let her talk him into sailing west. And it is Karlsefni's mother—who initially thought her son had not married well—who finally labels Gudrid a *skörungur,* a very stirring woman: bravehearted, high-spirited, remarkable, capable, bold, a winner, a survivor.

CHAPTER 4

The Terror from the North

One evening as Grettir was getting ready to go home, he saw fire blaze up from the end of the ness below Audun's farm. Grettir asked what it could be. . . .

"There's a barrow there," said Audun, "where Kar the Old was buried. . . ."

"You were right to tell me," said Grettir. "I'll come in the morning, so have some tools ready. . . ."

Grettir broke open the mound, though it took a great deal of effort. He did not let up until he struck wood. By then it was well on toward evening. He broke through the wood. Audun tried to stop him from going into the barrow. Grettir told him to hold the rope. . . .

Grettir went into the mound. It was dark and the air was foul. He poked around to see how things were arranged. He found some horse bones, and then he bumped into a chair on which a man was seated. Gold and silver lay piled up there, and a chest full of silver was under the man's feet. Grettir took the treasure and carried it to the rope. But before he could climb out of the barrow, he was seized fast. He dropped the treasure, and they grappled and wrestled with no holds barred . . . but finally the barrow-wight fell backward with a great crash. Audun let go of the rope and ran away, certain that Grettir was dead. Grettir now took his sword *Jökulsnaut* and cut off the barrow-wight's head. He set it by his buttocks. Then Grettir went to the rope with the treasure and . . . climbed up hand over hand. He had tied the treasure to the rope, and drew it up after him.

—*Grettir's Saga*

IN 1995 I WAS ON THE ISLE OF LEWIS IN THE OUTER Hebrides of Scotland, visiting an area that tradition links to Olaf the White, the Viking king of Dublin, whose failings as a war leader and a family man would shape Gudrid's life. The windswept *machair*, a sandy, grassy mix of peat lands and sheep pasture, gave way on the west side of the island to buttressed cliffs and arcs of yellow beach. Small islands made a sheltered harbor big enough for a Viking fleet. A shallow river wound for a mile through tidal flats before reaching a gap between two headlands. The place was called Uig, from the Norse word for bay, *vík*, from which comes our word *Viking*.

The Lewis chessmen, a cache of ninety-three late–Viking Age chess pieces exquisitely carved out of walrus ivory, had been found here in 1831 when a cow fell into a hole. A grave had eroded out of a sand dune nearby in 1979, providing a pair of spectacular gilded-bronze "tortoise" brooches—examples of the massive oval ornaments that Viking women used every day, like buckles or safety pins, to clasp the shoulder straps of their gowns. Six more Viking graves, adults and children, were found near Uig in the early 1990s.

One day, as I was walking back to my lodging across the sands beside the turquoise-colored tidal lagoon, I spotted two oddly shaped hills on a headland. I asked my host if anyone had excavated them. "A postdoc from Glasgow poked into one last summer. She found the prow of a ship." He added immediately, "It's just a modern wreck covered with sand." I wished I were more like Grettir the Strong: I would have asked to borrow a shovel and a rope.

For to understand Gudrid's desire to go to Vinland—why sailing west off the edge of the known world seemed to her a reasonable thing to do—we need to know first how and why her ancestors left their own homes in the late 800s and created a new society in Iceland. Some of the answers were here, on the Hebrides and across the rough waters of the Minch on mainland Scotland. According to the sagas, Unn the Deep-Minded—a Norse chieftain's daughter, and the discarded second wife of Olaf the White, king of Dublin—set sail for Iceland from one of these coves. Gudrid would have known the story of Unn the Deep-Minded as thoroughly as her own genealogy, for in Unn's ship, fleeing from Scotland, was a Gaelic boy, Vifil, who was Gudrid's grandfather. All her life, she would have kept Unn in mind as an example, a paragon of women.

To the Vikings, the Hebrides were the *Hafborðey,* the "Islands on the Edge of the Sea," or they were the Southern Isles, being south of Shetland and the Orkneys on the direct sea route from Norway to Ireland. That voyage took about a month, with an island rest-stop each evening. Well before 841, when the Norse established a trading post at Dublin, the route had become routine, and the havens along the way were in friendly hands, known by Norse names. No one knows if the first Norse settlers married into native families, or found no one there, or drove them out: The Viking homesites that have been excavated in this part of the world show signs of all three approaches. In Orkney, archaeologists found a Viking building that had been erected on top of an earlier Gaelic house, but the artifacts inside—particularly a distinctive style of bone dress pin—remained Gaelic. In Caithness, on the Scottish mainland, there is no sign of any settlement for a century before the Vikings came. But in Uist, everything Gaelic was destroyed when the Norse arrived—evidence, said the archaeologists, "as conclusively in favor of conquest as we are ever likely to get."

Anthropologist Agnar Helgason, on the other hand, finds "conquest" more likely closer to Norway—in Orkney—than as far south as Uist. Agnar, whom I met at DeCode Genetics in Reykjavik, compared the genes of modern people living in Scandinavia and the British Isles with those from the Shetlands, Orkneys, Hebrides, and Iceland. He found DNA markers, harmless mutations, that labeled a person "Norse" or "Gaelic." Tracking these markers in the mitochondrial DNA (passed down from mother to daughter) and in the Y chromosome (father to son), he could tell from which side, sword or distaff, the mutations had come. Men and women in the Orkney Islands, he found, are 30 percent Norse. In the Hebrides, the men are 22 percent Norse, but the women are only 11 percent Norse. The Orkney Islands, Agnar concludes, were settled by Viking families. In the Southern Isles, Viking men at loose ends took Gaelic mates.

Whether or not the women were willing, the genes cannot say, but once the Vikings were in the islands, we can assume they acted as they had in Norway. They were loyal to their king and considered anything in another kingdom fair game. Given that the coast of Norway alone had seven or eight "kingdoms" in the 700s, that made for some fairly loose rules. *Strandhögg*—literally "beach strike"—was a common practice: A party of Norsemen would row over to the next fjord, run their lapstrake boats up onto the beach, round up the cattle, slaughter them, load the boat, and row home. As historian Gwyn Jones puts it in his classic *History of the Vikings*, "Robbing your richer neighbors was a simple way of redressing the injustices of nature."

Sometimes these raids had aims other than cattle. Jones tells the story of Gudrod the Hunting King, who took a fancy to Asa, the daughter of another king in Norway. When his suit was refused, Gudrod gathered his men, descended on the kingdom, killed Asa's father and brother, and "carried her off with much booty." He then made her his queen. When their son was a year old, Queen Asa took her revenge: She furnished a servant boy with a weapon. "King Gudrod perished of a spear-thrust one dark evening," writes Jones, "gross and full of beer." The queen was not punished. Her son ruled both kingdoms in his time, and *his* son, Harald Fine-Hair, unified all of Norway's many kingdoms into one—his—and curtailed the local practice of *strandhögg*.

Conveniently, Norse shipwrights had by then solved the puzzle of how to make their light and efficient rowing boats carry a sail. With a wider beam, a deeper keel, and more draft, these first true Viking ships were carrying parties of Norsemen to *strandhögg* on farther shores. In Queen Asa's day, they made their infamous raids on the monasteries of Lindisfarne in northeastern England and the Holy Island of Iona, off the west coast of Scotland. They sacked churches in Wales, Ireland, and the Isle of Man. In 789 they were at Portland on the south coast of England. The *Anglo-Saxon Chronicle* for 792 says that "seagoing pagans with roaming ships" were harassing Kent, by the Straits of Dover. Vikings were plundering towns in France, Germany, and along the shores of the Baltic Sea in the early 800s, especially after the death of Charlemagne in 814, which left a power vacuum. By midcentury they had sacked Paris, Rouen, and Hamburg. They sailed south to Islamic Spain and sacked Seville (unwisely), then did the same to the Mediterranean port of Luna, which they mistook for Rome. They established bases in Russia along the routes to Constantinople (which they also attacked) and Baghdad.

They fought just as much among themselves. Vikings from Norway raided the shores of Denmark, and vice versa, while in the 850s, the "Black" Vikings drove the "White" Vikings out of Ireland (only to be evicted by that Olaf the White, king of Dublin, who married Unn the Deep-Minded).

That we can distinguish the Norwegians from the Danes from the Swedes (in order to say who gets credit for founding Dublin or Kiev or Normandy) in all this sacking is a fallacy, given the medieval penchant for using the names interchangeably. Adam of Bremen, writing in 1070, for instance, states helpfully: "The Danes and the Swedes, whom we call Norsemen . . ." That the monks throughout the Western world were chanting *a furore Normannorum, libera nos Domine* ("From the fury of the Norsemen, deliver us, O Lord!") is equally a myth. The closest thing any manuscript expert has found—and they've looked most diligently—is *ab incursione alienigenarum, libera nos Domine* ("From the invasion of foreigners, deliver us, O Lord!")

Even the famous entry in the *Anglo-Saxon Chronicle* about the destruction of Lindisfarne in 793 never names names. It reads:

> In this year terrible portents appeared over Northumbria and sadly affrighted the inhabitants: these were exceptional flashes of lightning, and fiery dragons were seen flying in the air. A great famine followed soon upon these signs, and a little after that in the same year on the ides of June the harrying of the heathen miserably destroyed God's church in Lindisfarne by rapine and slaughter.

That this entry, and the *Anglo-Saxon Chronicle* itself, is universally classified as "history" and therefore more true—in spite of its fiery dragons—than such "literary sources" as the Icelandic sagas is a debate I won't get into here. But the Vikings' reputation in the modern mind as paragons of brutality does need some qualifying. They may have been the Terror from the North, but there were many terrors in those days, both heathen and Christian, foreign and native. The Hungarian invaders of Germany, Adam of Bremen writes, "were burning churches, butchering priests before the altars, and with impunity were slaying clerics and laymen indiscriminately or leading them into captivity." The Irish Annals record at least thirty attacks on churches before the first Viking sailed "west over sea" from Norway; in 807 a fight between the monks of Cloufert and those of Cork ended in "an innumerable slaughter of the ecclesiastical men and superiors of Cork." In 878, Pope John VIII excommunicated Count Bernard II of Toulouse for ravaging church property.

Nor were the Vikings unbeatable war machines. Caught off guard, they suffered from the same brutal treatment as did their victims. That unwise sacking of Seville? When the Muslims retook the city, they hanged all their prisoners, two hundred Norsemen, from palm trees. When the Vikings harried the coastline by Constantinople, the emperor sent Greek fireships to meet them. As Luidprand of Cremona wrote in the mid-900s, "The Greeks began to fling their fire around, and the Rusi"—yet another medieval name for Vikings—

> seeing the flames threw themselves in haste from their ships, preferring to be drowned in the water than burned alive. Some sank to the bottom under the weight of their cuirasses and helmets . . . some caught fire even as they swam among the billows; not a man that day escaped save those who managed to reach the shore. . . . These were all beheaded.

In England, in 794, just a year after the raid on Lindisfarne, the Vikings had a stunning failure. They attacked the monastery of Tynemouth, but, says Simeon of Durham:

> St. Cuthbert did not allow them to depart unpunished; for their chief was there put to death by the cruel Angles, and a short time afterward a violent storm shattered, destroyed, and broke up their vessels, and the sea swallowed up very many of them; some, however, were cast ashore and speedily slain without mercy.

The English had no compunction about killing Norse women and children, either. In 1002, shortly after paying a Viking horde 24,000 pounds of silver in so-called Danegeld (essentially a bribe to go away), King Aethelred II issued an edict that every Dane in the country was to be rounded up and killed on St. Brice's Day (November 13). Historians have had some trouble believing that a civilized Christian king would define "Dane" to mean every man, woman, or child, craftsman or noble, merchant or homesteader, especially since by 1002 the Danes and all other Vikings were officially Christian. But in a royal charter issued a few years later, King Aethelred promises to pay for the rebuilding of the church in Oxford, England, which was burned by citizens pursuing Danes who "were to be destroyed by a most just extermination" and, "striving to escape death, entered this sanctuary of Christ."

Among the murdered, according to the much later history of William of Malmesbury, was Gunnhild, the sister of King Svein Forkbeard of Denmark, and her son, "a youth of amiable disposition," whom she watched die "transfixed with four spears." Though modern historians doubt William's account, it does seem as though Svein wanted revenge: He sent his army to ravage England during the next ten summers. In 1009 Oxford was leveled. By 1013 Svein was king of England. In 1018, when his son Knut the Great was proclaimed king of England and Denmark, the peace treaty was signed in Oxford. Knut ruled England until 1042, and there was only one other truly English king (Edward the Confessor) between him and the Norman Conquest in 1066. In the two battles that year that defined the future of England—at Stamford Bridge between Harald Hard-Rule of Norway and Harold Godwinsson of England, and at Hastings between Harold Godwinsson and William the Bastard (later known as William the Conqueror) of Normandy—both sides in each battle could claim Norse ancestry.

Still, the Norse legacy in the British Isles is mainly linguistic. Thousands of towns have Norse names like Derby, Kirby, Wadbister, Isbister, Winskill, Skaill, Laimiseadar, Lacsabhat, Heylipoll, and Kirkapoll, while from Norse the English language gained such words as egg, ugly, ill, smile, knife, fellow, husband, birth, death, cast, take, kettle, steak, leg, skin, lost, mistake, law, and brag. Not to mention ransack.

Why did Viking hordes suddenly descend on the Western world (and some of the Eastern) between 793 and 1066? The smart answer is because they could: They owned the best ships on the seas. But what was driving them? What inspired their technology?

Modern historians have not come up with any better explanations than did the medieval monks trying to see God's purpose in the burning of their churches. According to Adam of Bremen:

> On account of the roughness of its mountains and the immoderate cold, Norway is the most unproductive of all countries. . . . Poverty has forced them thus to go all

over the world and from piratical raids they bring home in
great abundance the riches of the lands. In this way they
bear up under the unfruitfulness of their own country.

He adds, charmingly, that "since accepting Christianity"—which
came to Norway in the late 900s—"they have already learned to
love the truth and peace and to be content with their poverty."
Dudo of Normandy, writing about fifty years before Adam, in
1020, thought the problem was population pressure caused by
lack of morals (as well as land). The Vikings, he says:

> . . . insolently abandon themselves to excessive indulgence,
> live in outrageous union with many women and there in
> shameless and unlawful intercourse breed innumerable
> progeny. Once they have grown up, the young quarrel
> violently with their fathers and grandfathers, or with each
> other, about property . . .

Those that are driven away fight in other lands for a place
"where they can live in continual peace," he concludes. The
Icelandic sagas also explain the Norse exodus as a response to
violent quarrels "about property," not within families, but between political factions. When Queen Asa's grandson, Harald
Fine-Hair, determined to become king of all Norway, he dis-
possessed a number of other kings and chieftains and noblemen. Some went to Denmark, some to Sweden and farther east.
Others became sea-kings, hoping to outlast Harald and retake
their old estates (without luck: Harald reigned a long time, from
about 870 to 930). Others went to the British Isles or took a
chance on the empty new island in the west: Iceland.

Ketil Flat-Nose, the father of Unn the Deep-Minded, was
one of those who sailed "west over sea," taking the sea route
through the Southern Islands toward Ireland. "He knew the

country well," one saga says, "for he had raided there extensively." It isn't clear when or why he quarreled with Olaf the White, king of Dublin, but Unn the Deep-Minded might have been the "peace cow" that brought these two Viking sea-kings to terms; her marriage to Olaf was certainly not a love match. A few years later, Olaf put her aside to marry the daughter of Kenneth mac Alpin, king of the Scots.

So it was not to Olaf that Unn turned when their son Thorstein the Red died in about the year 900, leaving her in charge of his six daughters and one son. According to the Icelandic *Book of Settlements,* which was written at the same time as the sagas but is considered to be more "historical":

> Thorstein became a warrior-king. He joined forces with Sigurd the Rich, son of Eystein the Chatterer, and they conquered Caithness and Sutherland, Ross and Moray— altogether more than half of Scotland. Thorstein became king of the Scots. But they betrayed him, and he died in battle. Unn was in Caithness when she learned of Thorstein's death. She had a ship built in secret, and when it was ready . . . Unn went in search of Iceland. She had in her ship twenty free-born men.

By this manly act, an elderly grandmother set in motion the events that make up many of the Icelandic sagas.

Thorfinn Karlsefni, Gudrid's husband, traces his lineage to Unn the Deep-Minded, as do Hallgerd Long-Legs, Olaf the Peacock, Chieftain Snorri of Helgafell, and three of Gudrun the Fair's lovers (Bolli, Kjartan, and Thorkel Eyjolfsson), along with many, many more saga characters. *The Book of the Icelanders,* the first history of Iceland, written in the early 1100s, calls Unn the Deep-Minded one of the four chief founders of Iceland.

Visiting the Hebrides, I could see at once why Unn had fled. The bleak, open landscape so close to enemy territory left nowhere to hide, nowhere for a cast-off Viking queen and her royal grandchildren to live in freedom from fear—the reason Karlsefni would give, a hundred years later, for leaving Vinland. Walking that landscape, I understood, too, why Iceland would have felt so homey to Unn and her shipmates once they reached it. In both places, the sky is the element in which people live. The views are immense—or shut off by fog. The wind is constant. Life and death hang on the balance of frost and sun. But what I most wanted to know about Unn the Deep-Minded could not be found here, nor in the histories written by monks and so painstakingly dissected by modern historians. What I wanted to know was this: What did she take in her ship when she sailed to Iceland about the year 900? What did she wear? I had a possible answer only because someone had eyed an oddly shaped hill and imagined that something was buried in it. Like Grettir the Strong, he got a shovel and started digging.

The hill was in Norway, on the farm of Oseberg in the Oslo Fjord. Eighteen feet high and over 70 feet long, it was known as the "Foxes' Mound." In 1903 the owner of the property took a shovel to it. Unlike Grettir, he paused when he hit wood. The piece he pulled out was elaborately carved in a twisted, fluid, snakelike style. It occurred to the farmer that he might have something more significant here than a fox's den. Twenty years earlier, a mound on the farm of Gokstad along the same fjord had produced the grave of a Viking chieftain, complete with a splendid ship. The farmer at Oseberg took the bit of wood to the director of the museum at the University of Oslo, who agreed: They had a ship burial on their hands.

Oseberg, says historian Judith Jesch, is "undoubtedly the richest and most sumptuous burial known from the Viking Age." The two skeletons found in the ship were both women. Because the name Oseberg could mean Asa's Fortress, the burial has been linked with Queen Asa, who revenged so completely her rape by the Hunting King. Tree-ring analysis of the wooden burial chamber, along with pollen found inside, tell us that the women died in the autumn of 834. (The ship was built in 820.) But we have no firm dates for Asa—the story was written down hundreds of years after she died—so no one can say for sure whether this was her grave.

Nor can we tell if the queen was the young skeleton or the old one, whose feet were swollen with arthritis. One or the other, scholars believe, was a servant who chose (or was chosen) to accompany her queen to the Otherworld. Neither skeleton was found in the burial chamber amidships. The large, carved bed, made comfy with blankets and feather pillows and eiderdown, and surrounded by wooden chests and a chair, lay empty. Someone like Grettir—someone who knew exactly what he was looking for—had dug into the mound long before the farmer. A hole had been cut into the chamber's roof. One of the three ironbound oak chests had been smashed open and emptied. The bodies had been hauled down the length of the ship to the entrance shaft that the robber had dug. There, where perhaps the light was better, they were stripped of their jewels and the old woman's right hand cut off, presumably for its rings. No royal treasure remained when archaeologists uncovered the Oseberg ship. But just as Grettir had no interest in the horse bones or the chair the barrow-wight sat in, the Oseberg robber left behind the very things that give us the greatest insight into the lifestyle of a Viking queen.

The Vikings believed that a queen would be a queen in the next world, and a slave would remain a slave. (That Christianity declared all souls equal was one reason common people were attracted to the new faith.) So that the queen's rank would be recognized, however, she needed to arrive in the realm of the dead in style. Thus the great dragonship in which she was buried, with its high coiled prow and the glorious carving all down its sides. Despite its beauty, it was a working ship, with thirty oars, a bailer, a sail (small bits of it remained, the ropes still attached), and a gangplank. Arne Emil Christensen, who directs the museum that was built around the Oseberg and Gokstad ships, calls it the oldest true Viking ship, the prototype of the rowing boat with a sail, the typical longship for raiders in the early 800s. Such a vessel could have made it to Ireland, in the summer, if the sailors were lucky with the weather.

But what if the queen's last journey was not on water? Buried with the queen were a spoke-wheeled cart and four sleighs, all richly carved, and teams of horses and oxen enough to pull them all. The queen also had her saddle horse, with its tack, and two dogs on a leash.

Unn the Deep-Minded, fleeing to Iceland with her family seventy-some years later, would presumably have taken fewer animals (and those alive and probably pregnant), and she would not necessarily have had the sleighs on hand (they were not as useful in Scotland, where the snow cover was much less, as in Norway). But the rest of the gear packed for the queen's death journey would just as likely have been on Unn's ship and, in another hundred years, on the ship that took Gudrid to Vinland.

Many of the queen's belongings were made of wood, exuberantly carved with beasts and faces and interlaced lines—and all crushed into muddy splinters when found. That this treasure can be seen, now, in the cathedral-like museum at Bygdoy, Norway, is a credit to the patience of the archaeologists in the last century who puzzled it back together. Besides the furniture in the burial chamber, they recovered two beds that could be taken apart and stacked for travel; two tents to set up for overnight stops; three large wooden barrels and several smaller ones, some sheathed with brass (probably used for serving ale); a bucket of wild apples and another, with a lockable lid, full of weaving tools; a kitchen stool; two iron cauldrons, one with a tripod; a kettle carved out of soapstone; an iron frying pan; a carved wooden trough more than six feet long and three smaller ones, one of which held bread dough; five dippers, four dishes, and some wooden spoons; more spoons made of horn; a carving knife and two choppers with wooden handles; and a bundle of spices, including cumin, horseradish, and mustard seed. Another leather bundle held cannabis—hemp seed, grown for rope—while a small box held seeds of woad, a plant that makes a blue dye. Some of these things were found in the oak chests. One chest was four feet long and 16 inches high, and decorated with iron plates and tin-headed tacks. It had an iron padlock, whose key the queen would have worn on a chain.

In addition to kitchenware, the queen's heirs had sent her and her servant off with four looms on which to weave their otherworldly clothes, plus a set of square tablets made of antler, for braiding the elaborately patterned ribbons the Vikings favored as borders and hems. The queen's tablet loom still held the threads of her last pattern, as if she might pick it up in a moment and finish her work. She also had scissors and spindles and flax beaters (for making linen), a yarn winder, and two yarn reels. Two carved wooden whistles and a bone comb are all that remained in a set of small caskets and boxes. Before the robbers came, the queen had most likely been well provisioned with trinkets and jewelry to buy her way out of difficulty.

This attitude toward death—that it was a mirror world in which a woman would need horn spoons and a frying pan, and enjoy weaving ribbons or playing the whistle—changed as Christianity entered the Viking world. The Church did not forbid grave goods (though it did ban the sacrifice of horses, dogs, and servants), but household furnishings were not necessary in the Christian heaven. The Christian dead were washed, wrapped naked in a linen shroud, and buried in a coffin, facing east—leaving us with much less information about who they were and how they lived. Happily, though, Christians also were never cremated. If this was why the Oseberg ship wasn't burned, we'll never know; similar ships were set on fire before being covered with earth. On the Ile de Groix off the coast of Brittany is a ship burial every bit as rich as Oseberg, with two male skeletons, one old, one young. It was torched. All we have to look at are bits of burned bone (including a six-sided die made of walrus ivory and a set of twelve gaming pieces), scraps of blackened metal, and one gold ring.

From Oseberg, we have not only wooden whistles and brass-covered buckets, but *cloth*. What did a Viking queen wear? Wool and silk and linen. Light, supple fabrics that clung to her form and draped elegantly, woven of several different textures in thread counts as high as 150 threads per inch. Norwegian archaeologist Anne Stine Ingstad writes in a book on the Oseberg queen that some of the Oseberg wool fragments were "so fresh and bright it is hard to understand that they've spent over a thousand years in the ground." Most, however, were caked together into stiff clumps and flakes made of many layers of different fabrics. Having teased these scraps apart, Ingstad found a "lovely red fabric" woven alternately of two different threads, one thick, one thin. "This must have been done on purpose, as it has given this fabric a beautiful muslin-like effect." It was once appliquéd onto another fine red tabby-woven wool; the gown had accents of silk, and all the seams were adorned with fine chains of embroidery. The other woman's gown was bright blue.

Based on the evidence of other burials, under their wool gowns the women would have worn an ankle-length shift or chemise of finely pleated linen, pinned at the throat with a small bronze or silver brooch. Linen, being made of plant fibers, decays more readily than wool, and little of it remains. But traces of linen are often preserved pressed into the backs of brooches, where contact with the metal has protected them. Archaeologists have also deduced that the Oseberg queen wore a linen headdress—impressed into a clump of feathers on the bed was the shadow of a lacy, open weave. The linen could have been white and glossy; linen smoothers have been found in many other Norse women's graves. Made by flattening a single fist-sized droplet of dark green glass, these smoothers were still used in Norway and Scotland in the nineteenth century instead of irons.

Some idea of the style of the gowns can also be learned from other finds. For many years, archaeologists thought a Viking woman's wool overdress was always sleeveless, like a pinafore or jumper, the straps held up with two "tortoise" brooches. These brooches are the most common piece of jewelry in female graves throughout the Viking world, from Iceland to the Volga. They are found resting on the skeleton's collarbones, not on the breasts—they were not nipple caps, like the bronze bustiers that costumers for Wagnerian operas favor. The brooches are oval, convex, intricately patterned, just like a small turtle's shell. They were mass-produced, made of bronze using the lost-wax process (many broken clay molds have been found in Viking towns). For wealthier clients, the bronze was gilded, or etched with acid to make it silver-colored, or both. Silver wire was sometimes applied to highlight the pattern. "The overall appearance of these brooches must have been quite 'baroque' by modern standards," says Michele Hayeur-Smith, who teaches "The Vikings and Their Art" at the Rhode Island School of Design. Gaudy gilded brooches "probably said a lot about the status, wealth, or family histories of the women who wore them."

The Oseberg queen wears no oval brooches. They could have been taken by the robbers, but Anne Stine Ingstad thinks not—as if a grave robber today would cut off suit buttons. But if the queen didn't wear a pinafore dress, what did she wear? Among the fabrics in the ship were scraps of tapestry. Many women are depicted, but only one is without a shawl concealing the details of her dress. She is large and prominent, leaning against a horse, and is dressed in what Ingstad considers queenly garb: "She is wearing a tight, full-length skirt. The upper body garment is another color, basically a faded red. This too is tight fitting, with long, tight sleeves. Around her waist she is wearing a wide, patterned belt. It is possible that we have here the Viking Age costume of the higher social classes. This costume seems strangely modern, but with a shawl over it, it would probably look just like the other costumes of these tapestries."

Ingstad began studying the Oseberg fabrics in the 1970s. In 1979 archaeologists drained the harbor at Hedeby, a famous Viking market town from the early 800s. (After the Slavs destroyed Hedeby in 1066, the nearby city of Schleswig, Germany, was founded.) A crossroads of Danes, Frisians, Saxons, and Slavs, Hedeby is mentioned in many medieval travel accounts. In the early 1900s, archaeologists rediscovered its location; by the 1990s, with less than 5 percent of the town uncovered, the tally of artifacts was up to 340,000, not counting bones. In the mud of the harbor, the workers discovered bundles of torn-up clothing, well preserved by the water; they had apparently been used as rags for wrapping trade goods or for tarring ships. When pieced back together, the women's garments seemed to justify Ingstad's vision: They were tailored at the waist to emphasize the woman's curves. Some were long-sleeved, with cuffs or plackets in a contrasting pattern or color. That some of these colors were bright—not the muted earth tones of natural wool—was discovered at York in England, when the Viking craftsmen's quarters at Coppergate were excavated in the 1980s. Subjecting tiny samples of cloth to absorption spectrophotometry and thin-layer chromatography, Penelope Walton of the British company Textile Research Associates found that it had been dyed with the plants madder, woad, and weld to produce brilliant reds, greens, blues, yellows, and blacks. Analyzing cloth from other digs, Walton has found purples (made from lichens) and rich browns (from tannin; a pile of walnut shells excavated at Hedeby was probably meant for dye).

As Ingstad saw in the Oseberg tapestry, most women wore a cloak or a shawl for warmth. But at Hedeby were also found bits of a long-sleeved, ankle-length coat made of loden twill, a heavy wool fulled with a hairy nap to repel rain. The coat was quilted with down and trimmed with embroidered ribbons. Other wool coats found elsewhere were lined and trimmed with fur—or fake fur, a wool cloth with lengths of unspun wool knotted into it, giving it the texture of a shag rug. The sagas make several mentions of rain-shedding cloaks made out of this shaggy cloth.

She would have had long hair, the Viking queen in the Oseberg ship, loosely knotted at the nape and falling in loops and coils, as do the images carved on the sleds. Silver amulets found elsewhere, of Valkyries or goddesses, show the same hairstyle.

And she would have worn at least one bead necklace. In

nearly every Viking grave, male or female, rich or poor—except Oseberg—archaeologists have found beads. Amber beads were favored by Freyja, the goddess of love. (Amber commonly washed up on the shores of the Baltic Sea.) But most beads were glass. They came in blue, green, yellow, red, or clear, in multicolor stripes or the mosaic-like millefiori, made by twisting glass rods of different colors together and then slicing them. The glass itself may have been recycled from broken drinking vessels, a famous trade-good of the Rhineland. Small cubes of brightly colored glass covered with gold leaf have been found near Viking bead-making workshops (marked by tiny blobs and threads of glass around a hearth); these tesserae were originally meant for Italian church windows. Strung along with the glass beads are charms and pendants and often silver coins. One famous necklace found in a Viking grave beside the market town of Birka in Sweden has been called "a microcosm of the town's business interests." Interspersed among its glass beads and circlets of silver wire are beads of rock crystal and the reddish gemstone carnelian; two pendants in the style of the Khazars, who lived along the Volga River; a fragment of an Arabian silver bowl; an English book-mount; two round pendants and a tiny silver chair (origin unknown); and a silver coin from the reign of Emperor Theophilus of Byzantium (829–842). Coins on other necklaces come from faraway Samarkand, Tashkent, and Baghdad, as well as from nearby Germany and England. It's likely Queen Asa bore such sparkles on her neck, and the grave robbers relieved her of them. It's likely, too, that the ironbound chest the robbers broke open was stuffed with silver coins, like the one Grettir the Strong fought the barrow-wight for.

Most Vikings didn't get a send-off as lavish as Queen Asa's, especially not those who went west. We find their graves not by poking into odd-shaped hills, but by chance. The only complete Viking cemetery in Iceland—with both Christians and pagans buried in the same area—was found in 2002 by a farmer with a backhoe.

Keldudalur, like many Icelandic farms these days, includes the tourist trade in its livelihood. It has thirty horses, fifty milk cows, ninety other cows, 160 sheep, and two summerhouses sleeping from fourteen guests (in beds) to thirty (on camping mattresses on the floor), breakfast optional. A "News" button on the farm's home page leads to photos of prizewinning stallions and rams. There's no mention that Keldudalur is also the site of a Viking Age graveyard, where one of the earliest Icelandic churches was built adjacent to an abandoned longhouse. It might seem tacky, since the church, graves, and longhouse are now under one of the guesthouses.

Digging the foundation for that house in August 2002, the farmer, Toti, saw a skull. By the time the third one rolled into his backhoe's bucket he realized he had trouble.

Gudny Zoega, the archaeologist from the Glaumbaer museum, purses her lips and glares, just thinking about it. "The *third* skull, you know." It was Gudny down on her knees in the mud that autumn, trying to prevent the skeletons from being further damaged by the elements. "It was raining, it was getting dark—it was not really ideal. We didn't see much of anything related to the structure of the cemetery itself that year. We didn't see the wall, or the church. It was a rescue operation. Unfortunately, that's way too often the reason for excavating bones."

She and her assistants dug thirty-four skeletons out of Keldudalur in two rainy weeks in 2002. They rescued an additional twenty, along with mapping the longhouse, church, and circular churchyard wall, in 2003, when Toti wanted to start landscaping around his new summerhouse.

"If you're thinking of Gudrid and her time period," Gudny told me, "these people would be her contemporaries."

Gudny, whose speciality is forensic anthropology, would spend the next several years learning what secrets they had to tell, for the level of preservation of these bones—even those of infants—was excellent. All had been buried before 1300; most were found under the shiny white tephra layer from the eruption of the volcano Hekla in 1104. By the style of burial, almost all were Christian. They were buried in coffins in neat rows around the foundation of a small wooden chapel: men to the south, women to the north, infants tucked up right beneath the eaves of the church. None had grave goods.

A nearby hill contained three or four pagan graves. The backhoe had ruined the most complete, an old woman buried with her horse and greyhound. "We got her skull and some bones from the excavator," Gudny said. To learn if she was related to those buried as Christians, Gudny has sent teeth from several skeletons off to a DNA lab.

The other pagan graves had been damaged much earlier. One was missing all but the heel bones. "You had the grave, nicely shaped, with a couple of beads in it and some horse bones, but only the heel bones of the skeleton." The rest may have been moved into the churchyard when the Icelanders converted.

Another skeleton lay in an intriguing—and eerie—position: the skull next to the pelvis. Placing the head beside the buttocks is the traditional way to incapacitate a witch, or, as Grettir's fight with the barrow-wight shows, to keep a ghost you've just robbed from coming after you. Resting on the skeleton was a delicate dragon-shaped bone pin.

This pin and three glass beads are all the grave goods Gudny found at Keldudalur. From the evidence of its 300–plus other pagan burials, Iceland never had a queenly burial like that at

Oseberg. According to *Laxdaela Saga,* Unn the Deep-Minded was buried in a ship beneath a mound with "a load of treasure." The more no-nonsense *Book of Settlements,* however, claims that Unn was "a devout Christian" and was buried at the high-tide line because "she didn't wish to lie in unconsecrated ground." Either way, we haven't found her grave. The four ship burials found in Iceland so far were not dragonships but rowboats. Instead of richly carved sleighs to carry them to the Otherworld, most Icelanders had only their saddle horse, with their dog for a guide. The most lavish Icelandic burial was that of the merchant wife at Kornsa with her set of copper scales and her six-sided bronze bell, identical to bells from Viking graves in England and Scotland. A typical Viking woman's burial, re-created under glass in the Icelandic National Museum in Reykjavik, is pathetically poor. A bronze trinket at her throat. A serviceable straight pin to close her cloak. Some scraps of iron that might have been a knife, and three large clamshells that she may have used as spoons.

Given the simple way they buried their dead, Orri Vesteinsson of the Archaeological Institute of Iceland concludes that the country's founders had nothing to lose in pulling up stakes and moving to an empty land. The saga accounts give some sense of this. They tell of families like Unn the Deep-Minded's, stranded in a hostile land, or warriors who found themselves on the losing side of a battle with Harald Fine-Hair or another ambitious king. Some had time to sell their land for silver, to fill their ships with buckets and looms and frying pans, to gather their livestock and children and friends, their servants and slaves, and to set a course for the west. Others were overseas when their Norwegian estates were confiscated.

The idea in the sagas that Iceland's settlers were Norwegian noblemen—while not wholly wishful thinking, given the cost of such a venture—is not backed up by archaeology. Archaeologists have found little of the "imposing architecture, artwork and expensive consumables, rich burials, and evidence of large-scale planning" that Orri suggests they should if Iceland's settlers had wealth or power. Queen Asa's lifestyle was simply not possible in Iceland, where there was no timber to manufacture her ship and sleds and furniture and household goods. Nor could the Icelanders make even the simplest type of bronze tortoise brooch to fasten a woman's pinafore dress. Assuming the craftsmen had a source of bronze (from old or stolen jewelry, perhaps; there is no tin or copper in Iceland), they still needed the materials to make molds and crucibles: clay, beeswax, and sand, peat, or manure. In Iceland you could count on the sand, peat, and manure, but the clay won't stick together to make a jewelry mold. Beeswax also had to be imported: There are no honeybees in Iceland. Having to import even the simplest materials meant that the finest craftsman could hardly have turned a profit.

The witness of the graves agrees. "In Norway," says Orri, "tools are frequently found in graves, while in Iceland they are as good as unknown. This suggests that specialized craftsmen could not make a living in Iceland in significant numbers, which in turn suggests that their patrons, the aristocrats, were absent as well."

Who were these people, then, who founded Iceland? When anthropologist Agnar Helgason traced the ancestry of modern Icelanders through their DNA, he found that the men were 80 percent Scandinavian, but the women were 62 percent from the British Isles.

"How do you come to a situation where you end up with this discrepancy? You get people going from Scandinavia to the British Isles, raiding, then trading, then settling," Agnar said. "These were younger sons, men who had nothing to lose and something to gain from going into uncertainty rather than staying at home. Usually it's difficult for young males to convince females to accompany them into uncertainty."

Irish and English sources, such as the annals kept by clerks in monasteries, corroborate the saga tales of fighting in the British Isles at the time Iceland was discovered. Vikings fought on both sides of these battles in the isles, and those on the losing side—whether native-born or Norse—had no choice but to flee. "One of them was Unn the Deep-Minded," Agnar said. "Stories of individuals like her are illustrating the pattern going on. Probably many other people had the same experience." For her father's misdeeds, Norway was closed to her. Through her husband's and son's failed ambitions, Ireland and Scotland were no longer safe. Unn needed to find a new haven.

"Iceland got the chancers, the losers," Agnar told me. "Going to Iceland was no package tour. It was not easy to go to a place with no infrastructure and where you had to start from scratch. The idea that they were chieftains who were miffed—that idea is wrong. There may have been some chieftains, but they were chieftains who were in trouble."

CHAPTER 5

The Land-Taking

With her to Iceland came many high-born men who had been captured by the Vikings. One of them was named Vifil. He had been taken captive in the Western Isles and was a so-called bondsman until Unn released him. When Unn gave farm sites to her ship's crew, Vifil asked why she didn't set him up with a farm like the other men. Unn answered that it didn't make any difference. He would be thought a man of quality wherever he lived. Still, she gave him Vifil's Dale.

— *The Saga of Eirik the Red*

THE DALES, UNN THE DEEP-MINDED'S LAND-CLAIM IN Iceland, looks today much like the Hebridean bay where the chessmen were found and where I wanted to poke into those oddly shaped hills: open moorlands, high, rounded hills, rivers tumbling to a fjord with a sandy shore. Only on some days can you see a distant ice cap. Hvamm, the farm Unn kept for herself, means "Grassy Hollow," and grass is the dominant theme—a windswept grass like the *machair,* thin and barely holding back the sand, interwoven with heather and blueberry shrub, sandwort and sedges, cinquefoil and creeping willow. Nearby are places with Icelandic names that mean "hot springs," "grain fields," "wooded mountain above the dark river," and "wooded mountain above the river through the hay meadows" (these last two names derive from Gaelic), as well as "salmon river," "fish lakes," and "ptarmigan hill"; "sheep hill," "horse lake," and "swine valley"—which gives you some idea of what Unn and her people had on their minds. They were Vikings, but first of all they were farmers. In their boats they brought not only bedsteads, swords, and treasure chests, but sheep, cows, horses, goats, pigs, hens, geese, dogs, cats, mice, lice, fleas, beetles, and seeds of barley and flax. Archaeologists have found signs of all these in the detritus of a Viking Age house.

They have also learned, by counting and comparing the various pollen grains found in different depths of bog soil, how these Viking farmers transformed the landscape, trying to turn a wilderness into the dairy farms of home. The sagas hint at this transformation. Ingimund the Old, for instance, spent the first winter in a place he named "Willow Valley," but decided it was "a poor exchange for Norway." Next summer he packed the family up and set off on horseback. Just as they reached a rushing glacial river, his wife suggested they make a stop. "I'm not feeling well," she said, in classic saga understatement, and promptly gave birth to a girl. Ingimund named the spot after his new daughter. Exploring the river valley, he saw "fine land with good grass and woods. It was lovely to behold." He built his house on the edge of Smithy Lake—though deficient in many things, Iceland did, at least, have bog iron, lumps of ore found in stream banks and turf bogs and raked up from lake bottoms that could be worked into scythes and swords, given sufficient wood to make charcoal. Says the saga, "The richness of the land in those days can be seen from this: The sheep could fend for themselves outside all year. Also, some of Ingimund's pigs disappeared and were not found until the following fall. By then there were a hundred of them."

That poignant comment, "The richness of the land *in those days*," tells us that the saga author, putting pen to parchment in the 1200s, knew things had changed in the three hundred years since Ingimund's day. The sheep had eaten the willows' buds and twigs, the pigs had rooted them up, and what the animals had spared fed the fires of the smithy and the family hearth. By the 1200s, Icelanders were burning sheep dung to cook, had given up on pigs as well as goats and geese, and spent much of the summer making hay, for the sheep could no longer feed themselves. The woods had not grown back. The bare hills collapsed in frequent landslides. The rushing rivers and ceaseless wind worried at the edges of the fields, erosion eating what the lambs had left.

The *Landnámabók*, literally the "Book of Land-Taking" but commonly called *The Book of Settlements*, is a compendium of fact and fancy about the first settlers of Iceland. Written at about the same time as the sagas, it reads like a series of saga abstracts linked by a thread of nostalgia for the richness of the land, and particularly for the long-lost woods. The first people to spend a winter in Iceland, it says, were a Swede and his clairvoyant mother, who had guided their ship there by second sight. "In those days," we read, the island "was wooded all the way from the mountains right down to the sea." Of a site claimed by an Irishman, the book says: "At that time there was such a great wood there that he was able to build an ocean-going ship from the timber." Botanists Throstur Eysteinsson and Sigurdur Blondal have determined that birch and rowan trees tall enough to make ship strakes could have grown in the lowlands before grazing animals were introduced. (Though there was never a tree in Iceland that would serve as the keelson of the Sea Stallion, the 98-foot-long dragonship retrieved from the Skuldelev harbor floor: That one vital part, which supported the mast, required a straight oak trunk almost 60 feet long.)

Once the virgin forests were cut down, the shoots grew scrubby and crooked for two reasons. One was the constant pruning by sheep. The second, in the case of the downy birch, was genetic introgression with dwarf arctic birch, which seldom grows taller than 20 inches high and is more resistant to grazing. The crossing is natural, but "in the absence of sheep," the botanists say, "hybrids would have been at a disadvantage at lower elevations and been shaded out by taller trees."

The settlers considered land covered with brushwood "useless for farming." In one saga, a wealthy Norwegian who bought a large tract of it is complimented for his industry: He "had lots of clearings made in the woods, where he started farming." The standard way to claim a plot of land, according to *The Book of Settlements,* was to "carry fire around it." That may mean the claimant rode around his proposed acres on horseback with a flaming torch in his hand. More likely it means exactly what the wealthy Norwegian did to clear his land of brush: He burned it. Archaeologists have found a layer of charcoal under two-thirds of the earliest Viking houses.

But Iceland was not like Norway, where a farmer fought constantly, with fire and axe, to keep the dark, encroaching forest from reclaiming his fields. Iceland's ecology was much more fragile. With the trees gone, the snow did not stick. Without this insulating blanket, the low-growing succulent herbs did not last the winter, leaving only tough, stemmy, cold-hardy species. The soil froze and thawed, bucked and heaved, and re-formed itself into the hummocks now so common in Icelandic fields that city-folk claim to be able to spot a farmer by the lurching, awkward way he walks down the street. In windy weather, sheep tuck themselves into the lee of these hummocks and munch on whatever grass they can reach without moving. Once they eat a patch down to bare dirt, the wind takes over, peeling the surrounding sod and whisking away the soil until the hummock is a pedestal. Unless someone intervenes—removing the sheep, creating a windbreak—the pasture turns to desert. Scientists estimate the wind has stripped off a quarter of Iceland's topsoil since the settlement. More than half of the landscape that was woods and grasslands a thousand years ago is now gravel and sand—and modern Icelanders are hard at work planting trees and experimenting with various grasses and legumes, like Alaskan lupines, to reclaim the wasteland.

Not all the blame for Iceland's "landscape of ruins" and her "nakedness," as scientists have named it, should land in the Viking farmers' laps. Climate change also played a large part. The Little Ice Age hit Iceland in the 1200s, dropping the summer highs just enough to hurt the haymaking and end the growing of grain, while the sea ice, creeping near in springtime—not autumn—put the new lambs at risk. The length of time the sheep could graze their summer meadows in the highlands grew shorter; overgraze by a week, and each year's grazing would be noticeably poorer until the pasture all but disappeared.

But the choices the first settlers made, of where to live and how to make a living, both in Iceland and, later, in Greenland, "had resonance for good or ill throughout all the subsequent history of political, economic, and environmental interactions in both islands," write archaeologists Tom McGovern, Orri Vesteinsson, and Christian Keller. "Over the succeeding 1100 years, these interactions proved intense and often disastrous."

A description of those choices and interactions can be found in *Egil's Saga*. Egil's father, Skallagrim ("Bald Grim"), was miffed, adventurous, and fleeing for his life—all three. He brought two shiploads of men and all the trappings of aristocratic Norway to a fjord in western Iceland, where he found wide marshlands and thick woods, with good fishing and seal hunting. He claimed the land "from the mountains to the sea." His land-claim later sufficed for four chieftains—and three hundred individual farms.

Like Unn the Deep-Minded, Skallagrim shared his land with the people who had followed him to Iceland, and the saga is clear that he didn't divvy it up haphazardly. He put a man at Swan Ness to collect driftwood and gulls' eggs, to fish, and to hunt swans and seals. At Grain Fields he sowed barley and set a man there to farm. Another was sent offshore to Whale Islands. Two men he established beside two salmon rivers. Finally, he set up a sheep farm in the highlands, having noticed the sheep that had strayed into the mountains were fatter than the ones kept close to home. He parked himself, with his cows and pigs, beneath a fortresslike hill in a little bay that guarded the entrance to the fjord; by the water he set up his smithy. He placed his closest friend on the opposite shore, so they could control both banks. He divided what was left of his land-claim among his seven followers and their families, with enough remaining to grant his father-in-law a sizable plot when he showed up a year or two later.

Orri Vesteinsson believes the saga's author got it right when he says, "Skallagrim's farm stood on many feet." The grandson of Ludvik Kristjansson—whose masterly compilation of lore, common sense, and natural history of the sea and all its creatures, *Sjávarhættir,* in five oversized volumes, is renowned throughout Iceland—Orri travels easily between his personalities as historian and archaeologist. He is as confident of his argument when he dissects a saga scene as when he describes Sveigakot, the barren little highland farm he has been excavating for seven years. On both counts, he takes delight in turning accepted theory on its head.

"The saga was written by somebody with a keen academic understanding of these processes, somebody who has put a lot of thought into what is necessary when you're starting a new colony," he told me. "And he was closer to these events than we are. He could imagine them better than we can. But it's clearly a model. It betrays its academic origins. It's too neat a picture. Reality is never like that."

Other sagas present a competing model of how Iceland was settled, one that was preferred, said Orri, by the Icelanders of the nineteenth and early twentieth centuries: "the single settler who claims a reasonable bit of land. This was *the independent farmer,* the man who seeks political freedom as much as economic prosperity. It's still a part of the Icelandic psyche, this idea that our origins are as yeoman farmers." Orri added, "That model comes with all sorts of baggage about democracy. I don't believe in it."

Orri's own model takes the Skallagrim story and gives it a cynical twist. A farm that stands on many feet needs many hands to keep things running. But Iceland was a hard sell. There were precious few ship-sized trees, and hardly many more tall enough for house timbers. Grain was not easy to grow; the rice, sugarcane, dates, lemons, and strawberries the Muslims at this time were introducing into Spain were unthinkable. Cows had to be kept indoors, some years, into June. Nor were there reindeer or bears or other woodland creatures to provide meat and skins and salable furs. There was no silver and no wine, two luxuries that drew Norse settlers east and south. The reports that came home to Norway were mixed. One of the earliest explorers, Raven-Floki, landed beside a fjord that was "teeming with fish," the saga says, but his people "got so caught up with the fishing that they forgot to make hay, so their livestock starved to death the following winter."

Unn the Deep-Minded and Skallagrim went to Iceland because they had nowhere else to go, having fallen afoul of the new king of Norway, and many of the later settlers named in the sagas were killers and troublemakers kicked out of the old country. Once the word got out that the new land was, as Ingimund the Old put it, "a poor exchange for Norway," peaceful farmfolk were not lining up at the Trondheim docks. "How do you get people to come?" Orri asked. "The bulk of the population was either enticed, duped, or *bought*.

"One of the archaeological results we have is that the settlement occurred extremely rapidly," he said, hurrying to back up his intentionally offensive statement. "The shittiest places were occupied just as soon as the best—even places at high altitude, with limited capacity, like Sveigakot up north, a place nobody in his right mind would have chosen to live in after coming a thousand miles. Even compared to the most horrible places in Norway, it's desperate."

Sveigakot today is a thousand acres of desert—just sand and stones and a marbling of moss, not a tree on the horizon—900 feet above sea level, more than 30 miles from the sea. The foundation stones of the Viking Age houses are barely covered with soil. Yet the site was occupied for over 200 years. Close by is a chieftain's farm comprised of almost 4,000 acres, with a 2,000-square-foot feasting hall, the biggest ever found in Iceland, its exterior decorated with the horned skulls of cattle knocked on the head to serve up at the feast. Nor was beef the only thing on the menu, as the archaeologists learned by sifting through the garbage heap. The point of holding feasts, Orri and his colleagues write, was "to cement bonds of friendship and dependence and to impress competitors." A feast that included codfish, eggs, milk and cheese, lamb, and beer was a clear declaration that "this farm stands on many feet."

Sveigakot was apparently one of the feet. The house itself was a small sunken room, 200 square feet in all, a so-called pit house—literally a pit dug a yard or less into the ground with a turfed-over roof, making the whole thing roughly tepee shaped. The Vikings generally used them as temporary shelters until a longhouse went up; at Sveigakot, that interval took two or three generations. Next to the pit house, however, they immediately built a large byre, with stalls for fourteen cows. "They seem to have begun very optimistically," Orri said, "but things didn't quite turn out the way they expected. These people seem to have been extremely poor in terms of material culture." The only artifact found in the pit house was a nail.

"I think it was a planned settlement," Orri told me. "Somebody organized it, and the greatest problem the organizers had was getting people to go. One easy solution is simply to buy them and transport them." The slaves, Orri believes, were not only Irish and Scottish, but Poles, Slavs, Balts, Frisians, Finns, English, and other Scandinavians—all of whom were for sale in the markets of tenth-century Europe.

"That would explain why people had to put up with this place," he said. "Once you're stranded in Iceland, it's hard to get away."

By 930, the sagas say, Iceland was fully settled and the new settlers had set up a system of government. Or at least, a few dozen of the richest and most powerful men (they were all men: Unn the Deep-Minded was one of a kind) had proclaimed themselves *goðar*, a word that is usually translated as "chieftains." These chieftains then worked out a way to share power. The country was divided into quarters, North, East, South, and West, and each landowner had to attach himself to one of the chieftains in his quarter. He could change his allegiance once a year, and was free (at least in theory) to sell his farm and move to a different quarter if he didn't like his options. Laws were made and customs established to even out inequalities in wealth and status, to make sure that no one chieftain grew strong enough to become a King Harald Fine-Hair. It was, for instance, dishonorable (and often fatal) to be labeled an *ójafnaðarmaður,* a man who was unfair, unjust, overbearing: a man who upset the balance of the world.

Each summer the chieftains and their followers—perhaps a thousand people in all—met in Thingvellir, the "Meeting Plains" in the southwest of Iceland, to reaffirm their laws and to handle any disputes that could not be resolved at a more local level. Their meeting, called the Althing, was also the social event of the year, where marriages were made, goods traded, tales told, ale drunk, and politics discussed. It was at the Althing, in 1022, that the Icelanders ratified a trade agreement with Norway, permitting them to cut as much wood in the royal forests as they wished; and at the Althing, in 1024, that they learned the king of Norway wished to be given the offshore island of Grimsey as a token of the Icelanders' esteem. They refused. Alone of their time, the saga people bowed to no king. *With law is our land built,* they declared.

Scholars have called the system they designed a democracy. In 1930, at the Althing's thousand-year fete, the United States spokesman lauded the first Icelanders for seeking freedom and democracy and equal rights. The representative of Britain's House of Lords called the Althing "the grandmother of parliaments" (the English parliament being the mother). These statesmen "told the audience what it wanted to hear," writes Helgi Thorlaksson, a historian at the University of Iceland. To the Icelanders of 1930—struggling for their own independence from the Danish crown—the people of the sagas were "democratic, law-abiding, peace-loving parliamentarians." To some, Viking Iceland still seems rooted in the values of America. In 1995 William Pencak, a philosophy professor at Pennsylvania State University wrote: "Iceland and its sagas depict a nation of free men, abetted by formidable women."

To anthropologist Paul Durrenberger, also of Penn State, this romantic notion is bunk. When he read the sagas, he saw no "nation of free men" but an aristocracy of chieftains who "had no inclination toward egalitarianism." The balance of power among them broke down within a hundred years—well before Gudrid's birth. By then the Icelandic settlers had learned three things. One, their only crop was hay. Two, their only export was wool cloth, but the number of sheep a farm could keep over winter was fixed by the amount of hay the farm's laborers could bring in. And three, a man ate just about as much as his labor was worth. There was no profit in keeping slaves, so they were freed—that is, kicked out of the chieftain's longhouse. Some of these freedmen made a go at farming on small rented plots, perhaps like the desperate Sveigakot. Their sons worked summers for the chieftains or other large landowners; winters, the family fended for itself. With seasonal labor so cheap, some chieftains saw a new way to increase their power: Take the neighbor's hayfield. It was against the law—land-claims were "holy," sacrosanct—but the law, writes Durrenberger in *The Dynamics of Medieval Iceland,* couldn't be enforced. Iceland had no king's men (or police) and no castle dungeons. "Law or no, courts or no, decisions or no, one could do just as much as one's influence, cunning, and power at arms allowed," he writes. Rather than "farmers at fisticuffs" (as one eighteenth-century writer described the plots of the sagas), or free men and formidable women, to

Durrenberger the sagas show the cunning and unprincipled rich out for as much power as they can grab, and happy to exploit the labor of anyone who can't stand up to them.

Like any good literature, the sagas support both view-points—what you get out of them depends on what you read into them. The chieftains are not static caricatures. Snorri of Helgafell, friend and supporter of Gudrun the Fair, sometimes seems democratic, law-abiding, and peace-loving, and some-times aristocratic, unprincipled, and exploitative. He is always, however, cunning, or, as Jon Vidar Sigurdsson of the University of Oslo puts it, shrewd. "Shrewdness is the characteristic which the sagas emphasize most in descriptions of the chieftains," Jon writes in *Chieftains and Power in the Icelandic Commonwealth.* Their battles were fought with wits more often than weapons. Fate, or "the will of God," never explains why one chieftain suc-ceeds and one fails. "The cleverest chieftains, who could also ignore the political rules when necessary, became the most pow-erful ones."

In the 1930s, scholars knew exactly what those political rules were. Icelandic schoolchildren learned them by rote: Each of Iceland's four quarters had three spring assemblies (except in the North, which was too big and needed four). At each spring assembly, three chieftains met. The chieftains appointed judges, who would hear both sides of a dispute and agree on a settle-ment. The loser might pay a fine in silver, goods, or land, or he might be outlawed: either kicked out of the district or out of the country altogether, for three years or forever. If a conflict was not resolved at the local spring assembly, it went to the appro-priate Quarter Court at the Althing. If that failed, there was a Fifth Court, a supreme appeals court.

This picture of Viking law is—like the description of Skall-lagrim's settlement—a rationalization. Historians used to think that the laws, known from a medieval lawbook called *Grágas* ("Gray Goose"), were exempt from the problems of veracity that plague the sagas. Yet the first lawbook was not written until 1118, nearly two hundred years after the fact, and it no longer exists. The two manuscripts of *Grágas* that remain for us to read were penned in the late 1200s, after Iceland had become part of the kingdom of Norway. They differ greatly. No one knows why both are called "Gray Goose," or what their purpose was. No one knows if they contain the actual laws of the land or, as Helgi Thorlaksson suggests, "simply learned reflections and speculations." In Jon Vidar Sigurdsson's view, *Grágas* is even less reliable than the sagas. The saga author, writing for the public, had to stay within the bounds of his listeners' prior knowledge of his characters and his story. Writing for scholarly colleagues, the editor of *Grágas* was free to settle on "the simplest explanation," the academic model.

In this case, the model is wrong. Only 10 percent of the conflicts in the sagas are resolved by courts of law; 90 percent hang on negotiation. "Farmers who felt that their rights had been infringed usually asked their chieftain for support," Jon writes. "The validity of the case or the underlying circumstances were of secondary importance; what mattered was the kind of support that could be mustered." Or, as Paul Durrenberger says, what mattered was the chieftain's "influence, cunning, and power at arms."

Paul argues that chieftains bought their influence, flattering and cajoling their neighbors with feasts and presents. Jon considers wealth just one of several important qualities. Without money a chieftain had no men, but a good chieftain was also "generous, helpful, and loyal," as well as shrewd. He made strategic marriage alliances and supported his kin. He maintained peace among his own men. He could be either "aggressive, keen, bold, decisive, hard, and ambitious" or "peaceful, clever, good-natured, moderate, and unassuming"—both strategies worked, or at least, each worked sometimes. For the most obvious characteristic of a chieftaincy in the sagas, according to Jon, was that they "did not last for very long." A chieftaincy was not a dynasty. A man could inherit, buy, or be given a chieftain's ring, but that alone didn't make him a chieftain.

Nor were there just thirty-nine of them, as the academic model of Viking law would tell us. From the settlement of Iceland until the time of Gudrid's death, about 1050, anyone could claim the title. One of the fifty or sixty chieftains that Jon suggests were knocking around Iceland in the late 900s could have been Gudrid's father, Thorbjorn Vifilsson, as *The Saga of Eirik the Red* claims. He just wasn't a very successful chieftain, and he was, by the time the saga begins, an old man with money problems living in territory claimed by the young and aggressive Snorri of Helgafell. Although a chieftaincy was not defined geographically, no chieftain liked to have a rival on his doorstep.

As *The Saga of Eirik the Red* tells us, Gudrid's father refused to shore up his tottering chieftaincy by wedding his young daughter to a rich—but slave-born—merchant. His only other source of wealth, as for all Icelanders, was the hay that fed the sheep that provided the wool that Gudrid and the other women on the farm could spin and weave into homespun cloth, the only goods Icelanders had to trade with Norway. By 985, when Gudrid was born and Eirik the Red convinced twenty-five shiploads of Icelanders to sail off with him to start over in Greenland, many of the first settlers' choices had already proved disastrous. Many farms had been abandoned; many settlers' hopeful expectations had turned to dust. There's no way to say if Gudrid's father's farm suffered from overgrazing a thousand years ago, but erosion is one possible explanation for his "money troubles."

As Icelandic historian Gunnar Karlsson writes, "Iceland may have been a good country for the first generations of Icelanders, but it was not equally good to all its children."

Gudrid's family were among those for whom it was not so good.

Some students of genealogy find it questionable that Gudrid could be the granddaughter of Vifil, the highborn captive from Scotland, as the sagas say. The problem is that this Vifil sailed in the ship built by Unn the Deep-Minded, while Karlsefni, Gudrid's husband, is Unn's great-great-great-great-grandson. That gives a difference of several generations between Gudrid's and her husband's ages. Yet it is possible. Unn was a grandmother when she sailed to Iceland, with two granddaughters of marriageable age. Her youngest grandchild, Olaf Feilan, may have been about five. If Vifil was Olaf Feilan's age, there would be only two generations' difference between Gudrid and Karlsefni. If Gudrid's father and grandfather were in their fifties when their children were born, and Karlsefni's were in their twenties, the age difference is erased.

Assuming Vifil was a tot when Unn took him along, what was his status? Some translators call him a slave, but it's clear that he and his sons didn't think of themselves like the poor folk at Sveigakot, stranded and struggling. What slave would challenge his owner, saying, "Why didn't you give me a farm, like everyone else?" as Vifil challenged Unn, some years after they had arrived in Iceland? And what slave owner would then give that arrogant upstart a whole valley, as Unn did? When Vifil's son, Thorbjorn, was considering the marriage offer for Gudrid made by the rich young merchant, Einar of the fancy clothes, he said to his friend Orm, "To think that *I* would marry my daughter to the son of a slave!" It was apparently a sore point with Thorbjorn.

Vifil may instead have been a royal hostage. When Unn's son Thorstein the Red was setting himself up as king of Scotland, he needed to guarantee the loyalty of the Scottish aristocracy. Throughout the Middle Ages, a common way to ensure loyalty was to take prisoner a nobleman's young son, and to tie the boy's life to his father's good behavior. Young Vifil's life was forfeit when Thorstein was betrayed and killed by the Scots, but Unn instead took him with her when she fled. It's likely he married late; it was difficult to start a farm from scratch when you had no assets but a sense of your own importance. Unn might have rented him a cow and some sheep, so he could build up his herd. He would have turned to her for help if his hay crop was scanty, and her grandson Olaf Feilan, when he became a chieftain, could count on his sword.

The relationship was reciprocal, though, and it seems Olaf Feilan—or Thord Gellir, the next chieftain at Hvamm—let Vifil down. *The Book of Settlements* tells us that after Vifil settled in Vifil's Dale, he quarreled with another of Unn's shipmates, Hord, who had been granted Hord's Dale, the seaward end of Vifil's Dale. Doubtless it was a border dispute. We know who won by the nickname given Hord's son—Asbjorn the Wealthy—and by the fact that this Asbjorn married Thord Gellir's sister-in-law, while his daughter married the rising young chieftain Illugi the Black. Asbjorn was not only wealthy, he was well connected.

Vifil's connections were not so good. His wife is not named in the sagas—she is clearly not a chieftain's kinswoman. His two sons, Thorbjorn and Thorgeir, married sisters, the daughters of a prosperous farmer named Einar of Laugarbrekka ("Hot-Springs Slope"), who lived on the farthest western tip of the Snaefellsnes peninsula, right beneath the Snow Mountain's Glacier. Neither of Vifil's sons continued farming at Vifil's Dale.

Hellisvellir, or "Fields by the Cave," the farm where Gudrid was born, was the dowry of her mother, Hallveig. Gudrid's Uncle Thorgeir and Aunt Arnora lived next door, taking over the main estate of Laugarbrekka after Einar's death. Gudrid had a cousin there of about her own age, a girl named Yngvild, who would later marry a son of the chieftain Snorri of Helgafell.

Gudrid's father was not happy at Hellisvellir. He was perhaps the younger brother, married to the younger sister and given the smaller farm. His wife seems to have died young—Gudrid was an only child, and she was raised next door at Arnarstapi by Orm and his wife. Besides, Thorbjorn and his brother did not always see eye to eye, especially when it came to Thorbjorn's friendship with Eirik the Red.

Eirik the Red is the classic case of the independent farmer, the seeker of freedom whose "don't tread on me" attitude gets him into trouble. He was quick-tempered and quick to draw steel, and seems to have had an inflated opinion of himself. He also seems to have been justified in thinking people were trampling on his rights.

He came to Iceland with his father "because of some killings," and they set up a farm in the far northwest of the country, in one of the last areas to be settled. It was not the kind of place Eirik thought he deserved. When his father died, Eirik quickly looked for a way out. He married a widow's daughter; his mother-in-law was the famously buxom Thorbjorg *Knarrarbringu*, or Ship-Breast, and when she remarried and moved south to the Dales, Eirik and his wife followed her.

Eirik's new father-in-law was an important man, related by marriage to Olaf the Peacock, the strongest chieftain in the district. But for all his importance, he was not overly generous. He gave Eirik the Red a small plot of land at the northeast tip of a big lake. The site is pinched between the river and the mountain, hard up against the neighbor's farm. Here at Eiriksstadir ("Eirik's Homestead"), Leif Eiriksson, discoverer of Vinland, was born.

Eirik's troubles start with a landslide. In the sagas, these are often blamed on witchcraft. We know now that when steep slopes are stripped of their trees and grass by grazing goats and sheep, they become unstable and landslides are more likely. Archaeologists working at Eiriksstadir have found signs of a landslide that destroyed Eirik's house, forcing him to rebuild. But this was not the slide that led to his being ousted from the Dales. That particular landslide wiped out a neighbor's farm (probably killing the neighbor). Another neighbor decided two of Eirik's slaves were to blame, and so killed them. Someone who kills another man's slaves had three years by law in which to pay for them, but Eirik retaliated by killing the neighbor and another man who stepped in to help. Influential men in the district then decided Eirik was a troublemaker. Eirik's father-in-law did not intervene, despite his influence with Olaf the Peacock, and Eirik the Red was banished from the Dales.

He decided to move to an island in the fjord nearby, but it took him a while to find the right spot; meanwhile, the saga says, he lent his "bench boards"—another translator calls them "bedstead boards"—to a man named Thorgest the Old. When Eirik was ready to build his new house, Thorgest refused to return the boards. Eirik lost his temper. He rushed into Thorgest's house, grabbed the boards, and rode off. Thorgest's two sons went after him. Eirik killed them "and several other men." After that, the two sides gathered their friends together into armed camps.

Thorgest the Old was married to the chieftain Thord Gellir's daughter, so all the "influence, cunning, and power at arms" of the Hvamm clan fell in behind him.

Eirik had no chieftain on his side, unless we can count Gudrid's father. For Thorbjorn, backing Eirik the Red was a bad move: Ranged against him were his own father-in-law, Einar of Laugarbrekka, and Einar's two brothers, one of whom was related by marriage to Eirik's enemy, Thorgest the Old. Even Thorbjorn's brother sided with the enemy.

The dispute was heard at the local spring assembly in about 982. Knowing he was overmatched, Eirik readied his ship and hid it in a tiny bay, deep within the many islands in the fjord. Outlawed for three years by the law court, he fled just ahead of his pursuers. (An outlaw could legally be killed if he was caught.) Gudrid's father escorted him out of the fjord in his own ship, as did his other supporters. Eirik promised to return the favor if they were ever in need of his help. He set his course west, away from Iceland, toward a mountainous land that had been glimpsed in the fog by another mariner—the land Eirik would name Greenland. With him sailed any possibility Gudrid's father had of becoming a true chieftain.

It's no surprise that Thorbjorn and his daughter ended up in Greenland, too. The only puzzle is why Thorbjorn waited so long to follow his friend. Likely it was because of Gudrid. She was probably born in 985, the year Eirik the Red returned from exile, bragging about vast green pastures up for grabs. His salesmanship convinced twenty-five shiploads of Icelanders to try to colonize this new world. Only fourteen ships, carrying three to four hundred people, made it there safely. Some ships were lost at sea—a poem from the period makes reference to a *hafgerðing,* an ocean "fence" described in one medieval sailors' manual as looking *as if all the waves and tempests of the ocean had been collected into three heaps out of which three billows are formed. These hedge in the entire sea, so that no opening can be seen anywhere; they are higher than lofty mountains and resemble*

steep, overhanging cliffs. Modern observers attribute these terrifying waves to an earthquake or the eruption of an undersea
volcano. A few ships in Eirik's flotilla escaped this catastrophe
by turning back to Iceland. Their reports of the journey would
have convinced Gudrid's father—or mother, if she had survived
childbirth—that the trip was too risky for an infant. It would be
fifteen more years before Thorbjorn, embittered and impover-
ished, miffed that a slave-born boy considered himself Gudrid's
match, would assuage his honor by emigrating to Greenland.

At their heart, Eirik the Red's troubles were not about honor,
but about house building. After spending a few days learning
about turf houses with Sirri Sigurdardottir at Glaumbaer and
Gudmundur Olafsson at Iceland's National Museum, I better
understood how much time and effort Eirik had spent clearing
the land and building his house—two houses, since the first was
damaged by a landslide—at Eiriksstadir, only to be kicked out of
the Dales. And I could guess how frustrated he was, after having
put considerable thought into where to build his house on the
island he had purchased, when his house building was short-
circuited by the man he'd trusted with his "bench boards."

As curator of the Skagafjord Folk Museum, for nearly twenty
years Sirri Sigurdardottir has been responsible for keeping the
turf roof and walls of the circa 1750 farmhouse on the Glaumbaer grounds in good repair. June 2005 was unusually sunny
and pleasant for Iceland, and Sirri spent much of the month on
the roof with a garden hose praying for the weather to return
to normal. "It was like a nightmare to keep the grass green on
the roof," she said. A sunburned roof will crack, letting the next
rainfall trickle down into the wall. A wet wall will eventually
freeze, buckle, and have to be replaced, which means tearing the

whole thing down to the layer of foundation stones and starting over again. Or walking away and rebuilding elsewhere.

Northern Iceland has quite a collection of slumped and crumpled, roofless turf ruins. Here and there a turf farmhouse is in better repair, crammed with tools and old toys, or turned into a sheep barn. There used to be many, many more: Before concrete was introduced in the 1940s, the most common house was owner-built of turf. Traditionally, a turf house was patched, rebuilt, expanded, and renewed, the new parts erected on top of, or adjoining, the old, sometimes changing the footprint every few years. Today there are only four men in Iceland who have lived in a turf house they had made.

In the 1990s, Sirri and her assistants took a camera and interviewed the oldsters on each farm. "We went through all of Skagafjord to learn where they got the turf, what kind it was, and how the timber frame was built. Most of these houses are gone now," she said. It was the same method Arne Emil Christensen had used on the coast of Norway to learn how Viking ships were built *while there is still time*. If the tools are the same, the technique must be the same.

Sirri and her brother went out into the bogs with the old men and their turf-cutting tools and tried it. "They use a spade and a short-handled scythe. It's difficult, let me tell you," Sirri said.

Just how difficult I heard from a friend who had helped build a turf house as a boy. "First you cut off the top layer using a shovel or a curved peat knife. The better turf is at a certain depth," he had said. "You need a sharp thin blade and a very firm grip. You use the weight of your body, plant your feet to press with your leg muscles, and saw into the ground—it's like cutting bread."

Sirri agreed. "You have to know how to do it. You need to have good iron edges on your tools—you can't cut turf with a wooden spade. This could be a problem. There wasn't much iron in the old days, and you had to take care of it. So when they cut turf, they cut as little as possible and thought carefully about how to cut it."

They also thought carefully about what kind of turf to cut, Sirri continued. "The best turf is called *reiðingur*. A *reiðingur* is a packsaddle, but also what you make one out of. We used the best turf, with the thickest root system, to make pads for the horses. And we used it as a mattress for beds. It's very soft."

To find *reiðingur* turf, you tramp along the edges of a bog, just beyond where the grasses give way to sedges, looking for the little white flowers of the bogbean plant. It flowers only if its roots are soaked. "The best turf was always in the water. When you dig it up, it runs with water. When it dries, it is all roots. No earth at all. No sand, no dirt. It's good for saddles—you cut it on the horse so it's the best shape for that horse when it dries. It fits perfect."

But while the old men all agreed that *reiðingur* was the "best" turf, they didn't use it for walls. They backed off from the bogbean a couple of paces, and cut building blocks from the firmer grass-and-sedge margin.

"*Reiðingur* is so wet you can't build the walls high," Sirri explained. "In a wall, it compresses every year more and more, and the roof comes down with it. It stops on the wooden frame. If you don't do anything about it, the frame will cut through the turf. It's good to have a little bit of clay in the turf because when it dries, it becomes a block, almost a stone. But not too much clay, or it will destroy the root system as it dries. When you cut turf in a bog, you cut living roots. They die in the walls, and too much clay makes the roots rot, then the wall breaks. So how to choose the perfect turf for the wall is not how you choose the perfect turf for the horse."

Sometimes there simply wasn't time to be so choosy—such as when half of your house had disappeared under a landslide. A block of turf needs three weeks to a month to dry out properly, and house building or repair was always on the to-do list beneath making hay. It was an eve-of-winter chore. "If you're in a hurry," said Sirri, "you pick the turf you have. You just do it. If you're lucky it will last for decades. Or if not, just for two years."

The shape of the blocks you cut also depended, to some extent, on time. The best walls are made of *klömbrahnaus*, "club-shaped hunks." One end is fat (called the neck), the other is thin and tapered (the tail). "The tail goes inside the wall, and you see the neck," Sirri explained. Each hunk is about a foot in length—but the wall is three to six feet deep. You built an inside stack of turfs and an outside stack, and filled in between with rubble. Old turf—the torn-down wall—was often used, along with gravel, clay, or dirt. You packed the rubble down firmly, "trampling it with a horse or a heavy man." Sirri said, "When you can't see the sign of your foot, it's done." Every few courses, a long straight piece of turf would be placed lengthwise across the rubble, to tie the two stacks together.

The faces of a wall built this way have a distinctive herringbone pattern. "It's good-looking and it's very strong. If the weather is not very wet, you have walls like that standing for eighty to a hundred years," Sirri said, "and I know much older walls made this way. Gudny saw *klömbra* in the walls of the longhouse that was found in Keldudalur, under the churchyard, so we know the people of Gudrid's time knew this technique."

Lazy housebuilders, or those in a rush, however, didn't always use it. They cut the simpler, diamond-shaped *snidda*, without the lagging tail. "If you weren't too clever with building, it was easier," Sirri said. "*Klömbra* is bigger and it's *very* heavy. *Snidda* is much easier to carry about. But the turf that's fastest to cut and easiest to build from is also the one that falls down first."

Finding, cutting, drying, and stacking the turf was only half the work of building a Viking longhouse—and not even the half that determined how big a house you would have. "When you start to build a house," Sirri told me, "you first look at the timber you have."

Although it looked like a low green hill—a hobbit hole— a Viking house was actually a wooden house tucked inside a man-made mound. The turf walls blocked the wind and kept in the warmth, but what held up the roof was a post-and-beam wood frame. The inside walls and ceiling were also wooden, the thick paneling sometimes intricately carved. A house in *Laxdaela Saga* had "glorious sagas carved on the wallboards and the rafters. They were so well done that people thought the hall looked more splendid when the tapestries were not hung up." The householder, Olaf the Peacock, had cut the wood he needed in the king of Norway's forests.

Gudmundur Olafsson believes that's where many of the Icelanders' house timbers came from, that emigrants—whether Vikings fleeing the king or those of their descendants who moved to Greenland—literally pulled up stakes and brought the posts and beams and paneling with them.

Gudmundur is the chief archaeologist at Iceland's National Museum in Reykjavik. Although he has been excavating Viking houses since 1972, he is disinclined to speculate; he often answers a question with *We don't exactly know yet.*

For six summers he worked in Greenland, excavating a Norse farm that had been discovered in 1991 when two reindeer hunters spotted a stick of wood protruding from the bank of a glacial river, close to the inland ice pack. Greenland is as treeless as Iceland; as one account of the discovery remarks, "the sight of large pieces of wood is not an everyday occurrence." The hunters called the authorities.

The stick was part of a Viking woman's loom. What now is a barren plain of sand had been, from Gudrid's day to the fourteenth century, an attractive Viking farm site, with grassy pasture, wet meadows, and a meandering oxbow river. Its name is long forgotten. The archaeologists, digging through yards of sand to uncover eight layers of houses, called it the "Farm Beneath the Sand." Each winter the river dumped a new load of sand onto their work site. All summer, while they dug, it threatened to wash their work away. In the seventh year it succeeded; the site no longer exists. But in those six years, archaeologists learned more about a Norse household than they ever had before.

"The permafrost makes all the difference," Gudmundur told me. "When you come down to the floor layer, you can smell the cows and sheep." The stumps of the roof-bearing posts, preserved in postholes, were a bit under six inches across, about the size of sturdy fence-posts. They had been reused again and again as the house changed shape over the centuries. Just as in Iceland, the great hall favored by the first settlers had given way to a warren of small, interconnected rooms, presumably to save on firewood. But the earliest house on the site gave Gudmundur a queasy feeling of déjà vu.

"It was almost the same size as Eiriksstadir," Gudmundur said, "a little wider, but the same length. We have no idea who lived at the Farm Beneath the Sand. It was not by the sea, but far inland. It was probably not anyone important. But it has led me to conclude that the people who went to Greenland with Eirik the Red were the same sort of farmer: middle-class farmers who wanted to get bigger, who wanted this opportunity to get rich. I think they lived quite similar a lifestyle as they had in Iceland."

And they lived in quite similar—even exactly similar—houses.

"If you're moving to Greenland or a new place, and you want to be a more important man, why wouldn't you build a bigger house than you had at home, if you had the means?" Gudmundur said. "I think the reason they are building the same size of house is that they took all the timber with them on the boat."

Gudmundur knows just how to do that. He helped design a Viking longhouse that was built in Iceland and then taken apart and shipped to Greenland. It was set up near Eirik the Red's farm at Brattahlid to celebrate the thousand-year anniversary of the Norse settlement in Greenland. He showed me a photograph of a standard 20-foot shipping crate about half full of lumber—a precut Viking house kit. "This is all the wood for one house. It took a couple of months for the carpenters to make it, but only a couple of days to take it down and pack it. And it took up so little space on the boat."

It was the second Viking house kit with which Gudmundur had been involved. In 1997 the Icelandic National Museum was approached by a committee of citizens from western Iceland who wanted to commemorate the thousand-year anniversary of Leif Eiriksson's discovery of Vinland by reconstructing the house where he was born in the Dales. There was no question here of discovering the house, as John Steinberg had discovered Gudrid's house at Glaumbaer. "It has never been lost," said Gudmundur. "According to the local traditions, this was the site where Eirik the Red lived. The sagas are very much alive with the local farmers. They know their saga heroes."

Eiriksstadir was first excavated in 1895 by Thorsteinn Erlingsson, an Icelandic poet. Archaeologists of his day had no feeling for turf. As Sirri had told me, "It was just turf and they threw it away. They dug down until they reached the foundation stones." As a result, Eiriksstadir was well and truly ransacked. Most of the information a modern specialist would read in the turf—such as when the turf was cut and whether it was long-lasting *klömbra* or the lazy man's *snidda*—was lost. In Thorsteinn's drawings and descriptions, Eiriksstadir is square. The house is divided longitudinally into two parallel rooms, with an offset door connecting them.

"In 1938 Eiriksstadir was revisited by the state antiquarian, Matthias Thordarson," said Gudmundur. "He discovered there was no room in the back. It was a landslide that had formed the depression. So that's what we knew in 1997."

Gudmundur told the committee he would have to reexcavate the ruins before he could help with the replica. In his experience, the Vikings in Iceland before the year 1000 built two kinds of houses: longhouses and pit houses. A longhouse, or *skáli*, was a single rectangular room with a longfire, a narrow hearth running longways down the center. Earthen sleeping benches flanked the fire. The walls were slightly bowed out in the middle. The door was off-center, on a long wall close to one end. Longhouses are generally about 65 feet long and 20 feet wide.

Most longhouses had a pit house nearby. The much smaller pit houses—about 13 by 10 feet, roughly square, and sunk 18 inches into the ground—had benches along three walls, a fireplace in one corner, and no apparent doorway. People may have come down by ladder through the roof, which was not high: The rafter tips rested on the ground.

Early archaeologists thought the pit houses were saunas. Today some think they were housing for slaves—as at Sveiga-kot in the north—or temporary quarters for traders: Two to four people could live in them. "These houses are found all over Northern Europe," Gudmundur explained. "They were probably quite easy to build. They don't need much material. These were the first buildings you put up when you came to a new country." Gudmundur believes the pit house became the women's weaving room once the longhouse was built. "We find loom weights, small knives, and other artifacts connected with women in them."

At Eiriksstadir, Gudmundur found both a longhouse and a pit house. Charcoal pieces from the longfire were dated, using the carbon-14 method, to between the years 900 and 1000; Eirik had presumably lived there around 980, so it could be his fire. But Gudmundur also found a second fireplace. It was hard to tell which was older because the floor layer had been dug away by the earlier excavations. He found three possible doors: two offset, front and back, and one in the center. He could not be sure where the western gable was; the end wall was indistinct, and the foundation stones may have been scavenged when a telephone pole was erected close by.

"There had been an earlier building destroyed by a landslide," Gudmundur told me. "Then it was put up again. It's quite small, but not the smallest longhouse we have found. Probably Eirik had no choice. He was living there on the mercy of his mother-in-law. He had no land. This house site was just on the border of the next farm. He was probably always in conflict with the neighbor because his sheep were grazing on the neighbor's land."

The basic floor plan Gudmundur arrived at shows one room, a great hall 41 feet long and 13 feet wide in the middle, narrowing at both ends. There is a central longfire and both a front and a back door—a good idea since Eirik the Red had so many enemies. What Gudmundur calls "a hypothetical reconstruction" of Eirik's house was built on the site in 1999. He explained, "If we did it again, it wouldn't look exactly the same because our knowledge improves with every reconstruction. We discussed what we knew about every little detail in the house— and what was possible. How big the posts should be. How high the roof should be. Sometimes we had to compromise, because the archaeologists didn't always agree with the architects."

The beds, for instance, are too short. The earthen benches along the walls on both sides of the longfire were boxed with wood and covered with furs and blankets to make comfortable seats by day and double (or triple) beds by night. Each bed was separated from the next by a footboard joined to the posts that hold up the roof. The length of the beds at Eiriksstadir, said Gudmundur, "was a compromise after long discussion. We had to speculate about the posts because the early excavations had destroyed the evidence. But they had drawn a map of where they had found stones that had supported the roof posts, so our house is based a little on that. We archaeologists wanted narrower posts. To get them we had to shorten the beds. The engineers wanted to be sure the roof wouldn't fall in. It's calculated to hold the maximum weight of snow. I don't think that was a problem for Eirik."

He paused. "All things considered, I think this is probably the best reconstruction of a Viking Age house that I've seen."

I took Gudmundur's advice and went to the Dales to visit Eiriksstadir. It was the weekend of the yearly Viking festival, Leif's Holiday, very much a family event. There was ring dancing and folksinging. A man worked a furnace and made trinkets out of nails. A woman sold bone flutes. Another played *hneftafl* or "tables," the Viking board game, beating all comers. A Greenlander sold walrus-ivory amulets. Other merchants hawked felt hats, cured skins, and soap. A man turned four sheep carcasses on spits over a fire. Wearing special straps around their waists and legs for their opponents to grip, boys and girls competed at *glíma,* or Viking wrestling. A group of young toughs tried to lift huge stones. (The smallest of three was marked 75 kilograms, or 165 pounds.) Young and old in Viking garb competed in a sort of tug-of-war: A long rope was tied in a loop and laid behind the necks of two contestants; the goal was to pull each other forward past a bone marker.

A Viking tent with carved wooden tent-poles was filled with reproductions of Queen Asa's housewares from the Oseberg ship: A Viking reenactor was living inside. The seven-foot-long bed was full of rumpled furs and blankets.

Up the hill, Eirik the Red's house looked tiny from the outside, an earthen hovel. Inside, it was snug.

The architects had put in two wooden dividers, turning the single open room of Gudmundur's excavation into three: a small entry room, with storage space for tack and farm equipment; the main living room; and a small pantry, with a grindstone and a food chest, at the back door. The two anterooms were rough, the turf walls exposed, and each had a loft. The great hall was completely paneled and very pretty in a blond Scandinavian way. Furs and skins hung on the walls and were draped over the wide wooden benches along the walls. Tools and weapons hung from pegs or on crossbars that ran from the posts. At the base of each post, a carved footboard divided the benches into sleeping berths—for children or midgets, but not six-foot-tall men. Gudmundur was right: The posts were too close together.

The longfire was small, just one stick of wood burning on a bed of coals, and the room was rather dark and smoky, though warm. Over the fire, on an iron chain, hung a big black pot full of soup, simmering slowly. As I sat on a bench by the fire, imagining Gudrid minding the soup, there was just enough room for the tourists to walk past my knees.

The ceiling was higher than I had expected. It made the lofts over the anterooms into usable space, but it seemed odd to send the fire's heat away from the people.

"According to the sagas," the docent told me, "houses were as tall as they were wide."

Presumably that was an architect's reading of the sagas. According to Gudmundur, the height of a Viking house was one of those things we don't exactly know yet.

I told the docent, who was dressed in a pinafore gown with tortoise brooches, that I was working with an archaeological crew digging up Gudrid's house in the north, at Glaumbaer.

"Then can you explain why the beds in this house are so short?" she asked.

A man listening in on our conversation replied, "Because Vikings slept sitting up."

"That's nonsense," she said.

I had heard that theory, too, but I wasn't sold. The sagas include numerous episodes in which husbands and wives were clearly stretched out full length.

But the docent didn't call on the sagas this time; she stuck to the archaeological record. "Have you seen the bed in the tent down there? The one from the Oseberg ship? No way would they sleep in those big beds while they were traveling and then come home to a short bed."

I repeated what Gudmundur had told me about the post placement and the snow-load problem, and she was reassured to learn that we don't exactly know the size of a Viking bed.

But because of this theoretical reconstruction of Eirik the Red's house, Gudmundur did know a few other things. For instance, it took the carpenters weeks to build the wall panels.

Based on the wall panels found in Greenland, they were over an inch thick, planed as smooth as a ship's strake, and then decoratively carved.

The crucial scene in *The Saga of Eirik the Red,* when Eirik's temper snaps and he kills his neighbor's sons in a rage—the murders for which he is outlawed from Iceland, forcing him to sail west in search of the land believed to be beyond—is due to a couple of these boards.

CHAPTER 6

Eirik the Red's Green Land

The land called Greenland was discovered and settled by
Icelanders. Eirik the Red was the name of a man from
the Breidafjord. He sailed from there to Greenland and
claimed the land around what is now called Eiriksfjord. He
gave the land its name and called it "Greenland" because
he said people would be more inclined to go there if it had
a nice name.

—Ari the Learned, *The Book of the Icelanders*

GUDRID AND HER FATHER SAILED TO GREENLAND IN
the year 1000. They carried along the posts and beams and wall
panels and bench boards of their house at Hellisvellir, and most
likely the timber frame from Arnarstapi, too, since Orm and his
wife emigrated with them. The two households—around thirty
people altogether—had their clothes chests and milk buckets
and cooking pots and seal-oil lamps, their looms and tools and
tack and weapons, their fishing boats and the best of their livestock. They carried food and fresh water for a voyage expected
to last less than a week.

They were not so lucky. Following the gentler version of
Gudrid's story—the one that doesn't end in shipwreck—they
were blown about the North Atlantic all summer, *hafvilla*, "bewildered by the sea." Half their people died, including Gudrid's
foster-parents, and the survivors suffered miserably from fear

and exposure in the open boat before they reached the south-ernmost tip of Greenland, just before winter, and found shelter with Eirik the Red's cousin.

"At last we came to the harbor, and it was a surprisingly good one," wrote another Icelandic traveler, on a much bigger ship, in 1835, "though the land here is far from what you'd call beautiful. Sheer ice-gray mountains ringed the harbortown—not a few of them, either, and all bare-naked." Greenland, he summed up, "is more gray than green."

It was academe's considered opinion, when I first read *The Book of the Icelanders* thirty years ago, that in naming Green-land, Eirik the Red had perpetrated a hoax. The sagas have very little nice to say about Eirik's colony.

> I see death
> in a dread place,
> yours and mine,
> northwest in the waves,
> with frost and cold,
> and countless wonders . . .

So goes a verse addressing a traveler headed to Greenland. Trolls and evil spirits descended on Eirik's Fjord in the winter, the sagas say, breaking men's bones and destroying their ships. One poignant scene describes a girl who came to Greenland accidentally, adrift on an ice floe; she stands on the shore on a summer's day and stares out to sea, dreaming of seeing the beautiful fields of Iceland again.

Writing *The Book of the Icelanders* in the early 1100s, Ari the Learned, Iceland's first historian, practically came out and said it: Eirik's "nice name" was salesmanship, simple bait-and-switch. Lately, though, scholars have reconsidered. The name Greenland "might have been bestowed honestly," one condescends to write.

"Eirik had not lied," others say more forcefully: "This name is not inappropriate"; it "reflected accurately" the land he had found.

Greenland is indeed "more gray than green" (as well as more white than gray, at least from the air). Yet the little pockets of green are as lush as Iceland must have been when the first settlers claimed their plots. Doubtless, Eirik saw the other similarity: Like Iceland once, Greenland was empty of inhabitants. As historian Gwyn Jones puts it, "For the first time in his life Eirik was free of constrictive neighbors."

Today the largest town is the capital, Nuuk, on the seaward edge of a handful of long, twisting fjords that probe eastward sixty miles to the inland ice. It was here that the Danish missionary Hans Egede came in the 1700s, three hundred years after the Viking settlement had disappeared, looking for lost Christian souls. Finding the culture totally Inuit, he reintroduced Christianity, wool clothing, wood-framed houses, and, so I was told, "good Danish food." I visited Nuuk in mid-May, a week after "spring arrived," according to my hostess, Kristjana Motzfeldt, an Icelander married to a Greenlandic statesman. Built on a rocky spit three miles from end to end, the city of 15,000—more than one-quarter of the country's entire population—sported no trees, no flowers. Old snow-piles, gray with gravel, hid behind the bright-painted houses bolted to the bare rock. The reservoir was still iced over. The mountains that overlooked the town were sheer and ice gray, streaked with snow. Yet the air did hold a springlike mildness as I climbed the steep wooden staircases that linked the winding streets, most of which dead-ended in water. The children certainly thought it was spring: They waded barefoot in the bay.

Kristjana had offered to take me to Sandnes ("Sandy Point"), a farm deep in the Lysufjord south of Nuuk. According to archaeologists' best guesses, Sandnes is the farm Gudrid owned with her first husband, Thorstein Eiriksson, or at least where they ended up after their failed attempt to get to Vinland, and where Thorstein so spookily died. But circumstances intervened, and Kristjana turned me and the Motzfeldts' boat over to Tobias, whom her husband had introduced as his chauffeur.

"You have a map, you know where you want to go, good, good," she said, brushing away my doubts. "Tobias will get you there"—despite the fact that he spoke no English (or Icelandic) and I spoke no Greenlandic (or Danish). His wife, Rusina, would be going, too, I learned as we reached the boat at 8:00 Saturday morning. "Beautiful!" she said, with an expansive wave of one hand, as we passed the dramatic mountains that marked the harbor mouth. It was her favorite (and almost her only) English word.

The Motzfeldts' boat was a seal-hunting boat, half enclosed. It had two seats, for pilot and copilot, a two-sleeper cabin in the bow, and an open rear deck large enough for landing a seal or two. It had two engines and a large gas tank. Cruising along at about eight knots, drinking coffee and eating Danish pastries, I realized that sailing to Sandnes in a Viking ship would have taken amazing skill. The narrow Lysufjord (named for a kind of cod) heads due east for most of its length, the ice-gray mountains falling straight into the sea, with no beaches, no harbors, no skerries, no bays, nowhere to find safety if the wind should turn contrary—or the ship should sink. The cliffs' snow-streaks and striations puzzle the mind; the eye wants to find a meaning in the pattern. I began to see huge faces as the hours passed and the view refused to change. The sky was overcast, the silver sea glassy calm. A sense of distance eluded me until I saw a boat the size of ours looking like a speck, a seabird, between us and the gray cliff face. Ahead lay endless iterations of the same humped mountain, hill upon hill: I could see no passage in.

Finally, after almost four hours, the fjord divided in two. A dome-shaped mountain lay straight ahead, a low rocky toe reached in from our left. As we turned the point into shadow, the boat began humping the waves, "swimming like a seal," as Kristjana had warned me it might if the wind turned against us. No Viking ship would have made it to Sandnes that day.

But the sides of the fjord soon softened. The snow had disappeared. Red-brown brush clung to gentler slopes, and here and there above a narrow beach were bright yellow-gold patches of grass that looked man-made: they were straight-edged, rectangular. You could spot Norse ruins from far away, I had read, if you looked for the lushest grass.

The water grew greener, more shallow. Birds were feeding along the edge of a sandbar, seemingly in the middle of the fjord. We went slowly onward, rolling sideways and, I soon realized, hugging the wrong shore. Across to the north I could see another great swath of winter-gold grass and the landmark I'd read about: "a small round rocky hillock . . . a fine vantage place for looking for scattered sheep in the valley."

Creeping along the edge of the sandbar, we had to retreat back down the fjord quite a ways before we could come close enough to shore to launch our rubber dinghy. Luckily the wind was calmer now, and by the time we scraped the white sand beach, the sun had come out.

Tobias and Rusina, each carrying a bottle of soda and a handful of plastic bags, sauntered down the beach to gather mussels. I hurried off the opposite way, knowing we had very little time before the falling tide would strand our anchored boat. I soon found, though, that the clear Greenlandic air had again deceived me: It was much farther to the Viking site than it had seemed from the vantage of the boat. Climbing above the beach, I found a forest—head high, but dense and tangled, the tiny leaves just unfurling—between me and the winter-gold grass. I crouched and wriggled through it on reindeer trails, the broken birch branches in my wake leaving a pungent scent. Under my feet were juniper bushes thick with last year's berries and the tiny pink flowers of saxifrage. Jumping a rushing stream, I broke from the tree cover, startling three reindeer that had been grazing in the old Viking pastures. As I watched them course off into the hills, dwindling to specks, I finally understood the size of Sandnes: It was easily a chieftain's farm, to be measured in miles, not acres. That landmark hillock would take more time to climb than the tide would spare me, while beyond it, I knew from the map, was mile upon mile of grassy river valley leading north to the next fjord, the way marked by a series of linked lakes known for the finest salmon run in Greenland. To the south, across the silty end of the bay, were two long green valleys stretching ten miles to the inland ice. Along one of them was the Farm Beneath the Sand.

Just as that farmstead was buried in sand by the river's changing course, the church built at Sandnes soon after Gudrid's time is now underwater. The Sandy Point has eroded significantly since her day. But the hip-high grass is still rumpled into hummocks by the turf-and-stone walls of Norse buildings. These were lived in until at least 1300, and beneath the largest, according to drawings from the first excavation, in 1932, are two walls of an older longhouse: the house Gudrid may have lived in that long horrible winter when almost everyone she knew died. The archaeologist found a corner hearth and flagstones at the front door. Thirty feet away were two small buildings "almost obliterated" by a later midden. In one was found a finely carved ship's tiller, its knob shaped like a dragon's head and its shaft decorated with a row of cats' faces. The name "Helgi" was written in runes on its side.

It was not clear to me, standing on the old stone walls and gazing at the view, why Gudrid should have wanted to leave Sandnes—once spring arrived and the winter's spooks had been put to rest—except to go in search of a more suitable husband than the old farmer who had tried his best to comfort her. It is a lovely green spot in an otherwise barren gray land. Other visitors have had the same reaction. The world traveler Arni Magnusson, the first Icelander to visit China, remarked on the richness of Sandnes in 1755. Tallying up its birch trees and grazing lands, beaches full of edible seaweed, reindeer, seals, salmon, seabirds, and birds' eggs, he concluded, "I thought to myself that it would be good to build a farm there on either side of that river," adding, "I have never eaten so many blueberries."

Sigurdur Breidfjord, who had found Greenland "more gray than green," changed his mind abruptly when he saw Sandnes in 1835. "It would have been good to live here," he wrote, "for the grassland is beautiful and lush, likewise there is a good forest and salmon fishing both winter and summer in the lakes and brook." (The churchyard had not yet been entirely swept away, for he writes with macabre detail of the yellowed human bones that fell apart in his fingers as he tried to pry them from the eroding beachfront.)

To Aage Roussell, the young architect-turned-archaeologist who excavated the spot for the Danish National Museum in the 1930s, the setting was more remarkable than the resources. "The farm is surrounded by much natural beauty and the view over the fjord is magnificent," he wrote. "Here, as at most Norse farms, the impression one forms is that the view has been one of the chief considerations when the *landnáms* man chose his site."

What apparently was not a chief consideration for that first settler was easy access. If we had been in a Viking ship, sailing or rowing, we would not have made it back to Nuuk that night—one reason no one lives at Sandnes now. We had hardly shipped our anchor when the wind turned against us again. The boat began to buck and thump; Tobias gritted his teeth and concentrated on steering her straight. Four bone-jarring hours later, we came to the mouth of the fjord, into a suddenly calm and sunny evening, an iceberg floating like a big pale-blue swan in the distance. At the foot of the *beautiful!* mountain, Rusina finally got a chance to throw out a fishing line.

Gudrid lived at Sandnes, at most, for a year, leaving it for good after her husband died. Her main home in Greenland, a good six-days' row to the south, is not such a lush and secret wilderness. Instead, boatloads of tourists cross Eiriksfjord from the international airport at Narsarsuaq to visit the Viking ruins at Eirik the Red's settlement of Brattahlid ("Steep Slope").

As at Sandnes, what is visible through the grass are the stone foundations of the houses, barns, and church that were here in the 1300s—over three hundred years after Gudrid left. Unlike at Sandnes, these ruins are carefully marked, with clear pathways for the tourists to keep to and a striking metal sculpture bolted to an overlooking rock. A metal plaque gives the archaeological interpretation of each rank of stones; another shows the probable layout of Brattahlid in Eirik the Red's time. The main longhouse, it says, was up the hill west of the modern church, in a spot that now contains a very well-groomed and flattened hayfield on a steep south-facing slope, as well as a large sheep barn.

Brattahlid is the center of Greenland's sheep industry. The settlement is about the size of the island Eirik the Red had been trying to build a house on in Iceland, when Thorgest the Old refused to return his bench boards; you can stroll end to end in about twenty minutes. Doing so, I counted twenty-two horses, loose along the road; several dogs, all of a border-collie type; a church, school, shop, and warehouses by the dock; a café and youth hostel (closed until summer); the cluster of Viking ruins; reconstructions of a Viking longhouse (made from Gudmundur Olafsson's Viking house kit) and a tiny Viking church; about thirty houses (many of them apparently summerhouses like the one I had rented); and six sheep barns, each large enough for 600 ewes and the 1,200 lambs they were expected to give birth to in the next week or so.

Climbing the pink-gravel road out of Brattahlid proper, I hiked for two hours until the sheep pastures gave way to a fjord filled with icebergs. There were no head-high thickets to wriggle through, and no thick stands of winter-gold grass; just scattered sheep and sturdy woven-wire fences standing four feet tall with a strand of barbed wire on the top. The rare birch I passed had been browsed back; nothing was budding here, though spring comes sooner at Brattahlid than Sandnes. I saw no flowers. The hills were smooth and groomed almost bare by the sheep.

Green valleys, full of modern sheep fences alongside Viking stonework, finger out all along the thirty-mile length of Eiriksfjord, with sixty farming families now providing 30,000 lambs a year to the abattoir in the market town of Narsaq, a three-hour boat trip south. The farmers in Brattahlid are descendants of Otto Frederiksen, who established a sheep farm there in 1924. As a guidebook published by the Danish National Museum notes: "The fact that the Eskimos who wanted to be farmers chose Brattahlid is due to the simple fact that they, like Eirik the Red, could see that the richest grazing areas in the whole country were to be found there." Between the time each spring when the lambs go up to the mountain pastures to graze and when they come down again in October, the farmers make hay. That I saw ranks of round bales wrapped in white plastic behind the barns in mid-May, after spring had arrived and the sheep were being turned out on grass, testified that there was more than enough hay to go around.

The same could not be said in Eirik the Red's day. The biggest difference between raising sheep then and now is the haymaking technology: Today's Greenlanders have tractors and balers and plastic wrapping. Eirik the Red had a short-handled sickle with an iron blade, and even those were scarce. Although a few Greenlandic bogs and brooks show the ruddy tint of iron ore, archaeologists have found no signs of ore smelting. All the iron in the Vikings' tools, they learned by looking at bits of nails and knives under a scanning electron microscope, came from Norway in the form of "blooms": ore that had been roasted, crushed, and cooked in a hot charcoal furnace until most of the impurities ran out. This lump of solid iron was squeezed and shaped into a ball, then split, while hot, into two or more "fingers" that were easily transported and sold. Eirik the Red (or his blacksmith) would heat a finger of iron over a charcoal fire in a soapstone hearth, purify it further, and then forge it into a tool. It was expensive, time-consuming, and essential to making hay. An iron sickle blade also had to be resharpened every day during haymaking, which required heating it in a bed of charcoal. If you were out of charcoal, you couldn't make hay—which is why the modern Icelandic phrase *úrkul vonar,* literally "out-of-charcoal hopes," means "hopeless."

The estimates of how many sheep a chieftain like Eirik the Red might have owned range from fifty to 3,000, depending on how wild the writer assumes those sheep were. If his sheep wintered in sheds and were fed hay during the worst weather, then fifty. If expected to "fend for themselves outside all year," as the sagas say sheep did during the first years of Iceland's settlement, browsing the ground cover entirely away, then 3,000, more like the numbers kept in Brattahlid today. But Eirik the Red not only kept sheep, he also raised cows, which modern Greenlanders have given up on, after a brief assay at dairying in the early twentieth century. At last count, there were sixteen cows in all of Greenland; the stores sell no fresh milk. Not cold-hardy like sheep, cows cannot survive outside, as the old Icelandic saying puts it, "between the devil and the frost." The Vikings built sturdy byres to protect their cows, with tall flat stones standing on edge to divide the stalls. Counting those partitions, archaeologists estimate that a chieftain like Eirik may have kept up to twenty cows. Since they had to stay in their stalls for 200 days of the year, they required 55 tons of hay, or 500 horse loads. Eirik needed some hay for his horses, too, though like the sheep they usually could fend for themselves. He also kept goats, which can digest brush and scrub even better than sheep.

As in Iceland, the amount of hay Eirik the Red could make each summer depended on the labor at his call—how many men cutting the grass with sickles, how many women raking and drying the hay, how many horses carrying it to the turf-covered haystacks or the barns. But it also depended on the weather and on what the sagas call the "richness of the land." Greenland has a more continental climate than Iceland, and the Viking sites were subject to summer droughts. Elaborate lidded stone channels have been found on many Viking farms, diverting rivers to irrigate the hayfields (and, in some cases, into the houses to provide running water). It is not known if the Vikings manured their fields systematically, but even if they did, the watered and fertilized fields were large enough to feed only five to seven cows through the long winter. The additional hay had to be cut and hauled from the natural lowland marshes—which meant herding the cows in summer, and the sheep much of the year, away from that grass and into the highlands, a job that called for both shepherds and dairymaids, for the sheep and goats, as well as the cows, were milked.

When she first came to Brattahlid with her father, Gudrid, as an unmarried girl of fifteen, would have been sent into the hills with the other young people to work as a dairymaid for the summer. This again would have been her summer chore when she returned to Brattahlid, a widow at age seventeen. In the hills, she lived in a small house, close to wood and water, and spent her days making butter, cheese, *skyr*—a thick yogurt-like dish—and whey to feed the household over winter. Based on Icelandic practice in later centuries, we can guess that both cows and sheep were milked once a day, the cows in the field as they grazed, the ewes after being driven into a pen. Records from the 1400s say three women should be able to milk twelve cows and eighty ewes. While working, they should keep an eye out for butter imps, little demons that sucked the teats of other people's cows. These imps not only stole milk to carry home for their master's butter, "they had a habit of crawling between women's legs and going about their business there, too," as one folklorist puts it.

The day's milk was filtered through a mesh strainer, knotted up from the coarse hairs of cows' tails. Then it was left in a shallow, square wooden trough for thirty-six hours, until the cream collected on top. By laying an arm on one lip of the trough, and tilting the trough, Gudrid could quickly skim off the cream—in Icelandic, skim milk is still called *undanrenna,* what "runs under" the arm. The cream was churned into butter, kneaded into a block, squeezed to get every last bit of butter-milk out of it, and stored in a box. Unsalted, it would sour, but keep for decades. Later landowners filled their treasuries with butter; in the 1500s, an Icelandic bishop amassed twenty-five tons of it. In Ireland a common archaeological find is a barrel of butter dug up from a bog; the Norse also stored butter this way. Bog-butter grows hard, gray, and cheeselike, but stays edible: The specimens in the Irish National Museum, dated to the seventeenth century, are still "quite free from putrefaction."

From the skim milk, Gudrid would have made cheese and *skyr*. To make *skyr*, she heated the milk until a skin formed, then cooled it to body temperature and added a bacterial culture from the previous day's *skyr*, along with rennet, an enzyme from the dried, crumbled stomach of a calf a few days old. If the *skyr* tub was kept warm, the *skyr* would curdle by morning. Then it was sieved through cheesecloth, the curds (the *skyr*) and the liquid whey kept in separate wooden barrels to ferment. Once the whey was sour enough, it could be used to pickle blood sausages and other delicacies like rams' testicles; mixed with water, it made a healthy drink, especially when the whey was made from sheep's milk, which has three times the vitamin C of cows' milk. A diet of fish and sheep's whey will keep a worker healthy "for a long period of time," an Icelandic writer in the 1800s noted, whereas people drinking water with their fish soon lost their strength.

Making cheese instead of *skyr* called for more rennet and none of the bacterial culture. Once hard, cheeses were stored in a cool, damp larder and washed frequently to keep down the mold. Or they could be carried up to a convenient snowbank and put on ice.

The essential tool for dairying, as important as an iron sickle blade to haymaking, is a watertight bucket. In the National Museum of Greenland—a series of handsome wooden warehouses clustered by the old harbor in Nuuk—Georg Nyegaard took me to the conservator's workshop to see the plethora of wooden artifacts that had been retrieved from the Farm Beneath the

Sand. Most were splintered bits of what he called "coopered vessels"—buckets and barrels, no doubt including milking pails, *skyr* tubs, whey barrels (large enough for a man to hide in), cheese forms, and butter boxes.

Wearing white cotton gloves, Georg opened a plastic bag and gently removed two wooden plates, one round, one oval, each hardly longer than my palm. "These are bottom disks," he said. "They put staves all around here and tied them together with baleen."

Opening another bag, he drew out a thin board about ten inches long. "Here is a very fine piece of a stave, with a groove at the bottom for the disk." There was a matching groove near the top, but Georg couldn't explain its purpose. "There are so many objects like this one that we don't know the function of. So many strange shapes."

The wood, he explained, was driftwood: It bore the telltale signs of shipworm. Driftwood comes to Greenland with the drift ice, "whole trees, roots and all," as the missionary Otho Fabricius wrote in 1807. The trees are knocked from the wooded banks of great rivers in Siberia when the ice breaks up in spring, and float north to the pack ice of the Polar Sea, in which they travel, soaked and ground, stripped of bark and branches, for five to twenty years, following the current down the east coast of Greenland and around the tip north as far as Nuuk. Wood is tossed ashore in West Greenland at a rate of eighty to 120 cords a year, and most of it, according to Fabricius, is "crooked, twisted, or full of cracks and wormholes, or rotten." Another author describes it as "intractable" and requiring "much ingenuity" to carve: "The wood has lost most of its original flexibility. It feels 'dead.'" Very rarely is there a workable log, but it was all the Vikings had besides head-high birches and spindly willows and juniper.

Upstairs in the magazine, the main storage room, Georg opened box after box. An iron knife, whetted to a sliver. A polar bear tooth. A horn spoon. A partial basket made of willow roots, twined in a spiral. Beads of soapstone and walrus tusk. A small soapstone pot. A large soapstone basin for watering cows. A wooden ladle, broken centuries ago and stitched together with roots. A whalebone butter paddle.

We peered at scraps of a dark, woven cloth through the clear lid of a plastic box. "I remember this weaving room we excavated," Georg said. "There were so many kinds of textiles. There were spindle whorls in different shapes made of soapstone—it's a very common find. You see a lot of implements committed to this industry. You get an impression they spent a lot of time at it."

He put the box back and opened one next to it. "Here's one of the most beautiful objects to find," Georg said, "because you get so close to history. It's a last for a shoe." He took out of the box a smooth, dark foot carved of wood and cradled it in both hands. "When you take such a piece from the soil, you feel so close to the person. It's made for *one* person's feet.

"These people were very busy," he said as we left the magazine. "During the summer they had a lot of activities going on. The economy was quite complex. They recognized themselves as farmers, but when you look at the bones, a major part of the bones were seal and reindeer bones, so they were hunters, too."

Looking at the bones dug up before the Farm Beneath the Sand was found, archaeologists created a story of this economy, a story whose ulterior goal was to explain the puzzle that captivates most people about Viking Greenland: Why, after surviving over four hundred years, did its people disappear without a trace? Jared Diamond draws on this work in his popular book

Collapse: How Societies Choose to Fail or Succeed, arguing that the livestock the settlers brought with them, based on the Norwegian "ideal farm," didn't suit Greenland's colder, drier conditions. Diamond writes: "Although pigs found abundant nuts to eat in Norway's forests, and although Vikings prized pork above all other meats, pigs proved terribly destructive and unprofitable in lightly wooded Greenland, where they rooted up the fragile vegetation and soil. Within a short time they were reduced to low numbers or virtually eliminated." For similar environmental reasons, he says, the Vikings were forced to limit the number of "honored cows" they kept and increase their herds of "despised goats." A main cause of the "collapse," in his view, is that the Norse refused to give up their unsuitable livestock altogether and become dedicated seal hunters like the Inuit, who began moving south into Viking territory in the 1200s. He also thinks they turned up their noses at fish.

Seal bones are found in significant numbers in late-Norse middens in Greenland, but most are from harp seals. A migratory carnivore, the harp seal followed the capelin into the fjords for a few weeks in the spring, and the sand eels in the fall. The spring run was particularly timely, coming when the stored milk products were running out.

Diamond argues that only people at "small poor farms" ate seal meat—that it was famine food. In one garbage heap from the last days of occupation at a small farm on the Lysufjord, 70 percent of the bones were seal. People at the large, upper-class Sandnes, next door, preferred venison, if they couldn't get pork or beef. But as the climate worsened and the fragile vegetation was destroyed by overgrazing, they failed to see that seal or fish were their only options. Rather than change their eating habits—and adapt to their environment, the way the Inuit did—the Vikings starved. Diamond doesn't blame them. He had forced himself to taste seal meat while he was in Greenland, and had not "gotten beyond the second bite."

Despite the attractive environmental message in Diamond's *Collapse*, I have problems accepting this model of the Viking economy. How do we know that Vikings prized pork and despised goat meat? Our main source for Viking culinary practices, other than scattered references to food in the sagas, is the volume of Old Norse mythology written in the early 1200s by the chieftain Snorri Sturluson. In Snorri's *Edda*, the cow is given pride of place: Her copious milk fed the giant Ymir, from whose body the chief god Odin created the world. Pork is the meat eaten in Valhalla, the great hall in the Otherworld to which Odin welcomes warriors slain in battle; the same old boar is boiled each night in a huge cauldron, and in the morning he comes back to life. The other pig mentioned in the myths is not eaten, but ridden—by the fertility god Frey. Odin himself is said to never eat, living on wine alone; yet in another tale, he and two lesser gods butcher an ox and roast it on a spit over a wood fire. A goat, meanwhile, produces mead instead of milk for the dead heroes in Valhalla to drink. Goat is also the favorite food of the war god Thor; the two goats that pull his chariot allow him to butcher and boil them every night. Provided that he saves every bone and wraps them up in the skins, unbroken, the goats will come back to life in the morning. Given the number of children named after Thor— one-quarter of the names in the Icelandic *Book of Settlements* are Thor combinations—his totemic animal seems unlikely to have been "despised." Finally, three gods, Thor, Loki, and Njord, are all associated with fishing. In particular, Loki, the trickster god, is said to have turned himself into a salmon and invented a net. Noticeably missing from the gods' meals are sheep.

Jette Arneborg, an archaeologist at the Danish National Museum in Copenhagen, pointed out to me the second problem with Diamond's model of the Viking diet. It assumes that the Vikings were tidy, that they carefully cleared the table and carried all their dinner scraps out to the garbage midden. But there were no tables in treeless Greenland. And bones were valuable. Housewives collected them back into the pot and boiled them to make soup, then pickled them in whey to make "bone-jelly porridge." Toys, dice, flutes, and game pieces were carved out of them, and needles and needle cases. They were crushed and dried and fed to cows as a calcium supplement. Or spread on the fields as fertilizer—still a common practice in northern Norway in the nineteenth century. Bones were often burned, although they gave off a bitter, foul-smelling smoke. In profligate households, they were tossed to the dogs or simply left on the floor.

Archaeologists have long bemoaned the "fetid," "squalid" conditions of the Greenland Vikings' floors. Layers of twigs, hay, and moss served an insulating function—they kept the permafrost from thawing and the floor from turning to muck. Sifting through samples of such carpeting, scientists have identified flies that feed on carrion and feces, as well as human lice, sheep lice, and the beetles that live in rotting hay. Shards of bone are scattered throughout, "a few clearly having passed through the gut of the farm's dog," as one excavator writes, others the detritus of whittling. On the floor of the Farm Beneath the Sand, archaeologists even found fish bones.

Archaeologists have been agonizing over Greenland's missing fish bones for over thirty years. Whereas piles of fish bones are found on Viking sites in Iceland, they are "extremely rare," "nearly absent" from the bone collections in Greenland.

Jared Diamond thinks they should stop worrying about it. He writes in *Collapse*, "I prefer instead to take the facts at face value: Even though Greenland's Norse originated from a fish-eating society, they may have developed a taboo against eating fish." His explanation draws on his own painful reaction to a batch of spoiled shrimp. "Perhaps Eirik the Red, in the first years of the Greenland settlement, got an equally awful case of food poisoning from eating fish. On his recovery, he would have told everybody who would listen to him how bad fish is for you, and how we Greenlanders are a clean, proud people who would never stoop to the unhealthy habits of those desperate grubby ichthyophagous Icelanders and Norwegians."

"That's not how it was!" laughed Jette Arneborg, when I relayed Diamond's theory to her. In her cluttered office at the Danish National Museum, a converted Renaissance palace in downtown Copenhagen, Jette seemed worlds away from her Job as codirector of the dig at the Farm Beneath the Sand. She had already described her days there: going in by helicopter, using sandbags to hold the river back, excavating three to four inches of soil, then waiting for the sun to melt the next layer of permafrost. Wrapping every bone, every chip of wood, in wet paper and bagging it in plastic, the glacial river roaring past inches away: *It was very fast, very deep,* she had told me. *If you fell into it, you wouldn't survive.* An open box on her desk held two animal bones from Greenland; they had been sent to the diet-analysis group, where someone saw a cross had been cut into each one and returned them to her, reclassified as artifacts.

"Of course they ate fish," she said. "We do have one fishhook. We have sinkers. We have pieces of what I think were nets. We have fish bones from inside the house. If we sieve very carefully, we find them." The Farm Beneath the Sand is the only house from Gudrid's time in Greenland that has ever been fully excavated. "For the rest of the farms," Jette said, "we have excavated only the top part," the part from the 1300s. She explained, "These farms are ancient monuments. The walls are still standing. They are huge and marvelous. You can't spoil them by digging under them. But here we could, because the river was taking it all away."

And when they did, they found 24,643 bone fragments inside the house. Inge Bodker Enghoff of the University of Copenhagen's Zoological Museum could identify 8,250 of them, representing four hundred years of occupation. Of these, 166 bones were fish bones—the largest collection of fish bones found at any Greenland Norse farm. (By comparison, Enghoff identified only one pig bone.) Because of the permafrost and slightly acidic soil, most bones were very well preserved, she writes, "with the exception of the fish bones." Why only the fish bones decayed she did not know, but their poor state of preservation led her to conclude that "fishing may have played a larger role than the sheer number of fish bones indicates."

The Norse name for the fjord close to the Farm Beneath the Sand is, after all, Cod Fjord. And the best salmon river in Greenland is a few hours away by horseback. Said Jette, "They fished. We have written sources talking about the good fishing spots. They knew where to catch halibut. There's salmon and a lot of trout. They lived so close to the water, the trout jumped out of the lake at them." Exactly that happened to C. L. Vebaek in 1949, as he excavated a Norse farm by a lake in South Greenland. "One day," he writes, "one of these awful *nigeqs* [southeasterly gales] arose (lasting three days), and it blew so much of the water from the lake situated to the east that the water level suddenly fell considerably. As a result, nearly all the water in the river disappeared, and a large number of salmon (as far as I remember more than a hundred) were stranded in small pools—you could just walk out and collect the fish with your hands!"

Counting animal bones can't tell us that Vikings in Iceland ate fish and their cousins in Greenland didn't. We can't "take the facts at face value," as Diamond argues; archaeology is not so precise a science. But it is clear that the Greenlanders didn't catch fish on the same scale. Icelanders bartered with it: A farmer with too much *skyr* could strap two bull's-hide bags of it onto a horse, travel down to the coast, and purchase a horse-load of dried fish. Clear signs of eleventh-century fish-processing sites on the seashore, as well as quantities of headless fish found high in inland farms, prove that some sort of fish business was going on in Iceland in Viking times. Still today, the way to dry fish is to gut it, behead it, split it open, and hang it on a rack by the sea, where the salt air permeates it. Light and long lasting, dried, headless fish travel well and make an excellent commodity. In Greenland, the similar farm-to-farm trade was between reindeer and seal. Bones of cheap, plentiful seal are found far from the sea, while the best cuts of reindeer seem to have traveled down from the highlands, where they were hunted, to the chieftains' farms.

Jared Diamond cites another line of reasoning to prove that the Vikings' dependence on livestock caused their culture to collapse: Jette Arneborg's own study of human bones, published in the journal *Radiocarbon* in 1999.

In 1961 workers digging the foundation for a school dormitory near Eirik the Red's Brattahlid discovered a tiny church surrounded by a circular graveyard. *The Saga of Eirik the Red* speaks of such a church. In the year 999 Leif Eiriksson abandoned pregnant Thorgunna in the Hebrides and sailed to Norway to meet the king, Olaf Tryggvason. King Olaf was at the time strenuously urging Iceland to become Christian—so strenuously that he impounded all the Icelandic ships and imprisoned all the Icelandic men who had visited Norway that year, including Kjartan and Bolli, the lovers of Gudrun the

Fair. King Olaf's arm-twisting led the Icelandic chieftains to declare Christianity the official state religion the next summer. Through Leif Eiriksson, Greenland followed suit: Leif returned home from his visit to the king with a priest, timber to build a church, and a vow to do the king's saintly will. His mother, Thjodhild, converted instantly and had the chapel built, over her husband's objections: "As a Christian, Thjodhild refused to sleep with Eirik the Red. This annoyed him greatly."

The site and dating of the church found at Brattahlid match the story, and in spite of being professionally wary of the sagas, archaeologists refer to it as "Thjodhild's Church." In the churchyard were 155 graves: men to the south, women to the north, children and babies to the east. Twelve men and a boy were buried in a common grave, their bones "in wild disorder" except for the skulls, which were lined up facing east. More than one commentator has remarked that these must be the bones of Gudrid's husband, Thorstein Eiriksson, and the men who died with him during that terrible winter at Sandnes. As the saga says, "The bodies were carried to the church in Eiriksfjord, and priests performed the proper Christian rites."

It is likely that the bones of Thjodhild, Eirik the Red, and Leif Eiriksson, too, are among the skeletons that now reside in a climate-controlled room at the museum in Copenhagen. It was definitely a family cemetery—a dentist can see the family resemblance in the skeletons' teeth—and in use for only a short time in the first half of the eleventh century. Studies of the bones show that Eirik's people were healthy and tall, the men averaging five-foot-ten, and the women five-foot-five. Their teeth are especially good, with no cavities and little tooth loss—overall, better than either the Norwegians or Icelanders of the time. Icelanders, in particular, lost three times as many teeth before death.

Their teeth did show some wear by abrasion, probably due to grit in their food. Because of a dearth of large iron pots in which to boil their pork and goat (as the gods would do), the Greenlanders generally roasted meat outdoors in pits, laying it on the embers and packing earth over it. Chewing air-dried meat was also hard on the teeth; air drying, in dry-stone sheds, was a common way to preserve meat for the winter.

To learn how the Vikings' diets might have changed between Eirik the Red's Land-Taking in 985 and the last word from Norse Greenland in 1408, Jette Arneborg and her colleagues drilled tiny samples of bone from twenty-seven skeletons, some from Thjodhild's cemetery and some from five other graveyards. These bone bits were then analyzed for their concentration of three forms of carbon: the radioactive carbon 14 and the two stable isotopes, carbon 12 and carbon 13. For comparison purposes, the scientists also analyzed bits of cloth found in the graves and an ox bone that had slipped into the mass grave at Brattahlid by mistake.

Carbon 14, or radiocarbon, has been used by archaeologists for half a century to date wood, bone, and anything else that contains carbon. Being radioactive, carbon 14 decays over time; its proportion in a bone tells you when that bone stopped taking in carbon—that is, when it died. By measuring the carbon 14 in the annual rings of ancient trees like the very-long-lived bristlecone pine, scientists have been able to create a carbon-14 calibration curve that extends back over 10,000 years. By matching your bone sample against the tree-ring curve, you can date it to within about thirty years. The problem with applying this technique to human bones is that it is affected by what the human was eating for the ten years before he or she died. If the food came from the sea, the tree-ring curve will give dates several hundred years too old. For example, when analyzed this way, one young woman in Jette's sample was 420 years older than her clothes.

The dates are skewed by what scientists call the marine-reservoir effect. While the ratio of carbon 12 to carbon 13 to carbon 14 in the air is more or less constant, seawater holds very little carbon 13. The amount of carbon 14 depends on the water's depth, with more carbon 14 at the surface and less in the deeps.

Carbon is drawn out of the air or water by green plants during photosynthesis, and gets into human bones through the food chain. A person who eats primarily milk, mutton, and venison will show in her bones the carbon taken out of the air by the grass, twigs, and lichens eaten by the cow, sheep, or deer. A person who eats primarily fish or seal will show in her bones the carbon taken out of the water by plankton, one-celled aquatic plants that feed the fish fry and larvae on which ocean predators ultimately dine. The ratio of carbon 12 to carbon 13 for these two skeletons will not be the same.

Carbon-14 dates can be corrected for the marine-reservoir effect—so that a skeleton matches her burial clothes—if you know how much seafood the person ate. In reverse, skeletons dated by other means from cultures whose eating habits are known can tell us what ratio of carbon 12 to carbon 13 to look for to learn whether the Vikings buried at Brattahlid ate more mutton or seal meat.

The differences are very small. The tests are painstaking and tedious. But the bones from Brattahlid seem to show that Gudrid's diet while she lived there would have been between 22 and 50 percent seafood, including whale and seal. The later Greenland Norse, close to the collapse in the 1400s, ate up to 81 percent seafood.

Jared Diamond interprets this change to mean that the later Norse were having trouble making hay. They couldn't keep

enough cows to feed their growing population and were forced
to turn to seal or starve. Maybe. The paper she published in *Radiocarbon* in 1999, Jette told me, was only "a small project" to test
the method. She is unwilling to build an edifice, as Diamond
did, on twenty-seven bones. In the last six years, she and her
colleagues have tested many more bones, including those dug up
by Gudny Zoega at Keldudalur in Iceland. As Jette sees it, she
has "just started trying to make some human conclusions."

Georg Nyegaard, who dug side by side with Jette at the
Farm Beneath the Sand, thinks her 1999 results showed not a
chronological difference, but a geographical one. "Jette's article
had a very little number of individuals," he told me, "and the
later individuals are all from graveyards on the coast. You always
have more seal bones at sites on the outer coast." He expects her
results will change now that she has a larger sample size.

Georg's own research shows no change in diet during three
hundred years of Norse settlement in Greenland. When not
organizing exhibits for the museum in Nuuk, Georg has been
analyzing animal bones from a bog in the valley north of Brattahlid, beside a farm a mile and a half from the sea. Settled
in the second wave—about the time Gudrid and her father
arrived—it has a midden with a difference: In the bog water,
bones were very well preserved. And no one had disturbed it
before Georg came, which means that the chronology of his
samples, calculated from their depth in the bog, is better than
for any previous collection of bones.

Judging from the 50,000 mammal bones he has dated,
Georg said, "It was a small farm, but there seems to have been
very little change through time. We can compare whatever layer
we want to any other and we'll see the same overall picture, the
same ratio of cows to sheep. We have goat bones and pig bones
as well. Quite seldom do you find pig bones, but at this bog site,

we found them in all the different layers. There seems to have been a few pigs all the time—which is not what the theories say. They had a few horses, and they ate them, too. We see the cracked marrow bones. Then there's the dog bones in several sizes, big and small. And for the first time we found cat bones in Greenland. But at this site we see no change toward more marine adaptation. The marine part of the diet was a major part right from the start of the farm. We have many seal bones.

"They left the farm around 1300. In the final phase, we find the same percentage of cattle bones as at the beginning. If you have problems with the vegetation, with feeding the domestic stock, the first thing that would happen is a decrease in the number of cows. The cow is very expensive to feed in the winter. It's much cheaper to feed goats, and goats provide a lot of milk. But they go on with the same number of cows, maybe six or seven if you look at the cowshed, for three hundred years."

It's frustrating when a handsome theory like Jared Diamond's collapses, but the science simply doesn't support the idea that the Vikings ate themselves out of house and home and then starved, rather than lowering themselves to eating Inuit food. Georg Nyegaard's study argues instead that overgrazing in Greenland was not severe. The Vikings had no need to give up their honored cows. Nor did they hesitate to eat seafood.

Rather than dying out, they are more likely to have packed up and left, slowly, over a hundred years or more, the younger folk finding berths (or husbands) aboard the trade ships that still sailed fairly regularly from Iceland and Norway in the 1300s; by the early 1400s, the British were also plying Greenland waters in search of cod. The ships would have brought news of the Black Death, which killed half the population of Iceland between 1402 and 1404—or some 20,000 to 35,000 people, ten times the total Norse population of Greenland—

and left hundreds of valuable farms unoccupied. Doubtless Sigrid Bjornsdottir, whose marriage to an Icelandic ship's captain in the church at Hvalsey in 1408 is the last historical record of the Greenland Norse, was not the only heiress. The plague gave this young Greenlandic woman ownership of Stora-Akrar (Big Grain Fields), a wealthy farm in Skagafjord, Iceland, where, six hundred years later Sigridur Sigurdardottir, the curator of the museum at Glaumbaer, would grow up.

The sailors would also have told the Greenlanders that their caches of walrus ivory—Greenland's chief export—were now worthless. Elephant ivory became easy to get in the 1300s and, with the market flooded, all ivory had become cheap and unfashionable by the end of the century.

CHAPTER 7

Land of Wine or Walrus

A ship came to Greenland from Norway that summer. Its captain was a man named Thorfinn Karlsefni. He was the son of Thord Horse-Head, a son of Snorri Thordarson from Hofdi. Thorfinn Karlsefni was very rich. He spent the winter at Brattahlid with Leif Eiriksson and soon fell in love with Gudrid.

—*The Saga of the Greenlanders*

WALRUS IVORY BROUGHT KARLSEFNI TO GREENLAND. In the Viking Age, walrus ivory was as valuable as gold, and the only place to get it was in the north, where the seas are iced over nine months of the year, and mussels, the walrus's favorite food, seed the shallow bottoms of the bays. Five hundred miles north of Sandnes, the walrus congregated on the beaches each August. Eirik the Red's men would sail to Sandnes, replenish their supplies, and set out in hunting parties for Nordsetur—the Northern Camp. Then came the slaughter.

The Norse had no harpoons, so they trapped the huge beasts on land, where they were clumsy. They came at the animals with lances and spears, like Sir James Lamont did in 1858 in Spitsbergen, in northern Norway. "In all my sporting life I never saw anything to equal the wild excitement of these hunts," he writes. Sixteen men stole along the sea's edge, then rushed at the thousands of walrus lounging on the rocks, stabbing those nearest the water.

> The passage to the sea soon got blocked up with dead and dying walrus. When drenched with blood and exhausted, and their lances from repeated use became blunt and useless, [the men] returned to their vessel, had their dinner, ground their lances, and then returned, killing nine hundred walrus.

Even today, writes Robert McGhee in *The Last Imaginary Place: A Human History of the Arctic World,* the beaches of Spitsbergen are "carpeted with thick and heavy bones, the massive skulls with missing tusks."

The Vikings also left most of the bones on the beach. They took the skins to make a strong rope highly prized as sail rigging and anchor cables. Each skin could rig two or three ships. They cut off the penis. Walrus have a thick bone stiffening the male member; it made a good club. They knocked off the front of the skull, taking it home to do the careful work of extracting the valuable ivory tusks at leisure. And they took a joint or two for food.

Ivory was the perfect trade good. It was light, it kept indefinitely, and until elephant ivory nudged it out of the marketplace in the 1300s, it was essential to aristocratic Christian life. The finest reliquary boxes for holding the remains of saints were made of ivory. Crosses and crucifixes and bishops' croziers were intricately carved of ivory, as were the palm-sized religious plaques fastened to the covers of holy books. Nonecclesiastical uses included sword hilts, belt buckles, dice, and chess pieces—like the twelfth-century set found on the Isle of Lewis.

The Greenlanders kept very little ivory for themselves. The

bishop's crozier—a staff of office in the shape of a shepherd's crook—was retrieved from the bishop's grave when the church at Gardar in South Greenland was excavated; the designs on its curved ivory head date it to the late 1100s. The churchyard also contained thirty walrus skulls with tusks intact, some in a row along the church's east gable, others buried in the chancel itself. As Jette Arneborg deadpans, these totemic animal burials were "not quite according to normal Christian practice." Otherwise, archaeologists have found only a few ivory buttons and some tiny amulets. Two icons unearthed at one Norse farm were polar bears; a third might be a walrus. (It wasn't finished before it was lost.) A human figure thought to be a chess queen was found in an Inuit camp.

It may have been over a chess game played with ivory pieces that Gudrid first spoke to Karlsefni about Vinland. According to *The Saga of Eirik the Red*, Karlsefni was a sensible merchant esteemed for his seamanship—not an adventurer. He is described as wealthy and well connected, from a large and noble family, with kings in his lineage. His grandfather was one of nineteen children, so Karlsefni was related to most of the families in the prosperous valley of Skagafjord in northern Iceland. He was five or ten years older than Gudrid, having had time to establish himself in his profession, and he was an only son, owner of a substantial estate being looked after by his widowed mother.

As a good merchant, he would have been brave but also "discreet," according to *The King's Mirror*, a thirteenth-century handbook that gives this advice to businessmen: "On the sea . . . be alert and fearless. When you are in a market town, or wherever you are, be polite and agreeable; then you will secure the friendship of all good men." The writer, a priest who served three kings of Norway as chancellor and military adviser, asserts:

"I regard no man perfect in knowledge unless he has thoroughly learned and mastered the customs of the place where he is sojourning," chief among those customs being the language. He also admonishes any would-be trader to learn arithmetic, navigation or "how to mark the movements of the ocean," and the proper care of a ship. Finally, to be a good trader, you must "keep your temper calm" and "be not in a hurry to take revenge."

Karlsefni owned his ship in partnership with another Icelander, Snorri Thorbrandsson of Swan Fjord. This Snorri may have been ten or fifteen years older than his friend, and had certainly never heard *The King's Mirror's* advice. He and his brothers, along with Gudrid's father, were Eirik the Red's chief supporters in his feud with Thorgest the Old over those bench boards. After Eirik the Red left Iceland, the Swan Fjord brothers filled his role of district troublemaker. Besides being unruly and clannish, they were known for wearing tight, fashionable trousers. Snorri Thorbrandsson and one brother, Thorleif Kimbi, finally went to Greenland a year or two before Gudrid arrived, having forced their chieftain—the cunning and ambitious Snorri of Helgafell—to get them out of trouble once too often. One feud, for instance, started when Thorleif Kimbi grabbed a cooking pot away from another Viking, spilling the man's evening porridge, and was whacked with the hot ladle on his neck. In the last battle of this disagreement, two men died and the chieftain arrived just in time to save his foster-brothers' lives: Thorleif Kimbi had lost a leg and Snorri Thorbrandsson had taken an arrow through the throat. As proof of his manliness, we're told that he snapped off the shaft and didn't mention the arrowhead at the base of his tongue until he was sitting down to dinner that evening and noticed it was hard to swallow. Karlsefni's partner was tough and touchy, but he was a loyal friend—none of the feuds he fought in were his own. He had also lived in Greenland before setting up his trading route, and his friendship with Eirik the Red ensured Karlsefni's welcome.

The partners crossed the icy North Atlantic in convoy with a second trading ship crewed by Icelanders. They beached their boats in front of Brattahlid (a sonar survey of the fjord has found that the beach was 300 feet broader in those days) and unloaded their goods into Eirik's capacious warehouses, signs of which archaeologists can still see in the turf. *The Saga of Eirik the Red* next details the courtly dance of give-and-take that passed for a business transaction in the Viking Age. The two ships' captains invited Eirik to take anything he wanted from their cargoes. "Then Eirik showed them he was a great man, too," as the saga says, by offering to feed and house both ships' crews over the long Greenlandic winter. "They lacked nothing," the saga says, and enjoyed themselves until Christmas, when Eirik started going about the house with a long face. After a bit of polite prying, Karlsefni learned that Eirik feared he would tell everyone back home in Iceland that he had never had a poorer Christmas feast than that one at Brattahlid. Eirik was out of beer. "That's no problem," said Karlsefni. "We still have malt and grain from the ship. Take it and brew up a feast greater than any before." After a discreet pause, Karlsefni asked Eirik for Gudrid's hand in marriage, and this drunken, happy Christmas feast was extended into a wedding.

With Gudrid—at least, with the rich Gudrid of *The Saga of Eirik the Red*—Karlsefni gained half of Sandnes, her husband's farm. He got her father's farm, across the fjord from Brattahlid, and her father's ship. It's clear Karlsefni had no plans to put down roots in Greenland, given the value of his property back in Iceland. He would have sold Gudrid's farms in the spring for their worth in walrus tusks and hides, other skins (ox and goat for leather, polar bear for luxury), and perhaps one or two white falcons, which were highly prized by the Arabs. He would also have taken in trade whatever foodstuffs he needed to restock his ship for the return journey.

The haul might have been less than he had expected, divided up among his and the other ship's sailors, and he may not have had much of value left to trade. He had already donated his malt and grain to Eirik for the feast. He had probably given Eirik the other foodstuffs in his cargo, too—how else could Eirik have fed so many unexpected mouths over the long winter? Eirik would have chosen the iron tools and ingots in the cargo first off, when the captains gave him his pick of the goods. That left some linen or other fine cloth, wood for housewares or boat repair, candle wax and wine for the church, tar for sealing ships' timbers, and perhaps some bronze or silver jewelry and other finery. Fiddling with the arithmetic in his head, Karlsefni might have wondered if sailing through the ice and storms to Greenland had been worth the risk.

Yet even sensible merchants did not go to Greenland solely for gain. As *The King's Mirror* notes, they went to win fame, by sailing where others had sunk; and out of curiosity: "For it is also in man's nature to wish to see and experience the things that he has heard about, and thus to learn whether the facts are as told or not." And Karlsefni, as events would show, was both ambitious and curious.

Among the entertainments at Eirik's feast, and throughout that gay winter, the saga lists chess (or a game like it, *hneftafl* or "tables") and storytelling. Leif Eiriksson was easily cajoled into telling the story of his discovery of the rich new land to the west: Vinland. No one knows which version he related. He was blown off course, he may have said, on his way west from Norway four years ago. He spied a strange country and, landing, found it to be a paradise. Three things in particular struck him—three things which today no one can positively identify: fields of "self-sown wheat," well-grown "wine wood," and trees "big enough for house timbers" of a valuable wood called *mösurr*.

On the other hand, Leif may have told Karlsefni how he had cleverly retraced, backward, the route of another seaman, Bjarni Herjolfsson, who had been blown off course coming to Greenland and had refused to set foot on the three strange lands he had spotted farther west than any land ought to be. The northernmost land Leif named Helluland ("Flat Stone Land"). A little south was Markland ("Forest Land"). Then came Vinland ("Wine Land"), which had sweet dew on the grass, huge salmon, "wine wood" and "wine berries," and wide forests. In this story, Leif and his crew stayed the winter, first putting up "booths," or temporary shelters roofed by sailcloth, and then building large houses. They filled the ship with timber, and the towboat with wine berries.

Lured by Leif's stories of this land of riches, and inspired by Gudrid's eagerness for adventure—she had already gone looking for Vinland once before, she would have told him—Karlsefni made ready to sail when the ice went out in June. According to one saga, he took sixty-five people in one ship; in the other saga, his expedition had three ships (one of them Gudrid's) and 160 people. Says *The Saga of the Greenlanders,* they took along "all kinds of livestock," presumably from Gudrid's farms, "because they meant to settle there if they could."

Before he set sail, Karlsefni asked Leif to let him have the large houses he had built there to overwinter in.

"I won't *give* them to you," Leif said. "I'll *lend* them to you."

The sagas do not mention walrus, but likely they were on Leif's list of Vinland's riches. From Nordsetur, thought to be Greenland's Disko Island, you can sometimes see Baffin Island on the Canadian side, and the Vikings may have rowed well out into the Davis Strait to hunt the herds on the ice. This is the course Karlsefni and Gudrid took—north to Sandnes, north again to Nordsetur, west across the Davis Strait, and then south following the currents along the coastline of Canada. Gudrid may have warned Karlsefni not to head west too soon; that's how she and her previous husband ended up tossed about by the sea all summer. As a practiced ocean navigator, Karlsefni would have learned everything he could about the prevailing winds and currents.

They would have seen icebergs, and walrus, the whole way as they sailed south past Flat Stone Land or, as one scholar interprets it, "So-So Land," now thought to be Baffin Island; and Forest Land or "Useful Land," now identified with Labrador; until they arrived in Wine Land or "Luxury Land."

Where exactly is Wine Land? Georgia. Or between Pennsylvania and the Carolinas. Or New York harbor. Boston, on the Charles River near Harvard University. Rhode Island or Martha's Vineyard. Cape Cod or the coast of Maine. New Hampshire, New Brunswick, Nova Scotia, Newfoundland, Labrador, the St. Lawrence Valley, or back in Greenland. All of these places have been suggested in serious manner between 1757 and today. As the irrepressible BBC television host Magnus Magnusson said at a conference in Newfoundland in 2000, "Enthusiasts have twiddled the texts, selected from the texts, conflated the texts, and compromised the texts in endless attempts to create a coherent story that will 'prove' their particular hypothesis. But frankly, the sailing directions which dozens of eager researchers have tried to follow are not much more explicit than the old Icelandic adage for getting to North America: Sail south until the butter melts, and then turn right." Though folklorist Gisli Sigurdsson believes the Vinland sagas hold a coherent "mental map" of Viking explorations along the coast of North America, he concedes that "perhaps the most striking feature of the attempts to locate Vinland is that each and every person to have made one has disagreed with everyone else."

Some of the enthusiasts have evidence to back up their theories. In 1890, Eben Norton Horsford, a former professor of science at Harvard University, discovered what he believed to be a Viking city in Massachusetts, on the banks of the Charles River where it meets Stony Brook. According to Andrew Wawn, an expert on the Victorians' passion for Vikings, Horsford "came to archaeology late in life. His earlier publications had included works on phrenology, bread making, water pipes, coral reefs, glacial ammonia, tea ashes, and the problem of offensive odours from pig slaughtering. . . . His booklet *The Army Ration. How to diminish its weight and bulk, secure economy in its administration, avoid waste, and increase the comfort, efficiency, and mobility of troops* (1864) appeared just in time to become a best seller during the Civil War period."

On the banks of the Charles River, Horsford found the docks and wharves, pavements and terraced "places of assembly" of a city he called Norumbega and that he said was founded by Leif Eiriksson. He also found a turf house, "the outlines of which correspond with the outlines of an Icelandic house in the saga time," according to Horsford's contemporary, Rasmus B. Anderson. In the center of the house, Horsford's workmen found charcoal and fire-cracked stones. Digging along its rectangular perimeter, they found "a marked depression, as if there had been a door." In 1895 Horsford's daughter Cornelia funded the first excavation of Eiriksstadir in the Dales of Iceland in order to confirm her father's discovery. The outline of Eirik the Red's house there (later proved to look quite different) seemed to verify Horsford's find in Massachusetts.

Helge Ingstad, who claimed to find Leif Eiriksson's Vinland 1,500 miles farther north, at L'Anse aux Meadows, Newfoundland, in 1960, had a curriculum vitae almost as eccentric as Horsford's, if a bit more finely focused. He left a law career in his native Norway in 1926 to live as a fur trapper in the Canadian Arctic for four years. He came home only to be posted to south Greenland as governor of Eirik the Red's old settlement, which Norway was trying to extract from Denmark. Next he governed the Svalbard Islands, in the Norwegian Arctic, before ditching the political life to live among the Apache Indians in Arizona. He married archaeologist Anne Stine Moe in 1941, and during World War II served in the Norwegian resistance. In the 1950s, he and Anne Stine went to Greenland to study the Viking ruins, which resulted in his book, *Land Under the Pole Star*. He set off up the coast of North America in the spring of 1960, determined to locate Vinland. He started in Rhode Island and traveled north by boat, plane, and foot, asking people he encountered "about traces of old house sites."

At the far northwestern tip of Newfoundland, Ingstad fell into conversation with a man named George Decker who had "something bold and authoritative about him." Decker took Ingstad around to see the hillocks where he liked to cut hay, since the grass grew tallest there. The locals called them the Indian mounds.

As soon as he saw the mounds, Ingstad had no doubt they were houses, "and very old ones." Looking around, "I had a distinct feeling of recognition," he writes in his book, *Westward to Vinland*. "There was so much here at L'Anse aux Meadows that reminded me of what I had seen of the surroundings of the Norse farms in Greenland: the green fields, the rippling stream, the open country, the view of the sea, and perhaps something else that was not so easy to fathom. Here the people from the Arctic island would have felt at home."

Anne Stine settled in to excavate, and four years later Ing-stad announced, through an article in *National Geographic* magazine: "Vinland Ruins Prove Vikings Found the New World."

Serious Viking scholars had been tricked too often by such "cult archaeology" as Horsford's—whose Harvard ruins, un-datable, delivering no artifacts, could be Indian or early set-tlers'—to accept Ingstad's claim. Even when a spindle whorl, a small soapstone ring used for spinning wool, was unearthed, they tried to explain it away. No eastern Indians kept sheep or knew how to spin wool. No seventeenth-century French settler would use a spindle instead of a spinning wheel. But historian Frederick J. Pohl, writing in 1966, had an answer. L'Anse aux Meadows must have been an emergency camp, settled by one of the eleven ships lost in the storm in 985 on their way to Green-land with Eirik the Red. As Pohl wrote in an appendix to *The Viking Explorers,* the place simply couldn't be Leif Eiriksson's Vinland. "The L'Anse aux Meadows settlement does not by any stretch of the imagination fit the description in the sagas. It sat-isfies fewer than six of the eighteen geographical requirements. It is not up a river at the shore of a lake. There are no vines in Newfoundland. And so on."

Pohl's geographical requirements, drawn from his idiosyn-cratic reading of the sagas, are so vague as to match hundreds of spots on the Atlantic seaboard. Concatenating fourteen of them, we can say that Vinland is southwest of Greenland, with a prominent island thick with birds' nests, a wide shallow bay, a sandy cape, an amazingly long beach somewhere to the north, a river with tidal flats, and a couple of lakes. The sagas sometimes tell how long it took to sail from one spot to another, but scholars argue viciously over how to translate "a day's sail" into a distance. Is a "day" twenty-four hours? Twelve hours? The time when the sun is up? A Viking ship *can* sail at eleven knots per hour; we know from the replicas. It can also lie becalmed and be storm-driven backward. Some scholars take the wind into account. Others note that a cautious captain in an unknown sea with no hope of rescue might care to take his time, while an explorer, by definition, should poke into every interesting cove and bay.

A note on the length of a winter day in *The Saga of the Greenlanders* has been similarly dissected. It has "proved" that Vinland lay at a latitude of 31 degrees North (as does Jekyll Island, Georgia)—and at 50 degrees North (nearer to L'Anse aux Meadows). The saga says simply: "The length of day and night was more equal than in Greenland or Iceland," adding that the sun could be seen "during the short days" at *eyktarstaður* and at *dagmálastaður.* No one knows if those two terms apply to the places on the horizon where the sun rises and sets, or to times of day.

With the sailing directions and the day length both inscrutable, we are left with the Vikings' list of Vinland's riches. The land is called "Wine Land" so often, not only in the sagas but in other sources, that there must have been some berry from which wine could be made; the question of whether wine requires grapes has bedeviled generations of scholars. Although the words I've translated literally as "wine wood" and "wine berries" refer to grapevines and grapes in modern Icelandic, we can't be sure they did so in Gudrid's day. A related question is whether the Vin of Vinland has a long or short "i": *vín* (long "i") means wine; *vin* (short "i") means meadow. Although most scholars are convinced by linguistic arguments that Vinland is Wine Land not Meadow Land, and that the "Meadow" in the name L'Anse aux Meadows is a corruption of a French word for jellyfish or a ship's name, the other side of the debate still arises. The sagas do mention pastures "so rich that it seemed to them the sheep would need no hay all winter. There was no frost in the winter, and the grass hardly withered." There was also some kind of wild grain that resembled wheat. Eider ducks nested on the offshore islands, whales washed up on the beaches, and fish, including large salmon, could be easily caught. There were bears and foxes and plentiful game. Finally there were those *mösurr* trees "big enough for house timbers." (Twenty feet would have been tall enough.)

On Green Island off L'Anse aux Meadows, according to George Decker, "were so many eider ducks that you couldn't put your foot down without stepping on an egg." (Helge Ingstad, who quotes him, doesn't say whether he had primed Decker by reading to him *The Saga of Eirik the Red,* where there's an island with "so many eider ducks you could hardly walk for all the eggs.") Decker's daughter-in-law Madge, who cooked for the bed-and-breakfast where I stayed in August 2006, told me the duck population is lower now, but I saw eiders as I walked along the shore. I also saw berries galore: raspberries, strawberries, blueberries, crowberries, red and black currants (whose name in modern Swedish means "wine berries"), lingonberries, cloud-berries, and cranberries. I saw stands of bleached grass with a wheatlike head. And I walked through acres of boggy pasture and spongy turf edged by impenetrable, head-high spruce woods, the twisted trunks and spiny branches a poor source of charcoal (the wood is not dense enough to burn hot) and absolutely useless as house timbers.

It was a windy, wide-open place, filled with the roar of the sea and the plangent cries of whimbrels. With the sun hot on my neck, I had, like Ingstad, the overwhelming sense that Karlsefni and his crew would have felt at home here. The bare rocks and mosses and low-growing juniper, the bog and black beach looked surprisingly Icelandic. A hill called Round Head was a double for Helgafell, at the mouth of Iceland's Swan

Fjord; it would have been a comforting, homey sight for Snorri Thorbrandsson. One of the islands in view recalled the blocky, steep-sided Drangey, the most prominent landmark of Karlsefni's Skagafjord.

It was warmer than Iceland the week I visited, as it had been the first year the Ingstads excavated the site, when the summer temperature averaged 55 degrees Fahrenheit. But the weather is not always so pleasant in northern Newfoundland. August is the only month in which freezing temperatures haven't been recorded—the jokesters say there are only two seasons in Newfoundland: August and winter. Although it lies on the same latitude as London, L'Anse aux Meadows abuts the cold Labrador Current, which brings icebergs down from Baffin Bay. The sea freezes solid in December. It breaks up into a jumble of pans and plates and boat-sinking bergs, blocking ships from the Gulf of St. Lawrence well into June, and scattered icebergs may linger into August. Snow can be expected from November to May. Is this Vinland, where "there was no frost in the winter, and the grass hardly withered"?

Birgitta Wallace, an archaeologist trained in Sweden, began working alongside Anne Stine Ingstad in the late 1960s and was put in charge of the dig—by then overseen by Canada's national parks service—in 1975. Though retired, she is still the chief archaeologist associated with the site. In 1998, she writes, there was no snow there at all, and only a dusting in April 1999. The average temperature that winter was one or two degrees higher than normal, just as it was in the eleventh century, according to scientists who have modeled the past climate based on data from the Greenland ice cores.

"I do believe Leif Eiriksson slept here," Wallace told me when I met her at L'Anse aux Meadows in 2006. But she is not about to argue that there were once grapes growing in northern

Newfoundland. "I don't understand why people want to make Vinland one *spot*. People have never suggested that Helluland or Markland is one spot. Of course Vinland is not a little spot, and L'Anse aux Meadows can never be Vinland. It's *in* Vinland. Vinland is a much larger concept. I find it odd when people chastise me, 'You didn't find any grapes, so it can't be Vinland.' People don't think Brattahlid is all of Greenland.

"All I do is start with the archaeology. You can't deny that L'Anse aux Meadows is here."

The Ingstads had found three Viking longhouses, spaced evenly a hundred feet apart, on a grassy terrace above the shallow bay. Each house, built of turf in traditional Icelandic style, consists of a main *skáli* with a central longfire and wide sleeping benches along the walls, a large workshop, and one or more smaller rooms. Each house could sleep twenty-five to thirty people, or roughly one ship's crew. Two of the houses have small outbuildings, one of which is clearly a pit house. Across the brook is a tiny hut where iron was extracted from bog ore.

The walls Anne Stine Ingstad mapped are now outlined by low grassy ridges interrupted by door openings, so that tourists can walk through the original houses without destroying the last traces of them. Showing me the site, Birgitta darted from one wall to another, pointing with a pink-sneakered foot at the mistakes: "This room had a very clear door out to the west, toward the bog. That pit is not supposed to be here." The house outlines had been made in 1975; since then Birgitta has spent many years reanalyzing Anne Stine's work. "I've looked at all the photos, plans, and drawings—and I took notes at the time. I have gone back to the find bags and the earliest reports. They tend to be the most correct."

Next to the archaeological site, Parks Canada built a reconstruction of one of the longhouses—presumably the leader's, since it had the best location, closest to the brook. A spacious and sensible structure, it has four rooms in a line. At one end of the great hall is a snug sleeping room for the women; in the other direction, a doorway leads to a sizable workshop and an ample storage room.

But the turf ridges over the original dig show no central doorway—to go from the hall to the workshop, you have to go outside. Was that another mistake? No, Birgitta said. "The door isn't real. They needed it for traffic flow for the tourists.

"Though," she added, "I cannot be completely sure there wasn't a door. The first excavation was done under a very difficult situation. It was a tremendous job for Anne Stine to do this all by herself. And she had never dug turf buildings before."

Using the latest carbon-14 methods, the settlement has been dated to the year 1000, give or take thirty years. The tiny amount of trash uncovered—the midden is only about 12 feet long and 10 inches deep—proves the people did not live here long. (By comparison, the midden of a Norse farm in Greenland, occupied for 350 years, is almost 500 feet long and over five feet deep.)

Only a very few artifacts turned up, lost or broken in and around the houses, a lack that shows the Vikings were not run off, but left when they wanted to, after collecting and packing their things. The most impressive artifact is a bronze pin, used to clasp a dress or cloak, that was found in the longhouse beside the brook. The design was quite common in the tenth and eleventh centuries: a straight pin about four inches long, with a simple ring at one end. Thirteen like it have been found in Iceland alone, some in men's graves and others in women's.

The broken end of a bone needle used for a kind of single-needle knitting was dug from a fire pit, and a needle hone, a slip of quartzite about three inches long used to sharpen a metal sewing needle, was retrieved from the floor. A white glass bead (subsequently lost by the conservation lab in Ottawa) was picked out of the dirt by a doorstep. Beside a broken wall, in a pile of rubble George Decker had dumped when he was digging a hole for a fencepost (or looking for buried treasure, says another version of the story), was the soapstone spindle whorl, proof that a Viking woman was here, in North America, a thousand years ago.

"It had been a horrible, miserable day," said Birgitta, "cold and wet, one of those days when you work from teacup to teacup." A student found the spindle whorl by the northernmost house, just outside the attached shed where a Viking ship had been repaired. Perhaps the woman had come by to watch the men work, spinning as she walked, and something had made her drop or put down her spindle and forget all about it, leaving us her calling card. "I had brought a bottle of champagne in my backpack," Birgitta told me, "and you can bet it was cracked open that night!"

In a documentary movie shown in the park's visitors' center, Anne Stine Ingstad says, "Sometimes I identified myself with Gudrid of the sagas. When we found the spindle whorl, I thought it must have been hers. . . . And when I was longing for home, I thought of how she must have been lonely."

I asked Birgitta what she thought.

"I have no problem with Gudrid being here," she replied. "She was!"

One scholar has called the L'Anse aux Meadows artifacts "a rather disappointing collection." But Birgitta Wallace's analysis of some very uncharismatic artifacts—rusty nails, chips of wood, the slag from smelting bog ore—found around the houses and in the bog between them and the sea has answered the question, not only of *Where is Vinland?* but of what part L'Anse aux Meadows played in the Vinland story—Gudrid's story.

The Viking ship repaired in the shed where a woman lost her spindle whorl was not a *knarr,* but a small boat, a *knarr's* towboat. On the floor of the shed were the marks of a wooden form that had held the boat steady. Scattered inside and out were iron nails. Chemical analysis showed they had not been made from the local bog ore. X-rays proved their heads had been struck off with a chisel so they could be drawn from the wood they had once clinched.

The only whole nail, on the other hand, had been made from the local ore, which collects in ruddy nodules along the banks of the stream and clings to the undersides of turf blocks cut from the bog. The bog ore had been roasted in one of the outbuildings at the south end of the settlement. The iron had been smelted from the ore in a hut across Black Duck Brook beside a tiny tumble of rapids. The smelter was not very good at his job—the waste slag still held 80 percent of the iron in the ore. Nor did he practice: The furnace was fired only once, producing six to seven pounds of iron, enough for a hundred nails the size of those used in the Gokstad ship. The nails were fashioned in the workshop of the southernmost house.

So few nails would have secured only a very small patch—the total number of nails in the Gokstad ship is 3,500—and indeed, the broken floorboard of a small boat, with a plug of Scots pine, a European species, was among the hundreds of bits of worked wood that had been preserved in the bog's acid water. Some of the wood was worked with metal tools; experts saw marks of a knife and a broadaxe. The metal-worked debris seemed to fan out from the one west-facing door in the middle longhouse, the door that opened from its workshop. There were wood shavings and the cut-off ends of posts, tree-nails made of fir, and many slender skewers. (Skewers are commonly found at Viking market sites: They might be toggles for fastening bales of cargo.)

Other wood pieces had been shaped with stone tools. The layers of peat in the bog showed clearly that the people who cut with metal (the Vikings) and those who cut with stone (the native Inuit and Indians) had lived at L'Anse aux Meadows at different times. Stoneworkers were there from 4000 B.C. until 850 A.D., metalworkers for a few years around the year 1000, then stoneworkers after 1200 until colonial times. For at least 150 years before the Norse arrived, and again after they left, the peat that accumulated in the bog bore no trash.

The Vikings chose this spot precisely because it was long deserted. This settlement on the cold coast of Newfoundland—where, an Icelandic meteorologist has pointed out, the annual mean temperature was lower than at any Icelandic farm—was not a farm. It was an outpost, a base camp, a way to use and to control the resources of the whole Gulf of St. Lawrence from the Straits of Belle Isle west to Quebec and south to the forested banks of the Miramichi River in New Brunswick. About 2,000 miles from Greenland, the outpost could be reached in nine days (although the unlucky sailors in the unpowered replica Snorri took eighty-seven days to sail here from Brattahlid in "the windless summer" of 1998); the distance compared well to the standard twelve-day trip from Greenland to Norway. With the nearest Indian camp at Bird Cove, 75 miles to the south, the Vikings could safely winter here with full storerooms. They were safe from their own kind, too: Any sail entering the Gulf could be seen from here. And it was easy to find. With a few words, Leif could have told Karlsefni and Gudrid how to locate his camp. "There was only one thing for them to keep in mind on the southward journey: namely, not to lose sight of land to the west," writes Helge Ingstad, who more than once had approached by boat. "Great Sacred Island would then be an unmistakable landmark, and L'Anse aux Meadows lay just behind that island. It was as simple as that."

The camp at L'Anse aux Meadows was meant to last for many years and to serve many expeditions. The house walls are substantial and built with thoughts of winter—the walls to the west, where the wind blew off the sea ice, are slightly thicker than those to the east. Each house can lodge a full ship's crew—with private space for women in two of them—and each house has storage rooms to rival the warehouses at Brattahlid. The Vikings felled at least eighty-six tall trees to fashion the timber frames, and stripped 40,000 cubic feet of turf off the bog (essentially all that was available). House building would have taken ninety men a month and a half—not counting the time needed to cut, dry, and move the turf blocks.

Birgitta Wallace believes these were the houses Leif Eiriksson had agreed to lend—but not give—to Gudrid and Karlsefni. She writes in *Vinland Revisited:* "It is far too substantial and complex a site not to be mentioned in the sagas." It is like other gateways in the Viking world, where a king or chieftain will lay claim to a rich region and seek to funnel all its resources to one spot, where he or a trusted deputy can tax them more easily.

This gateway did have a strong leader, someone who divided the work of boat repair among the three houses: The men in the southern house smelted the ore and fashioned the nails. They worked the wood in the middle house. In the boatshed attached to the northern house, they pried off the broken piece and nailed on the patch.

But was that leader Leif, or Karlsefni? Leif did not have ninety men to build such sturdy houses; Karlsefni did. Then there's the jasper evidence. Among the artifacts were ten strike-a-lights—shards of jasper, a reddish flinty stone that, struck with steel, creates sparks to start a fire. Knowing that jasper varies in its chemical makeup, geochemists compared the trace elements in the ten strike-a-lights to jasper from Iceland, Greenland, and Newfoundland, as well as to samples from Norway, Nova Scotia, New Brunswick, New England, Pennsylvania, and the Great Lakes region. Four of the strike-a-lights came from Greenland. Five came from Iceland. One was Newfoundland stone.

The strike-a-lights had been recovered from the floors of the houses. The southern house held only Icelandic jasper; the middle house had Icelandic and Newfoundland jaspers; the northern house, Icelandic and Greenlandic. In *The Saga of Eirik the Red*, Karlsefni's expedition had three ships: two crewed by Icelanders, and one, Gudrid's ship, that was "mostly" Greenlanders. Just as the lost spindle whorl said *Gudrid was here*, those ten bits of jasper assert Karlsefni's claim.

Which does not push Leif Eiriksson out of the picture. His crew might have wintered here, building themselves a sturdy longhouse and some outbuildings. When Karlsefni and Gudrid arrived four years later, with three ships' crews to house, perhaps they enlarged the settlement. Birgitta Wallace agrees we will never know. "In archaeology, it doesn't really matter if the houses were built ten years apart—that's simultaneous to us."

Karlsefni called his base camp Straumfjord, "fjord with a strong current," an apt name for the Straits of Belle Isle. Entering the Gulf of St. Lawrence through the Straits, you might think you were in a fjord, for the Labrador coast pinches closer to Newfoundland just south of L'Anse aux Meadows; you would certainly have noticed the turbulent, unpredictable currents that have wrecked many ships.

From Straumfjord the next summer Karlsefni and Gudrid sailed south "for a long time," the saga says. They reached a river blocked by a tidal lagoon so full of shoals and sandbars that they couldn't continue until the tide rose. On the shores of the lagoon they found fields of self-sown wheat and hills covered with "wine wood." Every creek was full of fish, and the forest held all kinds of animals. Karlsefni called the area Hop, pronounced "hope" and meaning "tidal lagoon"; there is a region named Hop just west of Skagafjord in Iceland, well known for its wealthy farms and its wide tidal flats.

An oddity in the bog at L'Anse aux Meadows has given Birgitta Wallace a clue as to where in Vinland Karlsefni's Hop might lie. It has also confirmed—as far as archaeology can be expected to—that the Vikings found grapes and not some other wine-making berry in Wine Land.

She told me, "We sent all the wood, all the seeds, off to a botanist in Ottawa. I said, 'Look for what doesn't belong here, what's not here now.' He said, 'It's all what you'd imagine. Except what are those butternuts doing there?'"

To sample the bog, the park workers had dug a 200-foot-long trench five feet deep, along with twenty smaller blocks, or monoliths. In three different spots, each in the Viking layer, the workers turned up butternuts, or white walnuts.

Walnuts, white or black, do not grow in Newfoundland. The farthest north the butternut has ever grown is New Brunswick—some 800 to 1,000 miles south of L'Anse aux Meadows—and the currents along the shore of the Gulf of St. Lawrence run generally north to south. The only way three butternuts could have reached the bog when they did is by Viking ship.

As if to offer proof that the nuts had been picked by Viking hands, the bog also gave up a butternut burl, a wartlike growth from a butternut tree. Burls are prized by wood-carvers for their intricately swirled grain patterns, and a Viking whittler had indeed begun work on this burl, for it shows the cut marks of a metal tool. "Burlwood" is also one possible translation for the mysterious *mösurr* wood that Leif Eiriksson commented on; the English cognate *mazer* means a highly figured wood—usually maple, but occasionally walnut.

The butternuts prove that the Vikings who wintered at L'Anse aux Meadows had already traveled much farther south—to the Miramichi River in New Brunswick, up the St. Lawrence River toward Quebec, or into New England. All three areas lie within the ancient range of the butternut tree. And where butternuts grow, grapes are also found. Butternuts fall from the tree in early September, just when the grapes are ripe and ready to pick; when they collected these butternuts, the Vikings could not have avoided noticing the grapes.

Studying the range of butternuts and grapes, and consulting with botanists, Birgitta Wallace inadvertently solved another puzzle that has vexed saga scholars for many years: the translation of "wine wood." When Leif Eiriksson first discovered Vinland in *The Saga of the Greenlanders,* he set half his crew to "cutting wine wood" to make a cargo for his ship. Reading "wine wood" as "grapevine," Einar O. Sveinsson, who edited the manuscript of the saga for its publication in 1935, footnotes the phrase to say: "Wine wood is not a tree, and in any case is worthless without the berries." Counters Birgitta, "Where grapes grow wild, the vines look nothing like those in a vineyard. Instead they wrap themselves around any tree or bush that happens to be nearby, often all the way to the top of the trees. These are the *vínvið,* the grapewood-trees of the sagas, the lumber harvested and brought back to Greenland by every Vinland expedition."

That grapevine-laden trees were abundant is confirmed by later travelers. Jacques Cartier explored the Gulf of St. Lawrence five hundred years after Gudrid and Karlsefni. His 1534 description of the Miramichi River mouth is a close echo of the saga's:

Cartier points out its shallow tidal bay "skirted with sandbanks," its "beautiful fields and meadows," and its hilly northern shore, "covered with many kinds of lofty trees." In nearby Chaleur Bay, he saw "wild oats like rye, which one would say had been sown there and tilled." Along the St. Lawrence River, he saw the "finest trees in the world: to wit, oaks, elms, &c, and what are better, a great many vines, which had so great abundance of grapes that the crew came aboard all loaded down with them." He named an island by Quebec Ile de Bacchus, for the Greek god of wine. The first French settlers just south of the Miramichi followed suit, naming a little inlet there Baie de Vin, "Wine Bay."

The Miramichi area can make two additional claims to being Karlsefni's Hop—and part of Leif Eiriksson's Vinland. First is the salmon Leif noticed. The Miramichi River has the richest salmon run in eastern North America. The noise of fish jumping kept a visitor in 1672 awake all night. Another, in the eighteenth century, caught 700 fish in twenty-four hours. In the 1960s, the river's annual salmon catch was 30,000 fish. Catherine Carlson, an archaeologist who has studied the historical range of the fish, has shown that salmon did not spawn in Maine or farther south before the seventeenth century, which would make the Miramichi not only the best salmon grounds for the Vikings to find, but also the southernmost.

Second is the presence of the Skraelings, the native people who forced Gudrid and Karlsefni to leave Vinland. Because of the multitudes of fish, at the time the Vikings visited the New World the Miramichi River valley was home to the largest population of Native Americans in the Gulf. They were ancestors of the Micmac, whose totem was the salmon. These aboriginal Indians had "a rich and comfortable way of life," according to Kevin McAleese, a curator at the Provincial Museum of Newfoundland and Labrador. They lived in large villages in sheltered groves of the forest during the winter, moving closer to the water for the summer. They hunted caribou and moose, and they fished, drying or smoking their catch before packing it into birch-bark boxes to store in underground caches. They made stone knives and projectiles, but also clay pots—being one of the few ancient peoples in the East to do so. They made canoes of stretched moose hide, as well as ones clad in birch bark. They used their canoes to fan out over the countryside in small groups, traveling thirty to forty miles from home to gather birds' eggs and berries. Some traveled farther to trade with neighboring tribes: Excavating their ancient camps, archaeologists have found copper beads and exotic shells, probably from Ohio, as well as pieces of Ramah chert, a prized flintknapping stone found only in far-northern Labrador. It was most likely on one of these summer trading expeditions that they stumbled upon the Vikings.

Karlsefni and those with him had stayed at Hop half a month, *The Saga of Eirik the Red* says, "enjoying themselves" and, ominously, "not keeping watch."

> Then one morning, early, they looked out and saw a great troop of skin boats. Sticks were being waved above the ships—they made a sound like flails threshing grain. They were all being waved in a sunwise direction.
>
> "What could that mean?" Karlsefni asked.
>
> "It could be a sign of peace," Snorri Thorbrandsson answered. "We should take white shields and go down to meet them."
>
> They did this.
>
> The others rowed toward them and came to land, staring at them in amazement. They were dark and ugly-looking, with ugly hair on their heads. They had huge eyes and broad

cheeks. They stood there and stared for a long while, then suddenly they left and rowed away southward around the point.

The next spring, the strangers in their skin boats returned, waving their sticks sunwise as before. This time they brought bales of gray furs. They offered to trade for the Vikings' knives and axes, but Karlsefni brought out red cloth instead, which pleased them. They tied strips of it around their foreheads. All was going well until the Vikings' bull rushed bellowing out of the forest and the strangers fled. Three weeks later they came back, their numbers much increased, swinging their sticks against the sun this time, and howling. These noise-making sticks may have been like the "whizzers" Farley Mowat encountered among an Eskimo tribe in the 1940s. The Eskimo, Mowat says, used them as a defense against supernatural beings. Three feet long and swung on a tether, they made a "strange and disturbing noise . . . as if unseen giants were muttering in a wind-filled tunnel, and it seemed to come from all sides of me." Overwhelmed, the Vikings fled into the woods.

At this point in *The Saga of Eirik the Red*, Gudrid has disappeared, and another woman—strong-minded, adaptable, brave, and pregnant—conveniently shows up. She is called Freydis and is said to be the bastard daughter of Eirik the Red. (There is a Freydis, a bastard daughter of Eirik the Red, in *The Saga of the Greenlanders*, too, but her path and Gudrid's do not cross. This Freydis prepares her own expedition to Vinland, arriving there after Gudrid and Karlsefni had left.) Freydis appears in only one scene, here, as the Vikings flee:

Freydis ran after them but fell behind because she was pregnant. She was following them into the woods when the Skraelings reached her. She saw a dead man in front of her. . . . His sword lay beside him. She picked it up and got ready to defend herself. When the Skraelings came at her, she drew her clothing away from her breast and slapped it with the sword. At this the Skraelings grew afraid and ran back to their boats and rowed away.

This fighting technique has a long history in Celtic lore—one that Gudrid could have heard of from her Scottish grandfather. In the ancient Irish epic, the *Tain Bo Cuailnge*, when the hero Cuchulainn attacked the fortress of Emain Macha, the women "stripped their breasts at him." Said the queen, "These are the warriors you must struggle with today." Shamed, Cuchulainn "hid his countenance" and was captured. Such an action is in character for the Gudrid we have come to know in *The Saga of Eirik the Red*. It might be too racy, though, for a role model in a saga written for young nuns. I can see a squirming churchman attributing it to another, lesser woman, the late-arriving Freydis. The two women were easily switched: "Some people say that Bjarni and Freydis stayed behind," one manuscript copy of the saga says, while Karlsefni explored to the south of Straumfjord. A different copy of the same saga puts it: "Some people say that Bjarni and *Gudrid* stayed behind." Providing another clue that Karlsefni would not have left Gudrid behind and taken Freydis, the saga says that just before the birth of Snorri: "The men were now constantly at odds, and all the quarrels were over women." The lonesome bachelors were pestering their few married friends to share their wives. Would Karlsefni leave Gudrid in another man's arms for a year? Would Gudrid stand for it? It seems clear to me that Gudrid was the woman with Karlsefni when he scouted to the south.

The Saga of the Greenlanders contains a very similar story of the Vikings' interactions with the Skraelings, one in which

Gudrid's role is clearer. In this version, when the bull bellowed, the frightened Skraelings tried to barge into the Viking houses and hide. But when they realized that the Vikings did not fear the bull, the Skraelings relaxed. Karlsefni offered them not red cloth but pails of milk, and the Skraelings were happy to trade their furs for this strange new drink.

Before the Skraelings returned, Gudrid gave birth to Snorri, and Karlsefni had a tall stockade erected around the settlement. The Skraelings were not alarmed by the Vikings' new defenses. They flung their bales of furs over the wall and waited to be invited in. Karlsefni did so, calling out to the women to bring more milk. It was on this visit that a native woman approached Gudrid, while she was rocking Snorri's cradle in the doorway of the house, and tried to speak with her. As the saga describes the woman, "She was rather short and had a band around her head. Her hair was reddish brown. She was pale and had very big eyes, so big that eyes that size have never been seen before in a human head."

Gudrid motioned for her to sit down. "My name is Gudrid," she said.

The stranger repeated her words: "My name is Gudrid."

Then came a great outburst of noise, and the woman disappeared. Following her out, Gudrid learned that a Skraeling "had been killed by one of Karlsefni's men because he wanted to take some weapons." It's easy to imagine the scene. Men of both groups were examining the furs. A curious Skraeling eased up to a Viking and, drawn to this exotic, shiny object, put a hand on the Viking's sword. Instinctively, the Viking drew his weapon and struck the man down. All hell broke loose. I can imagine, too, what Gudrid might have said to the killer: "Idiot. You and your mighty sword. We were making headway with these natives. Soon the woman and I would have understood each other.

Now we're at war." Karlsefni predicted correctly that the Skraelings would not be so peaceful the next time they came, and although the Vikings won the skirmish in this saga, they realized it was not safe to stay. This rich land had already been claimed by another people, and they were not welcome. No doubt Gudrid, who "knew how to get along with strange people," and who had a newborn son to protect, influenced this decision.

The word *Skræling* is sometimes translated as "wretch," but it may in fact be more of an observation than an insult. The suffix *"ing"* meant a person: A *Skagfirðing* was a person from Skagafjord; the *Ynglings* were the descendants of Yngvi. *Skræ* seems to derive from *skrá,* "dried skin," particularly the kind of wellscraped and stretched dried skins on which books were written. This kind of skin is not so dissimilar to the leather used by Native Americans for clothing, making a Skraeling a person dressed in leather clothes, as opposed to the Vikings, who wore woven wool and linen.

The description of the Skraeling woman who visited Gudrid may also be accurate. Fixating on her reddish hair, her pale skin, and her huge, inhuman eyes—as well as the saga's assertion that "no one saw her except Gudrid"—scholars in the early twentieth century argued that this woman with "an aura of strangeness about her" must have been a ghost or a fetch, an ancestral spirit, come to warn Gudrid that she was in danger.

Lately the scholarly weight has shifted away from the fantastic. The Beothuck Indians of Newfoundland, a now-extinct Algonkian-speaking tribe with the same ancestors as the Micmac, dressed their hair with a mixture of powdered red ocher and oil, giving it a reddish sheen almost like a modern henna rinse. They were pale enough that several Europeans remarked on it. A map from 1520 says that Gaspar de Cortereal, who explored the Gulf of St. Lawrence in 1500, "brought from this region men of the same color as ourselves." Another map, from 1547, says, "It is a fair race." The English geographer Richard Hakluyt, who in 1584 wrote an influential book summarizing the *Divers Voyages Touching the Discoverie of America,* called the Beothucks "very white. If they were apparelled as the French are, they would be as white and as fair." Their large eyes were singled out in 1523 by Giovanni da Verrazano, in 1612 by John Guy, in 1618 by Marc Lescarbot, in 1633 by Joann de Laet, and by numerous modern authors commenting on the portraits of two Beothuck women published by James P. Howley in his massive compilation, *The Beothucks or Red Indians,* in 1914. The two women had been "captured" by Newfoundland fishermen in the early 1800s. For their portraits, says a letter from 1820, they were bathed until their "light-copper" skin became "nearly as fair as a European's" and their black hair was combed and oiled. Says saga scholar Bo Almquist, "It would be difficult to find a better illustration of our saga episode than these women with their wide-open staring eyes expressing a curious mixture of wildness and surprise."

Because of three butternuts, and the work of archaeologists studying the pattern of Indian settlements along the shores of the Gulf of St. Lawrence, we can say with some certainty that the people with whom Gudrid and Karlsefni traded and fought, the people with whom they tried and failed to communicate, and the people from whom they ultimately fled, were the Algonkian ancestors of the Micmac and Beothuck. But what about the cows that provided the milk, and the bellowing bull, so prominent in the saga stories? The archaeologists saw no bones of cows or sheep or other domestic animals in the midden. Birgitta Wallace's reports are quite clear that "there are no traces of the barns or byres, fences or enclosures usually associated with livestock." She writes: "The buildings also lack the dairy pantries which were so common in Iceland and Greenland. Nor is there any other evidence of livestock in the form of floral disturbances, or of insects associated with domestic animals."

Standing in the chilly August wind at L'Anse aux Meadows, Birgitta reminded me again of the limitations of archaeology. They had found no barns, true, and no cow bones. But what kind of sign would be left after a thousand years if the cows had grazed outside all winter, and been milked but not butchered? Unless the Vikings had left behind a broken milk bucket or a butter paddle, the only proof would be the presence of pollen from an alien weed—a European buttercup, for instance—that had come, via hay and manure, from Greenland. This pollen could have been spotted when the bog samples were examined under a microscope. Pollen in bog mud is nearly indestructible, and pollen of different herbs differs by size, shape, and texture. But scientists can't examine every pollen grain in a bog. At L'Anse aux Meadows, they took twenty samples and divided those into blocks representing twenty to thirty years of sediment. Each of these small blocks held up to 500,000 pollen grains; the scientists identified 300. A few buttercups could easily have been missed.

The pollen analysis confirmed that the Vikings had lived lightly on the land, but a pollen count is not sensitive enough to say whether Gudrid brought her cows or not. "Five cows and a bull, even five cows per ship, if they grazed here for one year, wouldn't make any difference," Birgitta told me.

CHAPTER 8

The House of the Sagas

Karlsefni now sailed across the sea, and his ship came to land in the north, in Skagafjord, where he laid it up for the winter. In the spring he bought the farm at Glaumbaer and built a house. He stayed there as long as he lived. He was a great man, and many fine people are descended from him and Gudrid. And when Karlsefni died, Gudrid took over the farming with her son, Snorri, who had been born in Vinland.

—*The Saga of the Greenlanders*

GUDRID AND KARLSEFNI AND THEIR LITTLE SON SAILED from Vinland in midsummer, after the ice went out, their ship laden with timber, furs, butternuts, and grapes crushed and fermenting in baleen-strapped barrels or in leather bags made from the entire tanned hide of a deer.

They had hoped to sail home with the two other ships from their expedition, but one ship hadn't returned that year to the gateway at L'Anse aux Meadows. It was Gudrid's ship, with its mostly Greenlandic crew. While the third ship headed for Greenland, Karlsefni set off north to look for the missing one, until in a quiet bay one of his men was killed by a stone-tipped arrow shot by a one-footed humanoid—a Uniped—on shore. After that Karlsefni called off his search. Unipeds and other fantastic beings are standard fare in medieval travelers' tales (although they are usually found in Africa). But in 1936, an arrowhead was found in the eroding Norse graveyard at Sandnes; experts say it is "very similar in style and material" to the projectiles used by the Algonkian-speaking Indians of Newfoundland and Labrador. More than one writer has linked it to this saga episode.

Sailing home, Karlsefni came upon another kind of Skraeling, a small family group that fled from the Vikings. Karlsefni captured two young boys; the others "disappeared underground," perhaps into the kind of sunken house, with a domed roof made of a whale's ribs covered with sealskin and turf, that the Dorset Eskimos inhabited from Newfoundland north to Baffin Island at the time Gudrid and Karlsefni were adventuring. The Dorset were "probably the least threatening of the peoples the Norse encountered in the New World," according to Arctic expert Peter Schledermann. Efficient hunters, they made houses, boats, and sleds entirely from the bones and hides of animals. Fine artists as well, they carved intricate tiny amulets of antler, ivory, and bone to honor and entice their prey. The two captive boys were baptized, the saga says, taught Norse, and quizzed about their culture, but the account is brief and garbled, and what happened to the boys afterward is not told.

The saga does give news of Gudrid's ship. Traders who came to Greenland years later reported that the ship had been storm-blown to Ireland, where the survivors were "attacked and taken as slaves." The third ship in Karlsefni's fleet also failed to make it home, sinking off the Irish coast. The handful of men who escaped in the towboat—the choice determined by drawing lots—returned to Iceland with the tale.

The loss of two ships and their crews was a blow to the Greenland Norse. Around the year 1000, the whole colony numbered only 400 to 500 people. When the thirty Greenlanders among the adventurers at L'Anse aux Meadows failed to return, Greenland lost 5 percent of its critical laborers—the hunters who brought home the walrus tusks. It was not a fair exchange for one shipload of timber and luxuries. No further expeditions were sent to explore and settle Vinland, although occasional trips to Markland to harvest timber may have continued until the 1400s.

Karlsefni did not tie his own ship and crew—or Gudrid—to Greenland's precarious future. The next summer he sailed for Norway and, the saga says, "never had a ship so full of riches left Greenland before."

In Norway, Gudrid and Karlsefni were "made much of," the saga says, leaving out the details we would love to know. Who hosted them that winter? Who heard the news of the rich land and warlike people farther west than West? Two brothers, Svein and Eirik Hakonarson, shared the kingship from 1000 to 1015. In the medieval histories, they are given short shrift, wedged between two colorful missionary kings: Olaf Tryggvason, converter of six lands, and Olaf the Fat, also known as Olaf the Saint. After 112 chapters about the first Olaf (who reigned for five years), we get only one chapter on Svein and Eirik. They were baptized, we're told, but "while they reigned, they let each man worship as he wished. They upheld the old laws and customs and were wise and popular rulers." And Eirik got Olaf's famous ship, the Long Serpent.

That's it. No mention of Vinland.

The discovery and attempted settlement of the New World a thousand years ago had, as far as we can tell, absolutely no effect on the Old World. The only result of the Vinland voyages was to make Gudrid and her husband rich.

Though word of their explorations may have gotten out. As Karlsefni was readying his ship to sail home to Iceland, a man from Bremen, Germany, approached him and asked to buy his *húsasnotra*. No one knows what a *húsasnotra* was, but it was apparently made of wood, attached to the ship, and of some value. One scholar calls it a "carved gable end," another a weather vane, a third thinks it was an astrolabe. Karlsefni at first refused to sell. His *húsasnotra* was made of irreplaceable *mösurr* wood from Vinland. But when the German upped his offer to half a mark of gold, Karlsefni, like a true merchant, parted with his souvenir. Half a mark of gold was eight times the tax a shipowner had to pay to the king of Norway for permission to dock. As folklorist Gisli Sigurdsson notes: "Given the way that oral stories circulate, it is not hard to imagine, if there is anything in this story at all, that this *húsasnotra* might have been accompanied by some kind of narrative or other details of its origins and that this information may have been passed on by the Bremen merchant when he displayed his exotic acquisition back in his home port."

Coincidentally—or perhaps not—the first historical reference to Vinland was written by Adam of Bremen in 1070, who said his source was the king of Denmark. Although Adam professes to be truthful, you can't believe everything he says. Of Greenland he writes: "The people there are greenish from the salt water, whence, too, that region gets its name." While about Iceland he says: "Here also are good Christians, but on account of the excessive cold they dare not leave their underground hollows in the wintertime. For if they go out, they are burned by the cold, which is so extreme that like lepers they lose their color as the swelling gradually spreads. Also, if they happen to wipe their noses, the whole nose pulls off with the mucus itself and, having come off, they throw it away." Yet the king of Denmark's description of Vinland, as Adam relays it, matches that in the sagas:

He spoke also of yet another island of the many found in that ocean. It is called Vinland because vines producing excellent wine grow wild there. That unsown crops also abound on that island we have ascertained not from fabulous reports but from the trustworthy relation of the Danes. Beyond that island, he said, no habitable land is found in that ocean, but every place beyond it is full of impenetrable ice and intense darkness.

From Norway, Gudrid and Karlsefni and little Snorri sailed to northern Iceland, turning south into a great gray fjord, past the high, jagged peaks of Trollaskagi ("Troll's Cape") to the east and the gentler massifs of Skagastrond ("Cape of Beaches") to the west; between the jutting, angular Thordarhofdi, a headland named for Karlsefni's great-grandfather, whose nineteen children had peopled the region, and the island Drangey, the sheer-sided block where the outlaw Grettir the Strong would spend his last unlucky years. A green valley opened out ahead of them, the broadest and flattest in Iceland, its braided glacial rivers irrigating acres of grasslands. They probably moored at the mouth of a salmon stream, where a small island made a cove that sheltered ships from the north wind. On the rocky spit up from the harbor was a cluster of turf-walled huts with cobblestone floors; tented with sailcloth, they made good warehouses in which to store the foreign goods Karlsefni had brought to sell. Before he saw to the unloading, though, he may have sent a man upriver, past the gorge foamy with rapids, to the farm of Miklabaer, where a cousin of Karlsefni's father lived. Out of courtesy (and for a cut rate on Karlsefni's wares), the cousin, Arnor Old-Woman's-Nose, sent back horses to take Karlsefni and Gudrid and their essential luggage west to Karlsefni's estate at Reynines.

The harbor at Kolkuos—or the little bit that is left of it—has been under excavation since 2003. Most has eroded into the sea. But it was a busy place in the early eleventh century, according to Ragnheidur Traustadottir, the Icelandic archaeologist who leads the dig. Her team has found a pagan grave, an ironworker's shop, six stone-floored warehouses, and 4,000 bones from birds, fish, whales, sheep, goats, pigs, and fourteen different dogs, from small to large. "People were importing *lapdogs* just to show off," Ragnheidur said of Gudrid's peers. Skagafjord was not the hand-to-mouth kind of place Gudrid was used to.

Nor was her reception at Karlsefni's childhood home what she might have expected. Karlsefni's haughty mother "would not have Gudrid in her house that first winter," *The Saga of Eirik the Red* says. "In her opinion, Karlsefni had not married well." Chances are that Gudrid's questionable genealogy, particularly the captive status of her Scottish grandfather Vifil, played into the old lady's pique. She undoubtedly pointed out the fact that Karlsefni could trace his lineage to an Irish king—this was the sort of thing women of the day were supposed to know.

The other version of Gudrid's saga simply states that Karlsefni laid up his ship for the winter and, next spring, bought the farm of Glaumbaer and put up a house. The fact that Karlsefni owned Reynines, one of the finest estates in Skagafjord, is not deemed worthy of mention in this saga, although the estate seems to have stayed in the family until it was given to the church in 1295 by Gudrid's seven-greats granddaughter, Hallbera, who became abbess of the nunnery established there. *The Saga of Eirik the Red* may have been written for her.

No one knows who lived in Glaumbaer after Gudrid's day. Not until 1285 does it return to prominence, this time as the farm of an important chieftain not descended from Gudrid. This chieftain's grandson, known as Glaumbaejar-Hrafn, was the leading figure in Skagafjord around 1315, according to historian Helgi Thorlaksson of the University of Iceland, who believes the second version of Gudrid's saga was written down about then. He says, "It is tempting to see the reference in *The Greenlanders' Saga* to Glaumbaer as an attempt to valorize the farm and flatter the residents." He and most other historians prefer the view that Gudrid stayed at Reynines, which they see as the better farm.

Which farm was better a thousand years ago, however, is hard to judge. The landscape is different now. The braided, glacial rivers have undoubtedly changed their courses over the millennium, and the coastline has been reconfigured. The first settlers may have sailed to Reynines; it and other farms named "-nes," or peninsula, are now landlocked. They may have rowed or poled a boat almost to Glaumbaer: A farm between Reynines and Glaumbaer is called Marbaeli, which may mean "Edge of the Sea" (it could also mean "Place Where the Mares Lie Down").

By 1010, when Gudrid arrived in Skagafjord, the effects of overgrazing were being felt. Archaeologists have found many highland farms that were abandoned early, apparently due to erosion. Some lowland farms, on the other hand, were slowly being enriched. According to a study published by soil scientist Gretar Gudbergsson in 1996, since the Viking settlement began in 874, two feet of soil has been blown off the highlands and carried by the wind to the lowlands.

This blanket of relocated soil hides a lot of history. An archaeologist like John Steinberg, who wants to map and measure all the Viking Age ruins in the valley, to see where power once lay and when the social structure changed, can't simply walk over a farmer's fields, as his counterparts do in Greenland, and look for house-shaped lumps—although that's how archaeological surveys had been done here before. It works in Iceland's highlands. There a trained eye can see the scars of old habitations just as easily as in Greenland; though, once found, those highland houses have few secrets left. "They've all been blown out," John said. "It's so eroded. There's nothing that will tell us how this place operated. No artifacts, no hay, no tephra. Conversely in the lowlands you have all this soil. Combine that with the compression of turf architecture. . . . Turf is in fact mostly air. It's like a down comforter, that tangle of roots. When you bury it, it gets smashed. Add wind blowing a lot of soil off the highlands and you can't find a thing. It could be right out the window of your museum, and you won't see it"—as the house he had found, Gudrid's house, was outside the windows of the Skagafjord Folk Museum.

In mid-July 2005, after ten days of dragging the ground-penetrating radar machine five miles a day back and forth across Glaumbaer's field, John came to breakfast one morning with his laptop tucked under his arm. He poured himself a cup of coffee and leaned down to whisper to Antonio Gilman, a senior archaeologist from California State University, Northridge, "We've got it." Antonio raised his eyebrows, and the two of them slunk off to a back corner of the breakfast room, as if they shared a great secret. Half a dozen crew members tailed them.

"You need some imagination," John whispered, as he showed Antonio the previous day's ground-penetrating radar scans. Each scan was a map of the hayfield at a different depth. The top one showed the marks of the farmer's plow, a straight line revealing where he had begun planting a different kind of grass. At deeper depths, intriguing lines and dots in various colors could be seen. John pointed out these shapes and patterns as more of the crew crowded about. Two long parallel lines were outside walls, partly fallen in. Dots in a rough oblong could be stones around a long-fire. "This is a pavement of some sort," John pointed to a cluster of interlinked blobs outside the eastern wall. "This is probably the reflection of the entrance of the house. We're not going to see these stones because we're not going to go all the way down. We're going to dig down just to the top of the walls."

"Don't you want to dig all the way down and see Gudrid's house?" I asked.

"One morning I wake up and I want to excavate, the next morning I don't," he said. "Yesterday I wanted nothing more to do with this site, because it's a saga site. It's a huge responsibility with relatively little payoff for me in terms of my research interests. But it's the first house we found. This is where we've tried out all our techniques. People have used them all before, but we've put them together into a package. The package is the key. The soil coring, the remote-sensing, and the ground-truthing," by which he meant various forms of limited digging to test the truth of the remote-sensing maps. "I want to go with this to Sirri and Gudny and say, 'Here's what we're going to find,' so they can say in their letters to the National Science Foundation, 'John showed us the remote-sensing and then excavated, and he found exactly what the remote-sensing said he would.'"

By 9:30 that morning, John was in Gudny Zoega's laboratory in Saudarkrokur, having a second cup of coffee and going through the same picture show. He did not request her imagination.

"The tops of the walls are where?" Gudny asked.

John clicked through the sequence of scans to the one with the long parallel lines. "This is at 24 to 30 centimeters"—nine to 12 inches down.

"And how deep down is your pavement?"

John hedged. "Forty-six centimeters down is a conductive spot of the sort we normally associate with middens. I assume they're rocks. They're very strong reflectors. What I hope to find is an entrance. Isn't that what's usually associated with flagstones?"

"I think it's more important to see if these are turf walls or not," Gudny said. She was not willing to grant that those blurry lines were the floor plan of a longhouse, much less one with a stone-paved patio at the door.

John retreated. "I doubt that we'll see this entrance."

Gudny nodded. "It's too deep."

John said placatingly, "I wouldn't feel comfortable going after it, much as it would help us determine the structure."

"Then you'd be down to floor level, and you don't want to do that," Gudny agreed. If this *was* a house, floor level was where artifacts would be found, and everyone knew John's track record with those. While using a motorized posthole digger to ground-truth his remote-sensing map of Reynines in 2002, John chewed a hole right through the floor of the medieval nunnery. In the resulting dirt pile, he found the broken bits of a Viking Age bone comb. Luckily, a conservator was able to piece it back together.

"Congratulations! I'm glad the *tækni* is working." Sirri took off her phone headset as John came into her office at Glaumbaer an hour later. She gave John her sunniest smile. "I hear you have something to show me."

John propped his laptop on the corner of her desk and started his show-and-tell for a third time, this time referring to the possible pavement as "very flat reflectors in a matrix."

"Not stones?" Sirri asked.

"Yes, stones in a pavement," John said.

"At the door," Sirri mused. She pointed to a bright spot a stone's throw east of the door. "I wonder if this is the midden."

"We've been thinking about that," John said. "If you look at the old EM-31 data, you see it's an area of high conductivity, which is consistent with a midden."

"I wonder, when we find the door, if it is the door, if it could lead us to different things," Sirri said. She traced the line from the door to the midden. Looking over her shoulder, I followed an imaginary Gudrid tossing out her kitchen ash and garbage. What other paths could there be? To the barn, where Gudrid would have milked the cows in winter; to the hot spring, where she bathed and washed the family's clothes; to the river, where she fetched drinking water.

"This really looks like a good pavement," John said. "It appears suddenly, deep down. Unfortunately, you're not going to see it this year."

"No," said Sirri, "but we have plenty of years."

It was time for Sirri's brother to lift the turf off the hayfield so we could see if Gudrid's walls were where the gadget claimed. But he was busy. John worked his impatience off by hauling the GPR machine over the lumpy, weedy, sloping terrain on top of the beautiful burned-birch roof at Stora Seyla, the buried Viking Age house that had convinced the Icelanders his technique worked. I was recruited to move one end of a 50-meter measuring tape every half meter; between times, I sat on a tussock and tried to imagine what it would have been like in this valley in Gudrid's day: no car noises, no electric lines. I heard the faint whistle of a flying snipe, the *squick, squick, squick* of a redshank. Two ravens flew by making a racket. A dozen mares and foals grazed while two pintos squealed and played in a nearby field. Nothing else was moving in the landscape but a smattering of flies dancing on the breeze; no other noise but the grass blades whispering.

To the east, across the river, rose a line of pink mountains, all but one flat on top as if sliced off with a knife, and nearly snowless in July. Behind me, a rugged triangle marked the route south across Iceland, between the great glaciers to Thingvellir, where the Althing, the yearly assembly of chieftains, was held. West were more smooth, rounded mountains; the valley here was wide. There were no trees from one mountain range to the next, only a few bushes around the summerhouses at the bend where the river curled east. From mountain to mountain, I saw hayfields divided by drainage ditches and the wall-like mounds of dirt that demarcated them. In Gudrid's day, those dry, firm, tractor-ready fields would have been wet hay meadows, and the round bales, wrapped in white plastic, ranked beside each farmhouse would have been turf-covered haystacks.

On a bright, breezy, warm July day like this one, Gudrid would have been raking hay to dry it. I remembered the sound of an old man cutting hay at Glaumbaer the weekend before, during the museum's Haymaking Day. His scythe went *snick, snick* through the grass, *tack, tock* when he whetted the blade. Sirri went before him with a sprinkler: You didn't make hay while the sun shines in old Iceland; the grass cut more easily if it was wet. You hauled it, wet, up from the meadows to the house on horseback. Then, on a sunny day (and you hoped one came quickly, so not too much hay would rot), you spread it in the fenced-in homefield and raked it until it was dry. That was women's work. Gudrid would have gotten sunburned that day.

Two days later, the turf-cutters still hadn't come. With a couple of spades and some volunteers, John's colleague Douglas Bolender "de-turfed" a small square to see how deep the tops of the walls really were. Surprisingly, they were *right* below the grass roots. Doug had aimed the hole for a trench dug in 2002, so through the test square ran a straight canal of disturbed soil, a uniform brown with the texture of a well-raked flower bed; at the edges, landscape cloth peeked out. A turf wall showed up on either side of the trench as a line of hard-packed and mottled earth. Swirls and blotches of rust-red and black, caused by rotted grass, was the "turf signature," Doug explained. A stretch of fallen *snidda* wall also appeared in the section, the cracks between the diamond-shaped turves marked by a lacy pattern of shiny white tephra from the 1104 eruption of Mount Hekla.

Then the turf-cutters, two young men trained by Sirri's brother, appeared one Sunday and worked all day and night—they had to catch a plane to Copenhagen at 4:00 Monday morning. They cut the turf into 20-inch squares and stacked it into a three-foot-high wall running along the west side of the field, as if to hide our excavation from the tourists at the museum. They'd gotten a little sloppy after midnight, so the north end of the site was bumpier and rougher than the south, with deep ruts and tire tracks from a little tractor they'd used to move the pallets of turf. At 9:00 A.M. Doug passed out flat-bladed shovels and we got to work. Our job was to scrape the top three inches of dirt—or however much it took to reach the white 1104 tephra layer—off the 130-by-65-foot area above the longhouse. We used our shovels like spatulas to lift off a half-inch of dirt at a time and toss it ahead of us. If you hit the 1104 layer, the shovel would glide as if it were greased and the upper strata would just flake off.

Though it was sunny, the wind was fierce and cold; we worked in sweaters and rain jackets. The shoveling made itself felt in the shoulders right away. We were lined up like a chain gang, going west to east, all trying to keep pace with Doug, who scraped like a maniac. We had five shovels and seven people, so one person ran the wheelbarrow and another used a metal dustpan to scoop the loose dirt into buckets. We finished the rough north end just as the wind picked up and, without discussing it, turned and started working in a north–south direction, our backs to the wind. At lunchtime the wind whipped up to gale force—it would blow the buckets away unless they had two scoopfuls of earth in them. We were all covered with fine dirt by then, with black grit in our eyes. Everyone was painfully polite, saying "thank you" each time someone dumped a bucket or brought over the wheelbarrow.

By the afternoon, my blistered hands had lost the feel for the tephra layer and in the low sun's glare I could not see the color changes in the soil that Doug had pointed out. I traded my shovel for the dustpan and tried to carry the buckets to the dirt pile without straining my back.

When we left at 5:00 P.M., Doug could trace out half of the walls by the soil color alone. I could see small stretches of wall if he pointed at them. The different textures of dirt and turf had dried differently after we exposed them, and if I stood off to the side and looked north-to-south along the east wall, one part was distinctly redder and swirled with orange, yellow, gold, and black. Another patch of fallen wall looked like white fish scales on a reddish background.

After one final five-mile run with the ground-penetrating radar machine over the deturfed field, we traded our shovels for masons' trowels, triangular, flat-bladed steel tools that a brick mason would use to scoop and spread mortar. (Archaeologists prefer those made by the Iowa-based Marshalltown Company because they take a good edge with a whetstone.) The weather turned hot and dry and the wind stilled. Stripped to a T-shirt and jeans, I crouched on my knees, scraping not a half-inch at a time, but a teaspoonful, the trowel like an extension of my index finger. The task was to define the width of the walls, see where they were standing and where they had fallen down, detect any breaks for doorways or alcoves or halls into side rooms, and find the main door—preferably above the "pavement" the ground-penetrating radar had shown was a foot and a half farther down. John explained that I should look for where the distinctive turf colors ended or broke off. The series of breaks would line up to make the edge of the wall. "It's not a *line* you're looking for," he said, "but the breaks in the turf that *line up*."

Four days later, I was still on my knees. Now the weather was breezy, misty, and cold. I had put on my sweater, rain suit, stocking cap, scarf—and still I was cold. With Linda Rehberger, who was back in school getting a master's degree after working as a professional archaeologist for several years, I'd been assigned a spot where the wall seemed to disappear under a layer of ash from burning peat—a standard fuel for blacksmithing. We drew a map of the peat-ash lens, a distinctive pale rose-pink color, and started to scrape. The lens seemed small and self-contained. The ash was crumbly and so light that once, when I began to reply to a question Linda had asked, the wind picked up a hunk of it and tossed it into my mouth.

We scraped all morning and all afternoon, the cold fog giving way to splendid, brisk sunshine. The pink became mixed with dark streaks of charcoal, in which I found four or five strips of burned birch bark. Other patches were cranberry red with fine spots of moss green that might be tephra. The colors swirled, the same palette that Edvard Munch had used in *The Scream*—there was even a light orange circle, like the screamer's face, highlighted by white. We dug and dug in some places, chasing pink ash in and out of tumbled turves. The hot ash had obviously been dumped there after the wall had fallen; in places it had burned its way into the turf.

I was concentrating on scraping down to burned turf in one part, carefully removing tiny bits of pink ash, when Doug walked over, looked down, and said, "Nancy found the edge of a wall." When I readjusted my gaze, it popped out: a section of turf wall about a foot long, rising above the pit out of which we had cleaned the ash. On the side where I was working was a completely straight edge.

The next day was remarkable for the smell of cow manure—the neighbor was fertilizing his fields. I had a sore finger, blistered by my trowel, and a tired wrist from the sustained twisting action needed to trace the dips and furrows of fallen turves. I spent the day on my knees anyway, scraping out peat ash. A volunteer working near me talked nonstop about politics.

At the close of the day, Tara Carter, a graduate student, found the missing south wall, allowing us to finally get a measurement: Gudrid's house was 30 meters, or almost 100 feet, long. Doug sent John, surveying a different farm, a text message from his cell phone: "30 M." John replied: "29," the length the remote-sensing device had predicted. In ten minutes, John was striding across the field from the museum parking lot. Doug led him to the south end, pointed to a line he had scratched in the dirt, and said, "Put your toes there and then look up."

"Holy cow!" John said.

I stood on the same spot. I looked up and a Viking longhouse appeared, the walls completely defined by red flags placed every five meters (or 16 feet), the north and south gable ends perfectly parallel, the long east and west walls narrower at the ends and bowing out a little in the middle. The walls were a uniform six feet thick.

While I was marveling, John was quizzing Linda on our peat-ash pit. Our excavation was now about eight inches deep, over three feet wide, and round. There were bones and large stones mixed into the ash. Linda had found several small stones that had been cracked by fire, showing black and red inside.

John, surprised and not entirely pleased that we had dug so deep, looked at our dirt pile and quietly mentioned that we ought to screen it for artifacts, which meant taking each bucket-load of dirt and forcing it through a wire mesh. (In the end, we didn't find any.)

Doug, who was responsible for our digging so deep, began to interpret what we had found. Based on the amount of peat ash dumped outside, the fallen inside wall I had uncovered, and the fact that the shiny white 1104 tephra layer was *always* on top of the peat ash, he figured the house had been abandoned by 1050, give or take twenty-five years, and purposely flattened. In 1050, I thought, Gudrid would have been sixty-five years old—a ripe old age for a Viking woman. This house it seemed, was demolished just after she died.

"A turf house will decay in ten years if there's a lot of rain, but this one had help," Doug said. The wooden frame and paneling had been taken out to be reused, and turves thrown into the hall to flatten it out. The fallen wall that I'd uncovered was too consistently flat and the same width all along its length for it to have just "happened." The house had been completely ruined by the time someone dug the pit and started throwing ash into it. From the pit, the ash had blown over to where I was digging, inside the house, as my deposits were much shallower.

For four more days I was assigned to the peat-ash pit. Linda had been moved to a site more in need of her excavating skill, and my new partner was our youngest volunteer, twelve-year-old Ayshe, who had a very light touch with a dental pick and a paintbrush. She spent the days brushing off a jumble of bones: a sheep's rib, the jawbone of a foal, a cow's tooth, four fish vertebrae in a neat line, and a mottled black lump that looked to me like a fossilized horse dropping. My knees began to ache, but I was feeling really comfortable with my trowel. I could get just the right amount of force to scrape off a dime-sized spot or to cut through an eight-inch-thick "nose" of peat ash. And the weather wasn't bad. I tried to remember to look up every now and then and take in the splendid view. The ash pit grew to the size of three bathtubs, extending from the house wall to the edge of the grass, where it disappeared out of our deturfed site.

Late on the last afternoon, having spent the day with my face five inches from the ground trying to find the southern edge of the ash pit, I stood up to empty a bucket and looked down at my work instead of off toward the mountains. Suddenly I saw two indentations in the side wall. I got out a tape measure and found that all three sides on both niches were exactly the same length—eight inches, or 20 centimeters. It looked as if somebody had pushed in a spade and cut away the dirt. I called over to Doug, who was on the east side of the house still trying to find the main doorway: "What size is a Viking spade?"

"Oh, about 22 centimeters," he said.

I said, "How about 20 centimeters?"

That got Doug off his knees. He came over and said, "Cool. This is really nice work." I'd found the marks of a thousand-year-old spade: Snorri's spade (or Snorri's hired man's spade), wielded just after Gudrid's death.

Or—an uncomfortable thought possessed me—could the two matching niches be the accidental result of how I wielded my trowel? I suddenly understood what John had meant when he said, *Archaeology murders its informants.* I knew why Sirri had urged caution in our ransacking of Gudrid's house, why Orri Vesteinsson described the progression of archaeological techniques as "increasingly comprehensive destruction." A complete beginner had been turned loose for days on a mysterious feature cutting into the wall of a Viking Age house on a historically important site. I had been told to scrape out and discard anything that was pink and had the texture of ash. I had also scraped out and discarded ash that was orange, red, and black, including those scraps I thought were birch bark and Doug, when I showed them to him, thought might be leather but in any case too small and fragile to save. I had discarded—as instructed—all stones smaller than my fist, whether fire-cracked or not. I had been the judge, when sifting my backdirt, of whether a bone should be bagged and cataloged or discarded. My untrained eyes were the only ones looking for artifacts. Would I have spotted a jasper strike-a-light, the artifact that proved both Icelanders and Greenlanders were at L'Anse aux Meadows? Or would I have discarded it as a shard of ordinary stone? Would I have recognized a thousand-year-old butternut, thereby establishing that Vinland had been named for wine grapes? What I called a fossilized horse dropping was roughly nut-shaped, but it disintegrated when Doug tried to pick it up for preservation, crumbling into bits of charcoal. No one knows what it actually was; future archaeologists have only our photographs and drawings to go by. No one will be able to excavate that peat-ash pit again. It is well and thoroughly gone, every bit of ash removed and sifted and mixed with dirt scraped from elsewhere in the house. Only the shell of the pit remains, some Before and After maps and photos, and my word that it had been uniformly full of peat ash.

The Glaumbaer dig went on for two more weeks. Doug and Tara were alone on the site some days (the rest of us were moving mud at Stora Seyla, where John had laid out two square test pits), troweling at opposite ends, looking for the details of corners and doors and internal walls. The geese began flocking, preparing for their winter migration. The fields turned red as the pasture grass went to seed. It was dark by 11:00 P.M. now, and much colder, with spitting rain, a hard north wind, and temperatures below 40 degrees Fahrenheit. Doug thought the rain was an advantage: It made the colors and patterns of the turves stand out better. You could plainly see the herringbone pattern of *klömbrahnaus* turf in some walls, the diamond-shaped *snidda* in others.

On Friday, August 12, I was enlisted to help Doug map the site. Bundled up in long underwear and two sweaters under my rain suit, I still had to huddle behind the stacks of turf, out of the wind, to warm up every so often with a thermos of tea. Doug stood hatless in the cold drizzle, hour after hour, penciling his thoughts onto waterproof charts designed by the Icelandic Institute of Archaeology (for which John had swapped a carton of Marshalltown trowels). Cross-referenced to the GPS grid and compiled by computer, Doug's drawings would be the main result of our season's work. Under the most unpleasant working conditions of the entire summer, he was creating the scientific story of the Viking house at Glaumbaer, each line on the map his interpretation of the colors and patterns in the dirt.

Even without the shivers, seeing what you hope to see, as I had seen the marks of Snorri's spade, is inescapable in archaeology. I remembered Icelandic archaeologist Steinunn Kristjansdottir arguing in her 2004 doctoral dissertation: "Is it thus ever possible to reconstruct lost reality without making interpretations?" Material culture "is a text that can be read." The archaeologist's job is to read that text and then to write his own, "to generate a narrative about his subject, not merely describe it." Yet to tell a story, you must draw conclusions and make interpretations based on what you think you see. You must fill in the gaps. An archaeologist, she concluded, "should be aware that the search for truth is like a story that never ends."

As a check on Doug's storytelling ability, John took copious photographs, which meant we spent Saturday shovel-scraping the whole site once again so the turf lines would be clean and crisp for the camera. John borrowed a front-end loader and stood in the bucket to shoot down on the site, but he wasn't satisfied with how the pictures looked from that angle, so for Sunday he rented a cherry picker. Sunday morning, in cold misty rain, we scraped the 8,000-square-foot site clean again, this time on our knees, with trowels.

In the end we had found four rooms: one large, one small, and two whose size we could not measure because they extended past the edges of our excavation. It was now clear the house was longer than 30 M. Its eastern wall stretched, unbroken, for 37 meters—121 feet—from the northeast corner until it disappeared under a plowed and planted field.

The main entrance was on this eastern wall, toward the north end (not quite aligned with the flagstone pavement the GPR had seen). It opened into a great hall or *skáli* 72 feet long and 16 feet wide, providing almost 1,200 square feet of floor space. This room was twice the size of Eirik the Red's house at Eiriksstadir (41 by 13 feet, or 530 square feet) or the *skáli* at the Farm Beneath the Sand (40 by 16, or 640 square feet), on which the reconstruction of the chieftain's house at Brattahlid in Greenland was based.

At the south end of Gudrid's hall, a doorway led to a small room, about 10 by 16—perhaps Gudrid's weaving room, if the layout of her house was like others of the period. A test trench from 2002 cut through the center, nearly destroying the doorway into the room and a second possible doorway out of it. Beside the trench, the farmer's dog had uncovered the skull of a horse, inspiring Sirri to reflect that perhaps this building wasn't Gudrid's longhouse, but her stable. No one wanted to dig deeper—not with the field season running out—to see if there were human bones buried with the horse, as there had been in the pagan graves across the river at Keldudalur. Another small room, about 12 feet wide, shot out the back of the hall to the west and disappeared under the grass.

To this point, the size and layout of Gudrid's house were much like the house called Stong (meaning "Pole" or "Stick," its ancient name now unintelligible) in southern Iceland. Stong had been abandoned in 1104: The volcanic eruption that had provided our handy white dateline at Glaumbaer had completely buried some twenty farms that lay within sight of Mount Hekla. Several had been excavated in 1939, and a reconstruction of the largest house was built in 1974. It is often pictured in coffee-table books as the quintessential Viking longhouse. Looking from the outside like a long green hill, inside it has a high-ceilinged, wood-paneled hall 52 feet long and almost 20 feet wide, bisected by a longfire, with wooden sleeping benches along the walls and an enclosed sleeping closet for the master and mistress of the house. (Experts like Gudmundur Olafsson believe that the ceiling is too high, but the floor plan follows the archaeological evidence.) In the smaller room (26 by 13) that extends from the hall, a loom has been set up, identifying it as the women's "bower" or weaving room. The outshot off the back of the main hall was the dairy: Archaeologists found traces of barrels for *skyr* and other liquids, and workbenches for preparing food. Unlike Gudrid's house, Stong has a second outshot at the hall's north end, with a drain running down its length: This room has been identified as a lavatory, a place to keep a cow over winter, or a place to wash wool (and perhaps all three).

Instead of the northern outshot, Gudrid's house has a sizable room opening to the south, off the possible weaving room, and disappearing under the grass. None of John's remote-sensing devices had discovered this southern room, so we had not deturfed the full length of the house. The part we could see and measure was almost 20 feet long and 16 feet wide, a significant room. With several rooms in a line, the layout of Glaumbaer reminded me of the southernmost longhouse at L'Anse aux Meadows, the one with the choicest location, being closest to Black Duck Brook, where Gudrid would have gone to draw fresh water every day. It was even more similar to the layout of a house at Sandnes in Greenland, where Gudrid's husband Thorstein had died. This house, excavated in the 1930s by the architect Aage Roussell, is thought to be much later than Gudrid's day, but archaeologists today realize that several layers of houses were built on that spot, and Roussell's archaeological methods could not distinguish among them. The floor plan he drew shows three rooms in a row (two large, connected by a smaller one, as at Glaumbaer) and a single outshot off the back.

After the photos were taken came the strenuous and melancholy task of "putting the site to bed": covering the excavation with landscape paper and heaping the dirt back on top, so that Sirri's brother and his workers could reset the turf and turn it back into a hayfield. We were all smeared with mud by the end; the rain had not let up. I gathered a handful of muddy tools and followed the others back toward the van parked behind the museum, willing myself not to look over my shoulder to say goodbye to Gudrid's house.

"Here," Tara Carter called, "hand me those shovels." She was standing in the drainage ditch between two fields, scrubbing clean a wheelbarrow in the outflow of a pipe, sleeves rolled up, pant legs soaked.

"Aren't you freezing?" I asked.

"You kidding? This water's hot!"

I climbed into the ditch with her and stuck my hand under the pipe. It was indeed as hot as dishwater. I wondered where up the slope the water originated. Gudrid would have had a bathing pool there, like the one Grettir the Strong had thawed himself out in after his long, cold swim from the island of Drangey. Hot-spring pools were social places: Young men hung out there, making themselves seductively clean and flirting with the women who were doing the laundry; men met there to make deals and talk politics, knowing if a fight broke out everyone was unarmed. It was a matter of pride among the Icelanders that they were cleaner than their Norwegian cousins, who had to heat water with wood and bathe in little tubs.

Now I remembered John, when we had first arrived at Glaumbaer, discussing the name of the "Farm of Merry Noise" with Pastor Gisli of the Glaumbaer Church. An expert had told Gisli she thought the *Glaum* was the noise of iron being hammered on an anvil. John concurred that there had been a smithy on the farm—they had found plenty of waste slag in the soil cores, and the remote-sensing devices had picked up an iron pan off the south end of the house, where bog iron would have been extracted. His theory of the name, however, compared it to Steamboat Springs in Colorado: The *Glaum* was the whistle or bubble or chirp of the hot spring.

But now that the water's piped, we will never know what it sounded like.

CHAPTER 9

The Farm of Merry Noise

They passed Glaumbaer at the close of the day . . . and
when they had gone on a short way, a man came to meet
them. He was tall and thin, and had a big head. He was
poorly dressed. He greeted them and they exchanged
names. He said his was Thorbjorn. He was a wanderer, not
one to work much, always chattering and boasting. Some
people thought him amusing. He was very friendly and
started telling funny stories about the people of the nearby
farms. Grettir thought him great fun. Thorbjorn asked if
they didn't need a man to work for them. "I would gladly
join you," he said. He told such good stories that they
let him tag along. . . . And because he was such a talker
and joker he'd earned himself a nickname and was called
"Glaum," or "Noisemaker."

—*Grettir's Saga*

O F ALL THE HOUSES GUDRID LIVED IN DURING HER LONG
and adventurous life—at Arnarstapi under the Snow Mountain's Glacier; in Greenland at Eirik the Red's Brattahlid and
farther north, at Sandnes; at L'Anse aux Meadows in Vinland
and somewhere near the Miramichi River on the Gulf of St.
Lawrence; at Reynines with her haughty mother-in-law—the
house at Glaumbaer was her only true home. The others were
owned or overseen by someone else. Glaumbaer was hers, unfortunately, alone.

The sagas say almost nothing about the years she lived at Glaumbaer, only that she raised her two sons alone. Karlsefni died before the eldest, Snorri, came of age. Chances are that Karlsefni was lost at sea soon after his second son was born— otherwise, we could expect Gudrid to have had more than two children. Nor, this time, did Gudrid inherit a ship. Perhaps Karlsefni was caught in a storm on a routine trading run from Norway, and sailed his ship down somewhere in the icy North Atlantic. Gudrid never remarried.

But barring loneliness, her life at Glaumbaer was not a difficult one. She remained wealthy enough to fund her final adventure—a pilgrimage to Rome, essentially a grand tour of Europe that would have taken at least a year to accomplish— with enough money left over to let Snorri, in her absence, build her a church on their property. And, like all of her neighbors, her only source of income was the cloth she could make from the wool of her sheep.

By tallying the sexes and ages of sheep's bones and teeth, archaeologists concluded that the sheep in Iceland in the Vi-king Age were not kept mainly for milk and meat, as they are now. Instead of being culled young, as tender lambs, males were gelded and allowed to become "aged," as one archaeologist puts it—up to eight years old. These wethers were "valuable assets," another expert writes. "They were the kind of property which the farmer could keep from one year to the next with limited risk." Sturdy enough to graze outdoors in most weather, they could be turned loose and essentially forgotten until shearing time, when they would yield twice as much wool as a ewe that was being milked. At the two farms studied, 20 percent of the flock was tall, wool-heavy wethers: the Viking cash crop.

One day I remarked to Sirri about the amount of pasture in

the area. "Is that why Glaumbaer was such a good farm when Gudrid lived here?" I asked her.

"*I* don't think Gudrid did live here," Sirri said, "though she may have died here. I think Gudrid lived in Reynines for a decade or two while Snorri was small. Reynines was Thorfinn Karlsefni's heritage. It was the best farm in the district. I think Gudrid and Karlsefni lived there, but also owned Glaumbaer. Eventually their family owned the whole area. Snorri was the first farmer at Glaumbaer, but you can't tell when he started to farm—at age fifteen or at twenty-five—no one knows when Karlsefni died and Gudrid became a widow. Nobody will *ever* know that.

"But to answer your question," Sirri continued, "Glaumbaer must have been a very good farm when Snorri lived here. It's a very easy farm. You can cut grass wherever you like, everywhere in the area. You have good fodder for the animals all year long, even if you don't make hay. In normal years you didn't need hay. But of course you had to make it just in case.

"I suppose Gudrid would not stay at Reynines after Karlsefni's death," Sirri added, picking again at the old problem. "The saga says something about her mother-in-law not liking her. But this is just my theory. I have no way to say she lived at Glaumbaer or not."

"Doesn't the dating of the house John found suggest that she did?"

"No." Sirri pursed her lips, turning very serious. "All we can say, when archaeologists find something, is that the saga takes place at the same time. It's wonderful to see the old turf house that you found under the hayfield, because now we have the first generation of turf house down in the field and the last generation of turf house up on the hill, and people can see what has changed and what has not in a thousand years. The two houses are *real*. People really lived there. The sagas are not real.

"But it's quite entertaining to have them both," she added, smiling. "*You* can believe it was her house if you want. We have given her a place. And you can certainly place Snorri here. The saga says he built the first church here—though some people doubt that, too.

"But whether they are true or not, the sagas have a meaning for people. Icelanders have listened to them for a thousand years. They have the soul of the people in them, the image of the people. They name people, they name places. You can use them to learn genealogy, geography, history, to teach your children how to behave—"

"How do you use the saga of Grettir the Strong to teach children to behave?"

Sirri laughed, then sighed. "Oh, yes, Grettir. He did everything wrong. He was bad to animals, bad to people, he stole, he drank. He was in many ways crazy, an antihero. Many people would like to do what he did, but they don't dare."

The overarching theme of *Grettir's Saga* is that the Viking Age is over. The Viking values that Grettir embodies no longer apply: He was stronger than anyone, courageous to a fault, even a good poet, but his tragic flaw was hubris. Only when he learned to live humbly and love his brother was he happy. Until then he had no luck. He was outlawed in both Iceland and Norway for a good deed gone wrong: Seeking help after a shipwreck, he was mistaken for a troll, got into a brawl, and burned down a house, murdering several men. With a price on his head, he hid in caves and wilderness camps until his fear of the dark grew overwhelming, then convinced his fifteen-year-old brother Illugi to accompany him to Skagafjord to the island of Drangey, whose steep cliffs couldn't be scaled without a ladder.

It's on their journey through Skagafjord on a snowy day that Grettir's saga intersects with that of Gudrid the Far-Traveler, for at Glaumbaer they picked up a companion. He was a funny-looking fellow called Thorbjorn Glaum, meaning "Noisemaker" or "Chatterbox," and although his name might imply he had a connection to Gudrid's farm, he called himself a wanderer and spoke of the people there with no affection. He was a gossip and a boaster. His low status is clearly relayed by the phrase "he was poorly dressed." Clothing, in fact, seems to obsess him.

> "When you went by Glaumbaer, not even wearing a hood in this blizzard, they were pretty amazed," Glaum said. "They were wondering if being so cold-hardy made you any braver. These two farmer's sons, such big, strong men—when the shepherd told them to come out and give him a hand with the sheep, they couldn't pile on enough clothes, they thought it was so cold."
>
> Grettir said, "I saw one youngster in the doorway. He was pulling on his mittens. And the other one was going between the cowshed and the manure pile. I wouldn't be scared of either of them."

The two farmer's sons being lampooned would be Snorri and Thorbjorn, his younger brother. The year is about 1028, making Snorri twenty-three and master of Glaumbaer. Gudrid could have been away on her pilgrimage to Rome, for the years 1025 to 1028 saw a brief interlude of peace in the wars between Norway and Denmark, and King Olaf the Saint of Norway was encouraging Christianity in Iceland.

In these few words, the saga gives a good sense of the working farm of Glaumbaer a thousand years ago: two young men, a shepherd, sheep, a cowshed, a manure pile, work to be done on a cold winter day, and a painful awareness of the importance of hoods, mittens, and other warm clothes.

As *Grettir's Saga* continues, we get a wider picture of the neighborhood around Gudrid's farm. Grettir and his two companions walked on as far as Reynines, where Gudrid's mother-in-law may still have been in charge. She must have been generous and discreet, as well as haughty and capable, for the travelers spent the night there (without making any snide comments about it), and the next day traveled on up the coast to the farm with the hot spring now known as Grettir's Bath. There, by greasing a palm, the outlaws got a man to row them out to the island. They climbed up, secured the ladder, and settled in.

Grettir and Illugi were content on Drangey for five years. They had plenty of sheep to eat, with seabirds and gulls' eggs for variety, and they were safe as long as they hauled the ladder up each night. The only unhappy one was Glaum. He got the blame when the fire went out—causing Grettir to swim the four miles to the mainland, warm himself up in the hot spring, and rape the serving maid.

And how was Glaum to know that the great driftwood tree trunk he lugged home for firewood one night had been cursed by a witch? Her spell turned Grettir's axe, and he struck his own leg while chopping the log. The wound festered and turned black. While the hero lay feverish, Glaum forgot his duties once again and left the ladder down. Forewarned by the witch, Grettir's enemies clambered up and killed them all.

When I first read *Grettir's Saga*, I wondered if this miserable creature known as Thorbjorn Glaum was really Thorbjorn of Glaumbaer, Gudrid's second son. An impressionable eighteen years old, irritated by his older brother's authority, had he remembered how Grettir refused to do farmwork? Had he pulled on his mittens and run after the ill-starred hero, looking for glory? Had he joked about himself and his brother to cover his tracks? What finally convinced me the name was an odd coincidence—or a scribe's mistake—was the saga-writer's remark that the chatterbox was "poorly dressed." No matter how lazy or boastful, no son of Gudrid, living on the grass-rich farm of Glaumbaer, would be poorly dressed.

A housewife's chief duty was to see that her menfolk wore good clothes. Clothing was the most visible mark of her family's status, the main outlet for her creativity and industry, and the foundation of Iceland's economy. The sagas say little about such everyday tasks as cloth making, but this gap in our knowledge of Gudrid's daily life has recently been filled in by experimental archaeologists, like two I met at the University of Copenhagen. Using tools Gudrid might have owned, they make cloth that matches, thread for thread, the samples dug up from Viking houses and graves.

To clothe her family, Gudrid started in early summer, just after the lambs were born, with shearing the sheep. Their thick double-coated fleece could be pulled off by hand—called rooing—or snipped with iron shears, partial pairs of which have been found in several archaeological sites. Wool samples from the Farm Beneath the Sand in Greenland showed both rooing and shearing were done at the same time; no one knows which was better, or why. At Copenhagen's Center for Textile Research, Linda Martensson spread a full, sheared fleece, mottled black and gray, on the conference table. Beside it she lay a partial one in the rich, rusty color called "moor-red," after the tint bogwater takes on from iron ore. Eva Andersson, who is in charge of the Center's "Tools and Textiles" program, ran a hand over the gray fleece, as if it were a cat that had jumped into her lap.

"The process," Linda said, "is first you shear the sheep. Then you sort the wool."

The best wool, I had read, came from the neck, the sides, and the back; the worst from the belly and the legs. In between best and worst was a medium grade. To get a uniform thread, you would spin wool from only one grade at a time.

Linda touched the gray fleece delicately here and there, poking, squeezing, petting, fluffing. "The back leg is coarse and dirty," Linda said. "The back is a little dry. The sides I would see as a good quality to spin with. The front legs and neck are very felted. I would put that in another group."

"After you sort the wool," continued Eva, "you have to wash it."

She plucked a handful from the moor-red fleece and gave it to me. It was greasy with lanolin and slightly gritty. The washing step, I knew, we weren't going to get into here, in a glass-walled conference room. The Vikings washed wool in barrels of stale urine. When heated, urine, being alkaline, acts as a detergent—and it was certainly available. One scholar suggests that after the big milk tubs in Viking larders were emptied of *skyr* or whey during the winter, they were refilled with urine, little by little, especially on cold, windy days. *Modern sensitivities should not preclude the proximity of functions in the past now regarded as insanitary, such as the storage of urine and food in the same room,* he chides, noting, *it is less than a century since Yorkshire women used the chamber-pot contents to wash their face and hair.* The washed wool would be laid in the sun to dry, then stored in a wool crib until winter, when the work Eva and Linda were about to demonstrate would occupy every woman's day.

Linda had begun combing a hank of red wool with her fingers, teasing apart the mats and tangles, stretching it like taffy. "You can do a lot of work by hand, separating the different kinds of wool and hair, and opening it up." The handwork also warms the wool, softening and spreading the lanolin. She piled the fuzzier, woollier bits on the table, leaving the longer hairs in her hand. "Long hairs make a stronger yarn than short hairs. The warp of a loom is long hairs, but for the weft you can use short ones."

"You can't do too much by hand, though, or you start to make felt," Eva said. She got out a pair of wood-handled combs shaped like small rakes, with one row of four-inch-long metal teeth—reconstructions of Norwegian Viking finds. "You put them next to the fire to heat the teeth. That melts the fat while you comb." She placed the worked hank of wool in one comb, the teeth through the woolliest part, the long hairs hanging down, and passed both combs to Linda. Keeping the loaded comb still, cocked up to provide tension, Linda used the other to brush out the strands.

"You're so calm," Eva commented. "I'm much tougher when I comb."

"I like to be meditative," Linda said, with a flash of a smile.

After a moment she put down one comb and waved the other, letting the well-brushed wool ripple in the wind. "Doesn't it look like angel hair?" she said. With her fingers, she then pulled very slowly and gently on the dangling end. The hair lengthened magically until it was a yard long, from a beginning length of about four inches.

If she had been working, not just demonstrating, she would have wound the combed wool onto a stick—or distaff—accumulating a full reel before moving on to the next step, spinning.

But now Eva simply took the handful of combed wool, twisted it a little, and tied one end to the top of a spindle stick, securing it in a notch like that on a crochet hook. At the bottom of the stick was a conical weight, the spindle whorl. Holding on to the wool, she flicked the stick between finger and thumb to set the whorl twirling like a top in air. It dropped toward the floor, slowly as a spider on its silk—except the thread was being produced from the top, from Eva's fingers feeding the wool down, pulling and pinching it, while the spinning whorl stretched and twisted it into thread. When the spinning slowed, but before it could stop and reverse, she flicked the spindle again. When the whorl reached the floor, she caught it, wound the new-spun thread around the stick, and started over. The motion was so simple, the tools so light, that she could have spun—as Viking women did—anywhere, sitting or walking. Spindle whorls are often found in odd places, like the boatshed at L'Anse aux Meadows; at one farm in Greenland, out of twenty-five whorls, nine were in the kitchen and two in the church.

The whorl could be placed either at the bottom of the stick or at the top, without affecting the thread quality. The shape and substance of the whorl—whether amber, soapstone, ceramic, or bone—also didn't matter. But the size and weight of the whorl did.

For her doctoral dissertation in 1999, Eva studied the textile tools from Viking Age houses in southern Sweden. "I found that whenever there was more than one spindle whorl found in a house, they were of different sizes. Why? So I got these four spindles reconstructed, all copies of whorls found in Hedeby in Denmark. They're 30, 20, 10, and five grams." (Thirty grams is a bit more than an ounce.) She recruited Anna Batzer, who runs the weaving house at the Lejre Experimental Centre, a living-history museum outside of Copenhagen, and both women, the expert and the novice, spun thread with the same wool. "With the big spindle," Eva said, "we got 40 meters of thread for 10 grams of wool. When we spun with the five-gram whorl, we got over 200 meters from the same amount of wool." (Forty meters is about 131 feet; 200 meters is 656 feet.) The size of the spindle whorl determined the gauge of the thread. "When we look at Viking textiles, there are many types of quality. Of course, there would be different types of thread for different types of cloth."

Spinning with the tiny whorl was much more difficult than with the bigger ones. "You have to concentrate a lot. You have to have few, few fibers in the thread, or it won't turn around," Eva said, still spinning while she talked. You also have to have the right spindle stick. "They had found some little sticks in Hedeby, but they were not interpreted as spindle sticks because someone said they were too short, they wouldn't function. But when we started to spin, we learned we couldn't use a long stick on a small spindle. It wouldn't turn. So I looked at those sticks again, and they were perfect." The smallest spindle whorls had also been mislabeled. "The classical archaeologists were very surprised that you could spin on a spindle under 10 grams. They were sorting all the little spindle whorls out and calling them beads." She wound up the thread and dropped the spindle down again. "Sometimes it is hard to see the difference. The hole has to be absolutely centered, so the spindle is balanced. And the hole should be quite big so you can put a stick into it. That's what I went after when I reregistered them. There are some spindle whorls made of amber—they were called 'beads,' but they had a very big hole."

Linda leaned over and pointed at a minuscule bit of fuzz on the thread Eva had spun. "Here you can see it wasn't combed enough," she said. "If there is any underwool, any fuzzy wool in it, it will look like this. And it will break."

Eva laughed. "Even if they had slaves to do their spinning, Viking women had to watch. They had to know it was good enough. What is Gudrid's status? If she was rich, she would be doing mostly sewing and embroidery. Rich women did some spinning, but they never did weaving—at least, they were not producing the everyday textiles. But I'm quite sure Gudrid learned how to do it all. We see, historically, that it's important for all women to know how to produce fine cloth. Textiles are often used as gifts. It's a sign of a woman's status that she could produce excellent textiles."

In addition to choosing the right whorl for the job, the spinner also chose the direction of spin, the twist she would give the thread. On two samples of thread wound flat onto a paper card, the twist was easy to see. Reading right to left, the angle of the first sample went from high to low, like the midline of an S; the other went low to high, like a Z.

"It's easiest for me to spin sunwise," Linda said. She did not say "clockwise" because Viking women didn't have clocks. Half sitting on the edge of the table, she didn't flick the spindle with her fingers to set it twirling, but rolled it down her thigh. Since she is right-handed, she explained, her thread is S-spun; if she switched hands, or rolled the spindle up her leg instead of down, it would be Z-spun.

The spin angle matters for two reasons. First, if you began spinning S and switched to Z, the thread would unwind and break. Second, the spin angle provided texture to the finished cloth.

Said Eva, "You can see in the archaeological excavations whether they wanted S-S or S-Z cloth," that is, whether they used the same twist for both the warp and weft of the loom, or not. S-S cloth has a fine nobbly pattern and gives a nice drape for a shirt or dress. With S in the warp and Z in the weft, the fibers will be going in the same direction, Eva explained. "It's much easier then to full the cloth, which you would do for a sail or an outer cloak." Fulling called for more hot, stale urine. When the cloth was soaked in it and pressed, the ammonia in the urine caused the lanolin to coagulate. Fulling shrank the cloth and tightened the weave, making it more waterproof.

Linda had begun transferring the spun thread to a reel, three sticks of wood connected into a crooked H. "When I get enough thread that its weight affects the spinning, I wind it off onto this other tool. The thread wants to tangle, so I put it on this reel for a few days to straighten it out. That's called 'killing' it."

She would next wind it up into a skein, twisting it almost as if doing a cat's cradle, holding it with her teeth and stretching it. From a hook on the frame of a loom leaning against the wall, she pulled off an already-prepared skein of white wool thread. It was a little longer than my hand and about as thin as my finger—more like a skein of embroidery thread than the plump skeins of yarn I would buy in a knitting store. It was 40 meters long, or 131 feet, and had taken Linda an hour to make.

"It's not strange that textiles were so valuable and that people appreciated them so much as gifts," Eva said. "For just two Viking Age costumes at Lejre, one male and one female, we had to produce 40,000 meters of thread. For one sail for a ship, around 100 square meters in size, we had to produce over 300,000 meters of thread. It's *endless* meters of thread."

The 1,000-square-foot sail, requiring almost a million feet of thread, took two women four and a half years to make. It used the wool of more than 200 sheep, each sheep the size of a large dog and yielding two to four pounds of wool.

The average Viking housewife like Gudrid needed to clean, sort, and spin the wool of 100 sheep a year to provide clothing for her husband and children and their servants and hired hands (who were paid in food and clothing), along with bed-clothes, wall hangings, tents for travel, packs and sacks, diapers, bandages, and burial shrouds. Most of this was made of undyed wool—"moor-red" or black were the most popular colors among men, while children's clothes were generally white or gray. But a man of means, like Gudrid's husband Karlsefni, would have worn bright colors, which meant that some of the wool had to be dyed.

When she analyzed bits of Viking cloth found in Green-land, Penelope Walton of the British company Textile Research Associates found that the most common color, a bright purple, came from lichens. Growing throughout the far north, these lichens were scraped off rock faces in early summer, dried in the sun, and steeped in more stale urine. The resulting blue-black mass was made into cakes and hung to dry in peat smoke, where it would last for years. Depending on how acidic the dye water was, this so-called lichen purple ranged from a bright crimson red to a deep blue. Another blue came from indigotin, the chemical found in indigo from India but also in a spindly yellow-flowered plant called woad, an "aggressive weed," accord-ing to the U.S. Department of Agriculture, that does well in Iceland. Other dye plants Gudrid might have used to make yel-lows and greens are Labrador tea, green alder, and dwarf birch.

Even with the wool of a hundred sheep, Gudrid could not have made Karlsefni or herself new clothes every year. The "av-erage housewife" calculation is based on a set of Icelandic in-ventories from the 1700s, which allots each person 11 pounds of new, unprocessed wool for clothing. But when Else Ostergard, a textile expert who retired in 2006 from the Danish National Museum, weighed a gown, a hood, and a pair of stockings from a Norse burial in Greenland and added to it a cloak and some underclothes, she came up with a weight of 17 to 22 pounds of finished cloth. Ostergard concluded that each suit of clothes must have been worn for at least two to three years before the family could afford to replace it. And yet, on top of all this, women like Gudrid produced enough extra cloth that it was Iceland's main export for two hundred years.

Cloth making was not just mindless drudgery. "You need to have a good head for mathematics to work textiles," said Eva, "just to calculate how much thread you need and to lay out the patterns."

But it was physically taxing. "If you're sitting and spinning for half a day, it hurts!" Linda said. "From spinning, it's the shoulders." She lifted her left arm into "spinning position," elbow cocked at shoulder height, hand dangling. "You have to hold yourself this way all day. It's the same when you're weaving, except both arms are up. And your fingers get stiff and swollen. From wool combing, it's the wrists that hurt."

Eva turned to the loom leaning against the conference-room wall. It was a vertical loom, also called a warp-weighted loom, known, in its many variations, from ancient Greece to modern Norway. The warp threads hang vertically, weighted taut with stones. The weaver passes the weft through the warp, shuttling from side to side, starting at the top.

"This loom is set up to make a tabby," Eva said, "the most simple weave. Even so, it takes a whole day to set up the warp. For a very intricate weave, such as a lozenge twill, it might take two weeks to set it up."

The process begins with putting together the loom. Tall and bulky, with two stout wooden uprights linked at the top by a heavy crossbeam, it took up too much floor space to keep out all the time. In summer it would be set up in a pit house next to the longhouse. Eva had doubted the archaeologists' theory that these were weaving rooms, until she worked in one at

Hogs Viking Village in Scania, Sweden, one year from March to October. "I now think these houses are really good for textile work," she said. Based on plans of Viking pit houses, she sited hers so that the door was in the southwest corner—at the edge of the roof, rather like a trapdoor—and the loom leaned against the northeast wall. "If the door was open, the light came into the house like a window in the roof. It was absolutely the best weaving light I could have had, so much better than inside the longhouse. I didn't even have a shadow."

Once the heavy wooden frame of the loom was in place, the uprights leaning at a gradual slant, the crossbeam held away from the wall in sturdy wooden brackets, the part of the process calling for good light and mathematical talent began: stringing the warp threads on the loom, fastening them to weights to provide tension, parting them with the shed rod, and knitting them to the heddle rods to make possible a pattern.

Each warp thread—of which there were hundreds—is one of Linda's 131-foot-long skeins. It is fastened to the crossbeam at the top and unwound until it almost touches the floor. In the simple tabby, every other warp thread goes in front of the shed rod, a fixed wooden bar that crosses from one upright to another in the bottom half of the loom. The still-wound end of the warp skein is knotted to a stone. These stones, or loom weights, have been found in dozens of Viking houses, sitting in neat rows as if their warp strings had just snapped. Archaeologists use them to say where the loom had been, but though weavers know a light weight is needed for light threads and a heavy weight for heavy threads, no one has studied how the stones' diversity of size and shape affects the cloth.

The next step in stringing the loom is the most painstaking. Half of the warp threads are hanging straight down, nothing impeding their drop from crossbeam to stone. The other half are hooked over the shed rod, pulled out at a slant in front of the loom for most of their length before gravity takes over. That gap, between the back threads and the front threads, is called the shed. Through this gap, the weaver will pass the weft, a long, loose skein. Before she passes it back a second time, though, she must change the shed.

Changing the shed requires heddle shafts—one for a simple tabby weave, up to four for some other designs. A heddle shaft crosses from upright to upright like the shed rod, but it isn't fixed in place. Its bracket has two options: snug against the uprights or a handspan forward. The shaft is looped to the back threads—each loop is called a heddle—so that when the weaver pulls the shaft out to the forward bracket, the back threads are all brought forward, too. They rise above the front threads and create a new opening—a new shed—for the weft. The heddle shaft's backward-and-forward motion is thus the key to weaving, catching the rows of weft in the changing pattern of the warp.

The loops that hold the threads to the shaft are all knotted from one long, strong cord, saved and reused again and again. Knotting the heddles is where a good head for math comes in handy. Mistakes are easy to make and hard to spot—until you've started weaving, and then the only way to fix them is to unweave it all and start over.

It's easy to imagine knotting the heddles for a simple tabby. Loop a thread, skip a thread, loop a thread, skip a thread. But tabby was not the most common cloth in the Viking Age. The standard was a plain twill in which the weft goes over two threads, under two threads, over two threads, under two threads—simple, except that the thread pairs chosen were not always the same. On the return journey, the weft goes over one thread from the first pair and one from the second pair, then under the remaining thread of the second pair and one from the third pair, and so on. "So you have to have three heddle shafts," said Eva. "If you have four threads, the first one goes to the first shaft, the second one to the second shaft, the third one to the third shaft, and the fourth one is not attached to a shaft. You can have two shafts in front and one in back, or two in back and one in front. You have to be very, very careful that you have the right thread tied to the right shaft."

Once the loom was strung, the work—and the walking—began. The weaver walked from right to left, slipping the weft through the open shed. Parking the weft in a hook on the loom frame, she lifted the left end of the heddle shafts from one bracket to the other. She walked back to the right side of the loom and changed the right end of the heddle shafts—the shafts are too heavy to pick up in the middle and change both sides at once. She walked back to the left side of the loom, picked up the weft, wove a new row walking from left to right, and changed the heddle shafts again. According to one calculation, a hardworking weaver walked 23 miles every day.

Added to the walking was the beating. Every two or three rows, the weaver would insert a weaving sword—a long sword-shaped tool made of whalebone or wood—into the shed and, using both hands, beat the weft upward, packing the rows of thread tightly together. The densest cloth required twenty thumps. A more delicate tool was the pin-beater, a slender finger made of bone or wood. Run along the warp from side to side, it evened out the spacing between the threads. The poets said it danced and sang—though the sound, to me, when Linda demonstrated, was more like that of a fingertip on the teeth of a comb.

"I am too tall for this loom," Linda said, showing how it forced her to bend to work. A woman who owned her own loom would have it made to fit her height—if there was ample wood available. A short girl working a tall loom might need a stool, particularly to get the necessary power into her beating strokes. In the weaving room at the Farm Beneath the Sand in Greenland, a large whalebone vertebra was placed flat in front of the loom, making a sturdy hassocklike stool.

When the finished cloth filled the top half of the loom, the weaver rolled it up around the loom's crossbeam—a stool would be helpful here even for a tall weaver, for the beam is heavy and clumsy to turn. Then, before she could begin again, the weaver had to get down on her knees to lengthen the warp threads, taking off the loom weights one by one, unwinding the skein, and retying the weights the proper distance from the floor.

All in all, weaving was an athletic task. By the 1400s, a professional weaver working on a warp-weighted loom was expected to finish about eleven yards of plain twill cloth a week. A more difficult weave would take longer. Among the fabrics archaeologists have found are stripes and checks and the fancy lozenge twill that required two weeks just to string the warp threads onto the loom. Unlike an ordinary twill, in which the fabric has a texture of diagonal lines, the lozenge twill has a pattern of rings.

The most distinctive cloth woven by Viking women was the pile or shaggy weave that imitated fur or fleece. The weaver strung her loom for a plain twill and used rather coarse thread in both warp and weft. But as she wove, she added in loops of unspun wool. These tufts were lustrous and wavy, untwisted locks of the sheep's long outer fleece. Added to every fourth row, with twenty warp threads between each loop, the tufts were long and thick enough to cover the cloth completely after they were brushed out. The fuzzy surface was excellent for shedding rain and sea spray. Even if soaked with salt water, the cloth remained warm and soft—unlike a true sheepskin, which would stiffen up. Dyed blue or purple, these shaggy cloaks were eye-catching; the sagas describe them trimmed with patterned ribbons or braid. Even in nondescript gray, they were popular on the export market—especially after King Harald of Norway, in about 960, accepted one as a gift, earning him his nickname "Graycloak" and starting a new fashion trend.

Historian Jenny Jochens points out that these shaggy cloaks became so valuable during Gudrid's lifetime that they were considered "legal forms of currency," one cloak equaling two ounces of silver. You could buy a cow, candles, or passage on a ship for shaggy cloaks. A law passed around 1100 fixed prices of "all imaginable items—including gold and silver" in terms of cloth, with "six ells new and unused homespun" equal to one ounce of silver, the Vikings' ell being the distance from your elbow to your fingertips, or about half a yard. One pound of beeswax traded for six ells; one cow was worth 120 ells. "By the end of the eleventh century," Jochens writes, "the previous silver standard, founded on men's violent and sporadic activities as Vikings, had been replaced by the homespun standard, based on women's peaceful and steady work as weavers."

CHAPTER 10

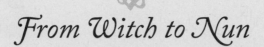

From Witch to Nun

But Karlsefni told the tale of these voyages better than
anyone else ...

—The Saga of the Greenlanders

THE WORLD WAS CHANGING IN OTHER WAYS AS WELL,
those years when Gudrid ran the farm at Glaumbaer. Not only
was wealth now counted in ells of cloth, not ounces of stolen
silver, but the Otherworld was not attained in a clinker-built
longship laden with beds and brassbound buckets, iron skillets,
whistles, looms, bells, brooches, merchants' scales, oxen, horses,
and dogs.

By then, almost all of the Western world was officially
Christian. In the north, the last Viking land to abandon the
old gods was Greenland, through Leif Eiriksson's efforts in the
year 1000. In the east, the Hungarian Magyars—as much a
scourge of the Church as the Vikings were—asked the pope
to bless their leader: Vajk was crowned King Stephen I in that
apocalyptic year and remembered by posterity as St. Stephen. In
the south, the grand Muslim city of Cordoba in Spain, with its
library of 400,000 books of Arabic science and Greek philosophy, was sacked and burned in 1013; by 1035 Sancho the Great
would call himself King of Spain, *by the Grace of God* (despite
the fact that Muslims would control large areas of the Iberian
peninsula until 1492).

A woman could not buy her way into Heaven by being buried with her treasures in a splendid ship. But she could earn entrance through godly deeds, the best being a humble pilgrimage to a holy site—Jerusalem (the way made safe by St. Stephen), Santiago de Compostela (Sancho of Spain's especial care), or Rome, where in 1027 Conrad II, king of Saxony, was crowned Holy Roman Emperor with Knut, king of England and Denmark, and Rudolph III, king of Burgundy, by his side.

At about that time, Gudrid's son Snorri, born in Vinland, reached manhood and married. Gudrid handed off her housewife's keys—and the heavy work of weaving homespun—to her new daughter-in-law and decided to take a pilgrimage to Rome. Whether it was to salve her soul or to serve her wanderlust we'll never know. It would be her seventh sea-crossing.

She may have had good company. According to *Laxdaela Saga,* a handsome young son of Gudrun the Fair set off in about 1025 for Constantinople to join the Byzantine emperor's Viking bodyguard. Their route much of the way would have been the same: from Iceland to the court of King Olaf the Saint in Trondheim, Norway. From there south by ship to Roskilde, Denmark, where King Svein ruled for his father, Knut the Great. There Gudrid would have seen the beginnings of the first stone church in the North, commissioned by Knut's sister Estrid, and completed in 1027. From Denmark, Gudrid and her companions headed south on foot, as was customary, on the Pilgrim Way. They lodged in hostels kept by monasteries and were protected not only by their numbers but by the *Pax Dei,* the Peace of God, which threatened excommunication to anyone who robbed a pilgrim, broke into a church, struck a priest (if he was unarmed), or harassed a virgin, child, or widow. (A few years later, merchants and their goods would be added to the list.)

No saga says what Gudrid may have seen on her yearlong sojourn south through central Europe. Certainly she would have been astonished by the cathedrals built of stone and wood in the stark Romanesque style, with their columns and arches and arcades, the high clerestory windows of stained glass, the towers and belfries, the frescoes of Christ's miracles, the candlelight and incense. She may have seen the books made in the scriptoria: the radiant Gospels with their illuminations in violet, red, blue, and green of fantastical birds and beasts and chimeras creeping through golden foliage, or of the Christ Child greeting the Three Wise Men under a sky of pure gold and a silver star streaming with colors. She would have marveled at the lifelike Madonnas carved from Greenland walrus tusk. And she would have descended into the sacred crypts beneath the sanctuary floor, where the relics—the foot of St. Andrew, a nail from the True Cross, the sponge held to the suffering Christ's lips, a shred of His coat, a scrap of His crown of thorns, a drop of His blood, the cord of Mary's dress—were kept in gold caskets encrusted with jewels. She may have met black-clad monks who lived simply, were kind to the poor, and never laughed. She may also have met the monks that Richer, a tenth-century French historian, described as "colored like peacocks," wearing habits so tight "that they exhibit the shape of their arse," and carrying "little mirrors on top of their shoes so that with each step they can admire themselves." She may have seen Princess Sophie, who ruled the convent of Gandersheim; there, a few years before Gudrid's birth, the nun Roswitha wrote plays modeled on the Latin comedies of Terence and an epic poem honoring the emperor. She may have stopped at Reichenau, on Lake Constance, where the crippled monk Hermann was working on his treatises on music, on astronomy, and on how to build an astrolabe. Finally, Gudrid would have heard, for the first time in her life, hymns and antiphons chanted in counterpoint by choirs, and the resounding chords of the pipe organs, whose design Pope Sylvester II had brought from Islamic Spain some fifty years before.

She crossed the Alps in the footsteps of Hannibal and his elephants, as well as Charlemagne and his knights, by the pass of Mont Joux. At the base of the mountains she probably met Bernard of Menthon, for whom the pass would soon be renamed the St. Bernard Pass. As archdeacon of Aosta, Bernard had for many years tended to travelers accosted on the pass by Saracens, who exacted murderous tolls. Gudrid may have sought protection by traveling in the train of one of the kings—Knut, Rudolph, or Conrad—on their way to Rome for Conrad's coronation as emperor. Or she may have crossed after Knut and Rudolph, annoyed by the harassment of their people, banded together to wipe out the Saracen fort and replace it with a pilgrim's hospice under Bernard's care.

Coming into Italy, Gudrid passed the white marble city of Luna, sacked in the 800s by Vikings who mistook it for Rome and, in 1016, by Saracens—an attack from which the city never recovered; in 1058 the last of its citizens abandoned it. Her route intersected the Pilgrim Way to Santiago de Compostela, and the number of travelers increased. They walked through the famous chestnut forests of Lunigiana and the vineyards of Montefiascone. They ate lamb and olives and beans and onions, bread baked from chestnut flour, mushrooms, sheep's-milk cheese, salami, and sweet cakes flavored with spring herbs.

Gudrid came to Rome during one of the few periods in the tenth or eleventh centuries when the holy city deserved the pilgrim's song: "O Rome, noble thou art and of the world ruler, / Of all other cities in glory exceeding." Pope John XIX was known for lavish spending, for courting kings and musicians, and for help-ing the Abbot of Cluny rein in the excesses (like those mirrored shoes) of monks. John XIX was not a priest and had no Church training. But like his brother, who was pope before him, he was a good statesman and a sensible man—a vast improvement on many popes of the time. John XII, for example, was a debauch, spending his days hunting with hawks or hounds, drinking, and playing dice. He so neglected the churches of Rome that rain dripped onto the altars. Female pilgrims shunned the city; the lascivious pope, they heard, would force them into his bed, whether wives, widows, or virgins. Boniface VII had two rival popes strangled or starved, robbed the Vatican treasury, and fled to Constantinople. Benedict IX, elected to the papacy as a teen-ager, sold the office to a priest so he could marry—then changed his mind and raised an army to take the papal throne back.

But the rot at the core of Rome would not have been ap-parent to Gudrid. Like her countryman, the monk Nikulas, who wrote a traveler's guide in the mid-1100s, what would have stayed in Gudrid's mind was the immensity of the stone and marble city. Four miles long and two wide, the city on the hill was a splendor of churches, sanctified Roman ruins, and the glittering bazaar, thronged with people dressed outlandishly and babbling in dozens of tongues.

If she spoke to Pope John or told her tale of Vinland to any churchman, we have no proof of it, although more than one writer has imagined a secret record of just such a conversation hiding in the Vatican archives.

When Gudrid returned to Iceland from this last eye-opening voyage, she found that her son Snorri had built a church at Glaumbaer—perhaps at her request—and she settled in as a nun. A few years later, on the nearby island of Drangey, Grettir the Outlaw was killed by Thorbjorn Ongul, aided by his foster-mother's witchcraft.

People despised Ongul, the saga says, for depending on a witch's spell. His own brother-in-law scolded that the killing was "not altogether of a Christian nature." The man who had outlawed Grettir refused to give Ongul the reward, saying, "I would rather see you put to death for your sorcery and witchcraft than pay you anything." At the yearly assembly, the Althing passed a new law forbidding witchcraft on pain of exile—Isleif, a chieftain's son who would become the first native-born bishop of Iceland in 1056, urged that the penalty be death—and Ongul was banished from Iceland forever.

The author of *Grettir's Saga* swiftly frames the moral of this story when Ongul first crashes into Grettir's hut and confronts the outlaw:

> Grettir said then to Ongul, "Who showed you the way onto the island?"
>
> Ongul said, "Christ showed us the way."
>
> "But I think that wicked old woman, your foster-mother, showed you the way," said Grettir, "for you have always put your trust in her."
>
> "It will be all the same to you," said Ongul, "whichever one we trusted in."

But not all the same, the Christian audience of the saga would have understood, to Ongul.

Grettir's Saga was one of the last classic sagas to be written, but behind its carefully crafted text lies a memory of the early eleventh century, when potential heroes didn't know where the path to honor lay. Ongul is truly astonished at his reception at the Althing: Instead of being praised for killing a notorious murderer and thief, he is outlawed?

Gudrid would have known Ongul and the other men who helped him kill Grettir. They were her neighbors, the chief men of her district; she was related to many of them through Karlsefni. She would have known Ongul's foster-mother, Thurid.

But to know what Gudrid the nun may have thought of old Thurid the witch, we need to understand what the Vikings believed in before they accepted Christianity—and how their beliefs changed. Unfortunately, not much remains to tell us about the old ways. Images carved on standing stones in the pagan eighth to tenth centuries seem to illustrate some of the entertaining stories Snorri Sturluson collected in the Christian thirteenth century in his *Prose Edda*, which modern writers have used to re-create a Norse mythology. These myths tell of the great ash tree, Yggdrasil, that linked the Nine Worlds, of the gods riding up the rainbow bridge to sit in counsel, of quests into Giantland after an enormous ale pot or a giant bride, of the thieving trickster, Loki, who pawned the golden apples of youth, of Thor's great strength and how Odin sold his eye for knowledge, of the eight-legged horse and the ship that folds up into a pocket, the gold ring that drops eight rings of equal value every ninth night, and the sword that wields itself. The myths are funny, shocking, and mind-bending, with their doors to other worlds—but how did a true pagan interpret the gods' quarrels and adventures? What did she think about Ragnarok, the end of the world, when good and evil would destroy each other and everything in between?

Take the story of Thor and the Midgard Serpent. One day, the burly, red-haired, and somewhat dim-witted Thunder God went fishing with a giant. They rowed so far from land that the giant was afraid. Thor baited his hook with the head of a bull and soon got a bite. He fought and fought with his catch, until finally he dragged its head up to the boat's gunwales—and found staring him in the eye the Midgard Serpent, the evil sea monster that encircled the earth like a living equator, biting its tail. Thor raised his hammer to slay the monster, but the terrified giant cut the fishing line and the serpent escaped. The moral of this story is . . . unknown.

One scholar interprets it as a clash between civilization (Thor) and the destructive forces of nature (the Midgard Serpent). Another sees it as the reverse: Thor is threatening the balance of nature and the giant must stop him. The fact that we can't agree whether Thor is good or bad in this tale provides us with one key to the Viking worldview: "Order and chaos, good and evil, may be opposite aspects of the same things, precariously balanced," as one scholar says. The gods may exist to give the chaos of nature some "shape and direction," says another. They create culture by taking things found in nature (or in the cave of the giants) and giving them meaning. In this way the gods gave men poetry and ale. But the Norse gods are strangely like their enemies, the giants. They have "limited powers. They are neither omniscient nor omnipotent. To know what is hidden from them they have to consult wiser beings," such as the mysterious old hag who lives at the Well of Knowing. And they are not to be trusted. They are grasping, duplicitous, vain, and brutal. Worse, they cannot defend themselves—or us—against the traitor among them, the half-god, half-monster Loki, bloodbrother to Odin, who will lead the ranks of evil at Ragnarok. Then, says the poem "Words of the Seer," Thor and the Midgard Serpent will battle to the death. One—the poem isn't clear which—"mauls in his rage all Middle Earth . . . Now death is the portion of doomed men."

In *Nordic Religions in the Viking Age,* Thomas DuBois shows how this mythology of doom could be converted into everyday rules to live by. All people, he says, citing Karl Luckert's

American Tribal Religions, divide the elements of the world, seen and unseen, into three sets: less than human, equal, and greater than human. The less-than-human are "handled." Animals, in Gudrid's culture, were generally less than human. The greater-than-human—Thor and the Midgard Serpent—evoke awe and surrender. Reports from Christian missionaries give some sense—distorted by the writers' disgust—of how people in pagan times expressed their awe. Adam of Bremen in 1070 describes a festival at Uppsala in Sweden, held for nine days every ninth year during the spring equinox, in which nine male animals of each kind were sacrificed, with the blood used to "placate the gods" and the carcases hung up in the trees of the Sacred Grove. "A Christian informant," Adam writes, told him that he once counted seventy-two carcases—of dogs, horses, and even humans—in the trees. Such sacrifices seem to be borne out by archaeologists' excavations, but these views through the eyes of outsiders cannot tell us why the Vikings conducted them.

According to DuBois, the elements of the world equal to humans are the ones that mattered most in Gudrid's time. People then, DuBois writes, "had a vast array of equals—human, near-human, and nonhuman, mobile and immobile, visible and invisible—with which they shared and competed on a daily basis." Among them were the dwellers in the mounds: the elves, the land spirits, the Hidden Folk. Mountains were declared "holy" and were not to be climbed by the unwashed, though beneath them the illustrious dead could be buried. Guardian spirits lived in caves and stones. "Some women are so unwise and blind about their needs," wrote a medieval Christian author, "that they take their food and bring it out to heaps of stones and mountain caves and consecrate it to the spirits of the land and thereafter they eat it in order to make the spirits of the land friendly and in order to have more luck with their farming than before."

In two sagas of the conversion to Christianity, the first missionary to come to Iceland, a Saxon bishop named Fridrek, made a bargain with a farmer: If Bishop Fridrek could drive the farm's "steward" from his stone, the farmer would agree to be baptized. This steward, the farmer said, was a good friend: He protected the cattle and gave helpful advice. The bishop advanced on the stone. He sprinkled it with holy water while singing psalms. That night the steward appeared to the farmer in a dream and cried: "Ill have you done to let that awful man pour boiling water into my house, so that it scorches my children. Oh, how hard it is to hear the screeches of my little ones!" He begged and threatened for two more nights, but the farmer held to his bargain with the bishop to see who proved more powerful, the elf or Christ. After the third night, the stone broke apart, and the steward was heard from no more. The farmer was baptized, believing that his new invisible friend, Christ, was stronger than his old one.

It was their belief in holy mountains, sacred groves, and in-habited stones that made the concept of pilgrimage so appealing to the Vikings (besides the fact that it was so similar to "going a-viking"). The holy city, the saint's shrine, were understood in terms of the steward's stone: a place inhabited by the new stronger "friend." At home, traditional holy places were resanc-tified by the addition of a cross or the mere blessing of a bishop. Gudmundur the Good, bishop in the twelfth century, erected a cross in a field. According to his saga: "People go there as they do to holy places and burn lights before the cross outside just as they would inside a church, even if the weather is bad." The reverse had happened in the early days of Iceland's settlement. When Unn the Deep-Minded and her Christian crew came to Iceland from the Hebrides, they marked their land-claim with a cross on a hill. There Unn prayed. Later, according to *The Book of Settlements,* "her kinsmen worshipped these hills." They built a pagan temple there, in which their chieftains were sanctified, and "believed they would go into the hills when they died."

The pagan belief in fortune-telling was also neatly co-opted into the Christian worldview, with soothsaying becoming a talent of Christian saints. Olaf Tryggvason, the missionary king of Norway credited with converting Iceland and Greenland, was baptized by such a one. When Olaf asked the hermit how he knew so much about the future, the hermit replied that the god of Christian men told him whatever he wanted to know.

In the old days, a person in difficulty would naturally turn, not to a bishop or holy hermit, but to a witch like Ongul's foster-mother. The sagas name seventy-eight witches, half of them male and half female. They are sometimes portrayed as good and useful neighbors, sometimes as wicked and hateful interlopers (who nonetheless had their supporters). One saga explains: "As Christianity was new to the country and had not fully taken hold, many people considered it an advantage that a person was skilled in magic."

A witch was a "fence rider," one who straddled the barrier between the fields and the wild lands, civilization and chaos, natural and supernatural, good and evil. (Over time, the fence turned into the broomstick on which our cartoon witches ride.) A saga witch could bring snow or fog to hide a hunted man. She could change the course of a river. In famine, she could fill a bay with fish or summon a whale. She could turn herself (or someone she loved) into a goat, a boar, a spindle stick, a walrus, a bear, or a bull's-hide bag filled with water. She could provide a shirt no sword could pierce and a helmet of invisibility. She could find a lost horse or family heirloom.

These otherworldly talents, too, were translated into the Christian world. Christ could raise the dead, turn water into wine, calm the storm, and feed the multitude. The early Christians highlighted not only Christ's miracles, but those of His followers as a way to prove God's might and His concern for His creation. Bishops of Iceland would become famous for ending a long winter or a drought, providing a calm breeze so young boys could sail home safely, turning aside a flood-swollen river to save a farmhouse, and causing a midwinter thaw so bodies could be buried properly at church. They found lost things, treated frostbite, cough, insomnia, and toothache, lessened women's labor pains, and healed crippled or broken limbs. One priest was said to be able to turn a bone into a horse that could carry a rider over the sea. Another had a whistle that could call up troops of demon workers to fetch in the hay before it was ruined by the rain.

The magical stones and potions and amulets a witch might have pressed on a client were replaced with saints' relics and holy water and all sorts of crosses, from silver pendants to two sticks tied with yarn. Even the story of a saint could be potent. In a small manuscript book of the saga of St. Margaret, the letters have been almost rubbed away on some pages. Such books were held against the legs of a woman in labor to ease her pains. The magical pagan songs that Gudrid sang so beautifully to call the spirits in Greenland, and the elaborate ritual surrounding the séance—the seer's jeweled blue dress and white catskin gloves, her cushion of hen's feathers, her meal of animal hearts—were replaced by equally beautiful and elaborate Christian prayers and rituals. The farmer who made the bargain with Bishop Fridrek had had no interest in Christianity—no desire to evict the farm's steward from his stone—until he witnessed a mass:

But when he heard the ringing of bells and the fair song of priests, and smelled the sweet fragrance of incense, and

saw the bishop clothed with splendid vestments, and . . .
the fair shining of wax tapers . . . then all this pleased him
rather well.

It was easy for the Norse to put a Christian gloss on their
old ways. In the saga of the Christian king Hakon the Good,
who ruled Norway in the mid-900s, the king is at a pagan feast
held by some rebellious nobles, and the sacred ale has just been
brought out.

> When the first cup was poured, Sigurd the Jarl spoke be-
> fore it and blessed it in honor of Odin and drank to the
> king from the horn. The king took it and made the sign
> of the Cross over it. Then Kar of Gryting said: "Why does
> the king do that? Will he still not sacrifice?" Sigurd the
> Jarl answered: "The king does as all do who trust in their
> might and main; he blesses the cup in honor of Thor. He
> made the sign of Thor's hammer over it before he drank."

What's important here is not that the T-shape of Thor's hammer looked like the sign of the cross, but the similarity of the
beliefs and rituals of the cults on a deeper level. Writes DuBois:
"The shared assumptions reflect a tradition of comparison, in
which the Christian Lord appears at first as just one more deity
of the sky, vying with the others for the best of adherents."

Christian doctrine does not allow for any other gods. Christ
cannot be "just one more deity." Yet both archaeology and history
imply that the Viking world failed to grasp this essential tenet of
the new religion for at least a hundred years, well after Gudrid's
death. Burial customs changed very slowly, with Thor's hammers
and Christian crosses sometimes found in the same grave. Thor

and his hammer appear on a Swedish baptismal font, alongside Christ and the cross. A jewelry mold found in Denmark could simultaneously cast a cross and a hammer. In one of the earliest Christian Norse poems, dated to circa 1000, Christ sits beside the Well of Weird next to the three pagan goddesses of Fate. The names of the days of the week were not changed in Icelandic until the 1100s—and were never changed in English: We still honor the gods Tyr (Tuesday), Odin (or Wodan, Wednesday), and Thor (Thursday), and the goddess Frigg (Friday).

Nor was the Christ who came to the Vikings the suffering, broken, abandoned, *blauður* Christ of Good Friday. He was the glorious, invincible, *hvatur* Christ of the Last Judgment, separating the righteous from the damned. He was the Christ in the letters of St. Paul, the "young hero" and "victor over evil." He was, in fact, "virtually a picture of Thor under the name of Christ," as one scholar writes. Crucifixes made in the newly converted North never show the dying, human Christ, but always Christ Triumphant, standing bolt upright, his feet on a footrest, his head held high and his expression regal, wearing a crown of gold, not thorns. In Old Norse poetry, he is called "creator of heaven and earth, of angels and the sun, ruler of the world." He is "king of the heavens and the sun and angels and Jerusalem and Jordan and Greece, master of apostles and saints." Wrote the poet Markus, "Alone the ruler of men, Christ can control all things." Said his colleague Eilif Kulnasvein, "The sun's king alone is finer than all other true glory."

One Icelander whom Bishop Fridrek tried to convert declined, saying he would hold to the beliefs of his foster-father who "believed in the one who made the sun and ruled all things."

The bishop answered, "I offer you the same faith."

———

What the sagas call the Change of Ways came to Iceland in the year 1000, while Gudrid was on her way to Greenland. The island was converted by parliamentary decree, with the Althing essentially blackmailed by the crusading King Olaf Tryggvason, who held many Icelanders and their precious ships captive in Norway until the outcome satisfied him. All Icelanders were to be baptized, but sacrificing to the old gods was not outlawed—if it was kept quiet.

Many of the Vikings' most ingrained values did not need to be Christianized. Men were praised for being peaceable, popular, and calm. They strove to be generous, hospitable, faithful, healthy, clean living, and tolerant. Among the advice in the pre-Christian poem *Hávamál,* or "Words of the High One" (the "high one" being the god Odin), are these stanzas:

> Mock not the traveler met on the road,
> Nor maliciously laugh at the guest:
> Scoff not at guests nor to the gate chase them,
> But relieve the lonely and wretched.

> Never laugh at the old when they offer counsel,
> Often their words are wise:
> From shrivelled skin, from scraggy things
> That hang among the hides
> And move amid the guts,
> Clear words often come.

> With a good woman, if you wish to enjoy
> Her words and her good-will,
> Pledge her fairly and be faithful to it:
> Enjoy the good you are given.

> These things are thought the best:
> Fire, the sight of the sun,

Good-health with the gift to keep it,
And a life that avoids vice.

As Russian saga scholar M. I. Steblin-Kamenskij complains, "What is taken for a Christian trait in the family sagas is usually 'Christian' only in the sense that it continued to exist after the introduction of Christianity."

The Change of Ways wrought no huge upheaval in society. Those who had been in power, remained in power. As Gunnar Karlsson puts it in *The History of Iceland*, the chieftains "just changed gods but went on with their social roles as far as they possibly could." The chieftains built churches as a mark of status. According to one saga, a chieftain could take as many of his followers with him to Heaven as could fit in his church. The chieftains declared themselves "priests"—rather like the pope, with no Church training (though when such training became available in the 1100s, they took it). Trade in wine and wax candles probably increased. According to Icelandic historian Helgi Thorlaksson, not until the 1100s did the Icelanders all learn to say the Lord's Prayer, cross themselves properly, and act "with reverence" in church. As late as 1150, the archbishop in Norway was still putting pressure on the Icelanders to "sanctify" marriage, by condemning out-of-wedlock births, the keeping of mistresses, and divorce—all ways to rein in that "aggressive authority" by which women in the sagas pursued their sex lives.

"It has been argued that Christianity was a disaster for women," writes Anne-Sofie Graslund, an archaeologist at the University of Uppsala, Sweden. In the old days, women were at the heart of the rituals. Housewives took the offerings to the "heaps of stones and mountain caves" and asked the spirits of the land to bless the farm. Women saw into the future, healed the sick with charms and potions, and prepared the sacred ale for feast days. Two women in *The Book of Settlements* are named *gyðja*, "priestess," though we do not know what their role entailed. Christianity, by contrast, has no goddess, and the Church is headed by men. When the Christian Church became fully established in the 1100s, these housewives and priestesses were shut out of the spiritual life, while wise women like Ongul's foster-mother were declared "of little use" and told to abandon their witchcraft. Many episodes in the sagas support this view; archaeology seems to show, instead, that women of Gudrid's day saw Christianity not as a threat to their social status, but as an attractive set of beliefs. After examining runestones and burials throughout the Viking world, Graslund believes that Viking women were the first converts.

During the time Gudrid was a nun, Christianity, Graslund says, was a religion of joy and sisterhood. Rather than limiting women's sexual or spiritual power, it enhanced their sense of worth. "Christ made no distinction between men and women," Graslund says. "His attitude toward women meant nothing less than a revolution." No longer was a woman's worth, high or low, defined by marriage or childbearing. Abandoned, orphaned, barren, kinless, a woman still owned a soul and a place in the world: She had rights from birth to death. A Christian father could not decide to set his baby girl outdoors to die. (Exposure had always killed more girls than boys in Viking Iceland, in spite of women's high status.) Shortly after the conversion, this practice, along with the eating of horsemeat (an essential part of pagan ritual), was declared taboo.

Graslund sees evidence of this new regard for the individual in the burial practices of early Christians. In the old days, families were buried together, under a holy mountain or on the boundaries of a farm, where their shades could watch over their successors. In the new churchyards, families were broken up: Women were buried to the north of the church, men to the south. By stressing the individual, not the family, notes Graslund, Christianity offered "the possibility of salvation for everybody. If you were a good person, you could affect your own fate and afterlife."

For women like Gudrid, this question of the afterlife—the Otherworld—might have been the biggest attraction of the new religion. Valhalla, the glorious feast hall of Odin, was open only to men killed in battle. Several other gods had halls that welcomed certain dead, but most women (and men who died of old age or illness) could look forward only to a cold, damp, dark, dreary, and depressing eternity ruled by Hel, the half-giant daughter of Loki. Hel's brothers are the Midgard Serpent and the wolf that will swallow the sun. Her hall, unappealingly named "Damp-with-Sleet," has "extraordinarily high walls and huge gates." Her plate is named "Hunger," her knife, "Famine." What woman would not choose Heaven—described in the *Old Norse Homily Book* as "delight and joy and all sorts of beauty . . . glory, and happiness without end"—over this?

In medieval Christianity, the Last Judgment—Doomsday— was just as cataclysmic as Ragnarok. In one Old Norse sermon, *The burning fire shall flow forth from Heaven and out of that fire the wide world shall burn. Hills and stones will then run as hot wax. . . . The stars will fall from the sky.* But in the Christian world, the men and women of Middle Earth were not doomed to die with their gods. Christ would walk through the destruction, leading His followers to eternal bliss, regardless of sex or status.

In the graveyard at Birka, the Viking market center in Sweden, Graslund notes, nine cross pendants and one pendant reliquary were found. All were in women's graves, and the fact that several are "very simple, plain, and carelessly made" indicates that they were prized as symbols rather than as jewelry. Elsewhere in Sweden, Graslund found prayers to the Virgin Mary—always referred to as "God's Mother"—on runestones memorializing a woman or raised by a woman in memory of her dead. The Church encouraged bridge building and road maintenance so that priests could keep in touch more easily with their bishops and archbishops and, ultimately, Rome. For these good and pious deeds, sins would be forgiven, paving the way to Heaven. A Viking Age "bridge" was not the arching span we're used to, but merely two stones marking a passable ford on a river. In both Uppland and Sodermanland, Sweden, runic inscriptions show that more than half of the bridge stones were erected by, or for, a woman. Based on this and other evidence, Graslund believes women were "prime actors" in the Change of Ways.

Among these prime actors in northern Iceland might have been Gudrid the Far-Traveler, just returned from Rome and living as a nun, tending the church her son built her.

John Steinberg speculates that we may have seen signs of Snorri's church without recognizing them when we excavated the house at Glaumbaer. Poring over the maps and drawings a year later, John noticed a similarity between the "strange alley" we had found in the southwest corner of the house, where the walls seem doubled with no space in between for a room, and something on the plans at Hofstadir. There, as Orri Vesteinsson and his colleagues at the Icelandic Institute of Archaeology indicate in their excavation reports, a plank-walled room was built, around which a protecting turf wall was later added—a construction method thought to have been used in the earliest Icelandic chapels. In the case of Glaumbaer, the two structures—house and chapel—seem to have been so close that the late-coming turf wall was snug against the house.

The chapel would have been quite small. The interior of Thjodhild's church at Brattahlid in Greenland is only 6½ feet wide and less than 12 feet long. In the center of the churchyard Gudny Zoega investigated at Keldudalur was a small, rectangular space free of graves. A few postholes were all that remained of the wooden church building, but if it were protected by outer turf walls, it could not have been larger than Thjodhild's church. Twenty or thirty people, "closely packed together," says one archaeologist, could worship inside these tiny candlelit rooms. Gudrid's chapel, built for a solitary nun, might have been even tinier, just a private space to light a candle before a simple cross and close a door on everyday cares.

Gudrid is one of only six Icelandic women called nuns before the first Icelandic nunnery was founded in 1186, and what the sagas mean by "nun" is a mystery. The Icelandic word translated as "nun," *einsetukona*—"woman living alone"—implies that she enjoyed the independence she undoubtedly had grown used to between Karlsefni's death and Snorri's coming of age. She may even have retained control of some of her wealth, instead of becoming her son's dependent. In later years, at least, when a church or chapel was built, all or part of the farm and its income were dedicated to it, with the proviso that the owner could continue to live on and manage the property. On a more personal level, Gudrid as a nun could not be expected to remarry and bear more sons, as Gudrun the Fair had done at age forty. Nor was she brushed aside as a *hornkerling,* the superfluous old hag sent to sit in the corner and be ignored—the fate Hallgerd Long-Legs had feared at age forty-five.

Being a solitary nun may have supplied Gudrid with a respectable—if unusual—position in society, one well in keeping with her history as a remarkable woman. It was not quite unprecedented. According to the sagas, Gudrun the Fair was the first woman in Iceland to learn the Psalter and call herself a nun; Gudrid the Far-Traveler followed her in less than five years. In *Laxdaela Saga* we have a brief glimpse of how Gudrun the Fair enacted the role of holy woman. She spent hours in her church at night by candlelight, on her knees, reciting her prayers so strenuously that a witch buried beneath the floorboards had cause to complain to Gudrun's granddaughter in a dream: "She twists and turns all night on top of me, and burns me all over with hot drops. I'm telling you because I like you a little better—even though there's something strange about you, too." When the church floor was dug up, Gudrun's people found some blackened bones, a brooch, and a staff. They reburied them far away, and peace returned to the church.

Gudrid the Far-Traveler may have learned to recite the Psalter—the 150 psalms, the Credo ("I believe in one God, the Father Almighty, maker of Heaven and Earth . . ."), the Paternoster ("Our Father . . ."), and perhaps other prayers and hymns. This was the first step in religious education and, as the sagas say, Gudrid was a good singer with a memory for poetry. But unlike Gudrun the Fair—who shamed her husband into killing his own cousin and foster-brother, the man she loved most—Gudrid had no great sins to atone for by grinding her knees into the church floor every night. According to historian Helgi Thorlaksson, "Gudrid was always Christian, behaved with great circumspection, and lived a thoroughly respectable and dignified life in a hazardous world." But what does this mean, to be "always Christian"? *The Saga of Eirik the Red* says she was raised a Christian, yet before the Change of Ways there were no churches in Iceland, and no priests to hear confession or perform mass.

No one knows what form of Christianity Gudrid might have practiced—or, for that matter, what form Unn the Deep-Minded brought with her from the Hebrides in the late 800s. It was "a strange and battered Christianity," says one historian;

other scholars tend to name it Celtic Christianity. Early churches in Ireland and Scotland were surrounded by circular church-yards like those found at Thjodhild's church and at Keldudalur. Norwegian churches of the time had rectangular churchyards. But what the difference in shape signifies, no one knows. We don't know how Gudrid prayed, or if wax candles, bells, and incense were as central to the rite as the sagas would have us believe. What little we do know about the church of St. Patrick puts it in direct competition with Rome. Already for hundreds of years, Rome had been trying to suppress what it saw as an offshoot of Druidism. When the British monk Pelagius debated theology with Augustine in the fourth century, the sticking point was free will. The Celtic Christian believed Divine Grace did not require the physical trappings of a church, or uniform rites such as mass, confession, extreme unction, and absolution; an individual with free will could achieve grace through his or her own actions. Such a theology would have appealed to an independent-minded woman like Gudrid.

The saintly actions available to her, as a nun at Glaumbaer, would have included caring for travelers and helping the poor. Along with these fairly obvious good deeds, however, Gudrid could also have sought Heaven by sharing her experiences. Wisdom is one of the four pillars of the Church, according to the *Old Norse Homily Book,* and the early Church in Iceland shows a surprising reverence for the wisdom of old women.

Christianity is a religion of the book, and one of the first and greatest changes the new faith introduced was this new tech-nology; it was as essential to the making of a Christian society as the technology of shipbuilding was to the Viking voyages to Vinland. In addition to the Latin alphabet, the Church taught the Icelanders how to transform the skin of a light-colored calf into a smooth vellum writing surface, how to create a long-lasting ink out of boiled bearberry and willow twigs, how to cut a goose feather to make a quill pen, and how to fold and sew the pages into a binding of wood or sealskin to make the book durable and portable.

The alphabet was not a new concept to the Vikings, merely an expansion of the runes they had used for centuries to mark their names on tools or trade goods, to keep tallies, to cut bridge markers and memorial stones, and to work magic. Perhaps because of their experience with runes—difficult to cut, difficult to read, limited to bulky materials like wood, bone, and stone—the Vikings were not immediately impressed with the technology of literacy. The human memory can file prodigious amounts of information. In storytelling cultures, people compose and share stories and poems, establish laws, preserve histories and genealogies, and investigate the sciences of medicine, mathematics, navigation, geography, and astronomy, all without books.

When the technology of the book came to Iceland in the 1030s, with the first Church schools, it had little effect outside religion. Says folklorist Gisli Sigurdsson, "The art of speaking and telling did not change, nor the art of composing poetry, and learned men continued to hold their honored position in society—at least to start with. It took a long time for people to accept the precedence of the written word over the testimony of the wise."

Gudrid, whose voyages had taken her from one end of the Viking world to the other, would have been counted among the wise. She had one grandson and three granddaughters whose names we know, and I can imagine the stories she told them: of the rich young merchant with the fancy clothes whose suit her father turned down; of the harrowing voyage to Greenland; of the séance and the songs she sang to raise the spirits, Christian though she was; of her marriage to Thorstein Eiriksson, their frustrated voyage to Vinland, and his spooky death at Sandnes; of Thorfinn Karlsefni and their three years exploring the New World, where Snorri was born and Gudrid tried, but failed, to talk to a Skraeling woman.

In 1118 Gudrid's great-grandson Thorlak became the bishop of Skalholt and, with his colleague, the bishop of Holar, commissioned Ari the Learned to write a history of Iceland. *Íslendingabók,* or "The Book of the Icelanders," was the first book written in the Icelandic language—not Latin—a critical step that made the Icelandic sagas possible.

Reading Ari's brief and sketchy book (only twelve pages in a modern translation) is nothing like listening to the lively tales Gudrid could have told her granddaughter Hallfrid, Bishop Thorlak's mother, as she sat spinning yarn by the fire, watching the younger woman weave. Ari cites his sources, making it clear that he got his information in the time-honored way—from the lips of old men and women—but his style is altogether new. It shows its Church origins in many ways. It's sprinkled with Latin words. It begins with a table of contents, and its ten sections (not counting a prologue and appendix) have subject headings: one on the settlement, one on the laws, one on the wise man who figured out why "the summer was moving backward into spring" (the old calendar had 364 days in the year). Local events are fitted into an international chronology. Iceland was discovered the same year that St. Eadmund, the English king, was killed, we learn, and that "was 870 years after the birth of Christ." Serious and straightforward to a fault, Ari only very occasionally lets a little gossip sneak in, such as when he refers to the Norwegian king as "Olaf the Fat" rather than "Olaf the Saint," or when he explains that Greenland got its name because Eirik the Red thought "people would be more inclined to go there if it had a nice name."

Three of Ari's six named sources knew Gudrid and could have told him about her travels. But although *The Book of the Icelanders* contains the first mention of Vinland in Icelandic, the discovery and exploration of the New World did not fit into Ari's tight outline. Unlike the Greenland colony, to which Ari devotes three paragraphs, Vinland had no effect on Iceland's history. He drops just one casual remark: In Greenland, he says, Eirik the Red and his settlers found some stone tools and the remains of dwellings that made them think that "the same kind of people had traveled through here as lived in Vinland, the ones called Skraelings." Ari assumes his readers know all about Vinland and its Skraelings, and Bishop Thorlak, who corrected a longer draft of the book (now lost) and made suggestions on shortening it, presumably agreed.

It would be left to another descendant of Gudrid, another bishop, to begin collecting Gudrid's stories into a book more than a hundred years after her death. Brand Saemundarson was bishop of Holar from 1163 to 1201. By his time, many books had been written in Icelandic, including books of law, sagas, and genealogies. The first sagas were lives of saints or translations of Latin works meant to inspire virtue. According to Icelandic literary scholar Olafur Halldorsson, who has made the Vinland Sagas his specialty, Brand compiled a life of his predecessor, the Bishop Bjorn Gilsson—also a descendant of Gudrid—when Bjorn became a candidate for sainthood. In addition to compiling a list of Bjorn's miracles, Brand needed to show that Bjorn had suitable ancestors and "saintly" bones. These were dug up and washed to see if they were bright and sweet-smelling—just as the prophecy said Gudrid's progeny would be.

Alas, Bishop Bjorn was not declared a saint. No "Life of Bjorn" remains. But some of the stories Brand collected, Olafur believes, made their way into *The Saga of the Greenlanders*, written early in the thirteenth century. The only copy we have dates from 1387. It is tucked into the saga of King Olaf Tryggvason in the splendid manuscript called *Flateyjarbók* or "Book of Flatey," named for the Icelandic island on which it was treasured until 1647, when its owner gave it to the bishop of Skalholt. It is a very large manuscript made from 113 calfskins. *The Saga of the Greenlanders* takes up the skin of just one calf.

Later in the thirteenth century, it became fashionable in Europe to make saints of common people who had lived exemplary lives. A *Saga of Gudrid* might have been thought the perfect way to celebrate the founding of the nunnery at Reynines, Karlsefni's childhood home, by Abbess Hallbera—yet another descendant of Gudrid—in 1295. Olafur Halldorsson believes that the abbess's *Saga of Gudrid* has come down to us, in part or whole, as *The Saga of Eirik the Red*. It exists in two vellum manuscripts and the two versions differ slightly; both were copied from a now lost original. The earlier of the two, *Hauk's Book*, was the work of Hauk Erlendsson, an adviser to the king of Norway, who spent two years, 1306 to 1308, in a monastery on the Icelandic island of Videy. Videy had a fine library, and Hauk read widely. As scholars did in those days, he copied what he read there and elsewhere to add to his own collection. The massive manuscript he compiled over the course of his reading life reveals an eclectic taste. Hauk copied a history of the Trojan War and the saga of how Christianity came to Iceland. He chose a saga about an Icelandic poet who died for love, and another about two blood-brothers who fell out over a woman. He includes the practical travel guide for pilgrims to Rome, written by the monk Nikulas, and the prophecies of Merlin, King Arthur's mage. Isidore de Seville's seventh-century encyclopedia of natural history, *Etymologiae* (which describes the Unipeds, a one-footed African tribe), is balanced by the *Algorismus,* the first mathematical text to use Arabic numerals.

Hauk's book holds one of five known copies of *The Book of Settlements.* The version Hauk copied had been compiled largely by his grandfather and, according to his critics, Hauk therefore felt free to embellish it with additional tales he had heard or read. Hauk also embellished *The Saga of Eirik the Red.* As well as smoothing out the style, he added two short passages. He did not add the strange account of Karlsefni seeing one of Isidore de Seville's Unipeds in the wilds of Vinland. Nor did he add the antiquarian description of the Greenland séance. These stories were already in the text he copied. Hauk's additions are plain and apparently factual. One traces Karlsefni's genealogy back to King Kjarval of Ireland, on his mother's side, and to the legendary Viking chieftain Ragnar Hairy-Breeks on his father's, making Snorri, born in America, royal. The second new passage traces Snorri's descendants through nine generations to Hauk Erlendsson himself.

For six hundred years, knowledge of the Vikings' voyages to Vinland was preserved in these stories about Gudrid the Far-Traveler, passed down in one form or another by her descendants. Then it was almost lost. The bishop of Skalholt gave *The Book of Flatey* to the king of Denmark in 1656. *Hauk's Book* and many other ancient manuscripts were considered worthless after printed books became available; they were torn to pieces and the stiff vellum was reused to make shoe soles, dress patterns, and bindings for newer books—one was even used to stiffen a bishop's miter. Rescue came in the person of Arni Magnusson, a young man from the Dales in Iceland, where Unn the Deep-Minded had settled, who became a professor of history at the University of Copenhagen. In the early 1700s, while in Iceland calculating the tax value of the farms at the behest of Iceland's

Danish overlords, he picked up every scrap of manuscript he could find. These he reassembled, based on handwriting and other clues, into books: One sixty-page manuscript came from eight different farms. Of *Hauk's Book*, Arni was able to find 282 pages out of an estimated 400-plus. *The Saga of Eirik the Red* was one story that survived.

Then came the Great Copenhagen Fire of 1728. Almost half the town burned, including the university. Arni and two other Icelanders saved the oldest manuscripts, including *Hauk's Book*. The rest of Arni's library was destroyed, as were all the saga manuscripts in the university's main library. The fire died out before it reached the palace, and *The Book of Flatey*, in the king's private library, was unharmed.

Legend has it that Columbus heard stories of Vinland before he sailed west in 1492, but the first serious attempts to locate the Viking colony began in the nineteenth century. The sagas containing the stories of Gudrid the Far-Traveler were then at the height of their popularity—they were translated into English more often than any other saga—due to the influence of such writers as Sir Walter Scott and the general romantic sense that "the old north was misty, mysterious, and sublime." (Scott particularly liked the séance in Greenland, using it in his book *The Pirate* in 1821.) These new Vinland explorers, all men, did not think they were retracing the travels of Gudrid. They identified instead with Leif Eiriksson, son of the doughty Eirik the Red. But their search led directly to the discovery of the Viking settlement at L'Anse aux Meadows and to those three butternuts that sent Birgitta Wallace south to the Miramichi River and the probable heart of the Land of Wine. Because of the two Vinland Sagas, archaeologists have also looked for—and found—Thjodhild's church at Brattahlid; the two houses of Eirik the Red, in Iceland and Greenland; the farm of Sandnes, where Gudrid's husband Thorstein died; and Gudrid's own house at Glaumbaer.

Digging that summer at Glaumbaer, I didn't find anything Gudrid had dropped. But as I explored the archaeology of Gudrid's days, the economy of the farms where she lived, the technology of her time—how to make cheese, how to weave, how to sail a ship and build a wall—I learned new ways to tell Gudrid's story, to pick up where the sagas leave off. Yet the last line of *The Saga of the Greenlanders* lingers in my mind. It sounds like Gudrid's own voice, carrying across a thousand years: *But Karlsefni told the tale of these voyages better than anyone else.*

ACKNOWLEDGMENTS

Among the many people I interviewed for this book, I am most indebted to John Steinberg, formerly of the Cotsen Institute of Archaeology at the University of California, Los Angeles, and now of the Fiske Center for Archaeological Research at the University of Massachusetts, Boston. John not only admitted me onto his archaeological team for the summer 2005 field season at Glaumbær in Iceland, but arranged for me to meet many of the other scientists and scholars quoted in this book. I am grateful to Paul Durrenberger of Pennsylvania State University for introducing me to John, and to everyone on the SASS team for answering my questions and keeping me inspired: Hans Bernard, Doug Bolender, Tara Carter, Brian Damiata, Suzan Erem and her daughter Ayshe, Antonio Gilman, Dean Goodman, Linda Rehberger, Kent Schneider, John Schoenfelder, and Rita Shepard.

Sigríður ("Sirri") Sigurðardóttir, curator of the Skagafjörður Folk Museum, meanwhile, kept me grounded in Icelandic history and led me to a deeper understanding of the farm of Glaumbær. Grétar Guðbergsson and his wife Guðný, as well as the family at Syðra-Skörðugil, taught me how to read the landscape of Skagafjörður. I particularly thank Eyþór for catching the horse I lost in the mountains. In Reykjavík, my friends Guðbjörg Sigurðardóttir and Stefán Jónsson opened their house to me on many occasions, while Kristín Vogfjörð was always there when I needed help.

For making my exploration of Greenland possible, I am grateful to Kristjána Guðmundsdóttir and Jonathan Motzfeldt, my hosts in Nuuk; although their boat was not ready when I arrived, their extraordinary library made the wait profitable. Thanks to Magnús Jóhannsson and Anna María Ágústsdóttir of the Icelandic Soil Conservation Service for introducing me to Kristjána, as well as for sharing their knowledge of overgrazing and desertification. In South Greenland, Jacky Simoud was an excellent tour guide (who didn't, in the end, "forget" me), while Ellen and Carl Frederiksen provided a beautiful place to stay on the edge of Brattahlíð and took time off from the lambing to explain how things were done.

I would never have made it to Greenland without the assistance of Matthew Driscoll and Ragnheiður Mósesdóttir of the Árni Magnússon Institute at the University of Copenhagen, and Kate Driscoll, my guide in Copenhagen.

Birgitta Wallace, now retired from Parks Canada, was extraordinarily gracious in agreeing to meet me at L'Anse aux Meadows in Newfoundland and in showing me around the site that she had excavated since the 1970s. Parks Canada guide Clayton Colbourne happily told me tales of George Decker's Indian Mounds, which Decker's granddaughter Loretta, the park superintendent put into context.

For my understanding of Viking ships, I am indebted to Ole Crumlin-Pedersen of the Viking Ship Museum in Roskilde, Denmark, and to Arne Emil Christensen of the Viking Ship Museum in Bygdøy, Norway (whom I interviewed in 1984); to Anton Englar, skipper of Kraka Fyr, who let me row around Roskilde harbor; to Gunnar Marel Eggertsson, Ottar S. Bjørkedal, Eggert Sigþór Sigurðsson, Ríkarður Már Pétursson, and Odd Kvamme, whom I met on board Gaia in 1991; and especially to Úlfur Sigurmundsson, Trade Commissioner of Iceland, who let me take his place for a short cruise in Newport harbor.

I thank Else Østergård for alerting me to the existence of the Center for Textile Research, begun at the University of Copenhagen in 2005. Her book, *Woven into the Earth* (2004), is an extraordinary source of information on Viking textile production.

Meetings with Carol Clover in 1991, when she was interviewed for a radio series I produced at Pennsylvania State University, and with Jenny Jochens in 1994, when we both took a course in Icelandic sponsored by the Sigurður Nordal Institute in Reykjavík, shaped my understanding of the status of women in the sagas.

Other scientists and scholars who contributed their time and expertise to this book are:

In Iceland:
Agnar Helgason of DeCode Genetics, Reykjavík
Elsa Guðjónsson of the National Museum of Iceland (with whom I spoke in 1988)
Gísli Pálsson of the University of Iceland
Gísli Sigurðsson of the Árni Magnússon Institute in Reykjavík
Guðmundur Ólafsson of the National Museum of Iceland
Guðný Zoëga of the Skagafjörður Folk Museum
Mjöll Snæsdóttir of the Icelandic Institute of Archaeology (FSÍ)
Orri Vésteinsson of the Icelandic Institute of Archaeology (FSÍ)
Ragnheiður Traustadóttir of the National Museum of Iceland
Sólborg Pálsdóttir of the Archaeological Heritage Agency of Iceland

In Greenland and Denmark:

Eva Andersson of the Center for Textile Research, University of Copenhagen

Jette Arneborg of the National Museum of Denmark

Linda Mårtensson of the Center for Textile Research, University of Copenhagen

Georg Nyegaard of the National Museum of Greenland

Finally, my thanks to my student, Daniel Saninski, who found Gudrid boring; to my teacher, Carey Eckhardt, who thought the Vinland Sagas were worth reading anyway; to my publisher, Rebecca Saletan, who organized my ideas about Gudrid and Glaumbaer; and to my editor, Stacia Decker, who found the hidden story.

NOTES

page 1—Viking longhouse: To say that the house at Glaumbaer is both a Viking longhouse and Gudrid's house, as I do, will strike some scholars as an oxymoron. They define "Viking" as "not Christian," and Gudrid was. I use "Viking" to mean anyone living in Scandinavia during the Viking Age from 793 to 1066. In this I follow Gwyn Jones, who writes in his *History of the Vikings* (1968): "Harald Hardradi, who waged war from Asia Minor to Stamford Bridge for thirty-five years, was a viking; so was his father Sigurd Sow, who stayed at home and counted haystacks. Hastein, who led the Great Army of the Danes into England in the early 890s, was a viking; so was Ottar, who came peaceably to his lord king Alfred's court with walrus tusks and lessons in northern geography. The men who destroyed churches in England, Ireland, and France were vikings; so were the woodcarvers of Oseberg and the metalworkers of Mammen. The men who said 'With law shall the land be built up and with lawlessness wasted away' were vikings; so were the practisers and curtailers of blood-feud, the profit-makers and those who robbed them of profit, the explorers and colonizers, the shapers of verse-forms and makers of legends. The kings and their counselors who brought the Scandinavian countries within the bounds of Christian Europe were vikings."

The definition of "longhouse" is also disputed. To Icelanders, "longhouse" is the translation for *skáli*, and can only be used to describe the earliest style of one-room Viking turf house. John Steinberg and I use "longhouse" more loosely, to include the later style of houses, such as those at Stong and L'Anse aux Meadows, in which additional rooms may branch off from the main *skáli*.

page 2—"Farm of Merry Noise": "Glaum" is a hard word to translate. It seems to describe classic Viking merrymaking—loud, drunken partying—with an emphasis on the noise, rather than the merriment. Yet it also can be translated as "joy" or "joyful noise," without the Christian overtones of that phrase. A third, archaic meaning is "horse," according to the Icelandic dictionary edited by Arni Bodvarsson (1983).

page 75—delights in reading the sagas: To untangle these connections, I collated six sagas: *Njal's Saga, Laxdaela Saga, Eyrbyggja Saga, The Saga of the Greenlanders, The Saga of Eirik the Red,* and *Grettir's Saga.* Genealogies show that many of the main characters in these six sagas were related. They also overlap in time and space. Several editors have established chronologies for individual sagas; these depend on the reigns of the kings of Norway and England, who are characters in many tales, as well as on estimates of the age at which a woman could bear children. For example, the sagas say Greenland became Christian at the instigation of Olaf Tryggvason, king of Norway from 995–1000, and that it was converted after Iceland, which became Christian in 999 or 1000. Gudrid's arrival in Greenland is intertwined with the story of the conversion. Since she was of marriageable age then, I arbitrarily chose 985 as her birthdate.

page 119—Hellisvellir, or "Fields by the Cave": Although Gudrid's father is known as Thorbjorn of Laugarbrekka, according to *The Saga of Eirik the Red,* he did not gain control of the estate when he married Hallveig, daughter of Einar of Laugarbrekka; he merely "acquired land at Hellisvellir in Laugarbrekka." His brother Thorgeir, who married Hallveig's sister Arnora, seems to have owned the rest of the estate, for it passes down to his daughter Yngvild, Gudrid's cousin. According to *The Book of Settlements,* Yngvild married Thorstein, a son of the chieftain Snorri of Helgafell. In *Eyrbyggja Saga,* Thorstein is said to live at Laugarbrekka.

page 119—the classic case of the independent farmer: The story of Eirik's outlawing, as told in *The Saga of Eirik the Red* and in *The Saga of the Greenlanders,* both derive from the version in *The Book of Settlements.* A different version appears in *Eyrbyggja Saga.* Eirik's relatives, and those of his enemy, also appear in *Gull-Thorir's Saga, The Saga of Gunnlaug Serpent-Tongue, Heidarviga Saga, The Saga of Bard Snaefells-ass, Laxdaela Saga, Njal's Saga,* and *Gisli's Saga.* It is not immediately obvious from the saga accounts why Eirik was outnumbered. To tease out a reason, I drew a large chart, tracing out the marriage and kin-ship alliances on both sides. It turned into a tangle of asterisks and increasingly finer print; even with three colors of ink, it was hard to see who was related to whom. Yet Eirik's line seemed the stronger. His wife, Thjodhild, is very well bred, with several important saga names in her genealogy.

Next I tried chronology. Thjodhild's mother, Thorbjorg Ship-Breast, must have been the youngest of her siblings, for her brother-in-law, Gold-Thorir, was making waves in western Iceland before the year 930. The big names in 982 are Snorri of Helgafell, Illugi the Black, Thord Gellir of Hvamm, and Olaf the Peacock.

The chieftain Snorri of Helgafell was then nineteen, just coming into his power. Eirik has a very slight connection to Snorri: Through his wife he is distantly related to Thorbrand of Swan Fjord, whose four sons are Snorri's foster-brothers. (How distantly? Her cousin's son married the sister-in-law of Thorbrand's wife.) Thorbrand's sons are Eirik's staunch supporters. Snorri will soon marry the daughter of Killer-Styr—another of Eirik the Red's friends—but the saga treats it as a great triumph of Killer-Styr's political skill simply to win Snorri's promise not to meddle in Eirik's case. Killer-Styr has no good reason to support Eirik the Red, and no one else in his large and aggressive family joins him.

Illugi the Black at this time was newly married and throwing his weight around. He had just trounced Killer-Styr and his kinsmen in a dowry dispute; young Snorri had brought the two sides to a truce, rather to Illugi's advantage, and Illugi had pledged Snorri his friend-ship. Illugi the Black did not take sides in Eirik's quarrel, though if pressed he would have recalled his kinship, through his mother-in-law, to Thord Gellir. His father-in-law was that Asbjorn the Wealthy against whom Gudrid's father, Thorbjorn Vifilsson, held a grudge.

Thord Gellir's power was waning (he may have already died; he fades out of the stories in the 970s), and his three sons were not living up to expectations. One, Eyjolf the Gray, had spent the last sixteen years hunting down Gisli the Outlaw—the chieftain Snorri's uncle, but also the killer of Snorri's father—and had just been repudiated by Snorri for setting on the man fifteen to one.

The bastard Olaf the Peacock, rather than any of Thord Gellir's sons, was now the leader of the Dales. He was the only chieftain on whom Eirik had any claim—through his wife's mother's second husband's son or through Killer-Styr's son's father-in-law, who was Olaf's half-brother—but since neither he nor any other chieftain took Eirik's side, the Hvamm clan's diminished power was enough to win the case and to outlaw Eirik from Iceland for three years.

page 135—two households—around thirty people altogether: The average size of a Viking household circa 1000 is hotly disputed by scholars. Thirty is the number of "friends" *The Saga of Eirik the Red* says went to Greenland with Gudrid's father. Orm of Arnarstapi and his wife are the only ones named. In my reading of the sagas, as well as my discussions with archaeologists Birgitta Wallace, John Steinberg, and Mjoll Snaesdottir, I find thirty to be one large household or two smaller ones. In *Eyrbyggja Saga,* for example, we learn of a sickness that killed "more women than men." In the translation by Hermann Palsson and Paul Edwards (1973), we read: "Six people died one after another, and the hauntings and night-walkings drove others away from the farm. There had been thirty servants there in the autumn, but eighteen of them died, five more ran away, and by mid-winter there were only seven of them left." The word translated as "servants," however, is *hjóna,* which means "the domestics, family, household," according to the Cleasby-Vigfusson dictionary. The dictionary notes that modern Icelandic distinguishes between *hjón* meaning "man and wife" and *hjú* meaning "servants," but Old Norse doesn't. So the thirty would have included the unmarried farmer and his mother, who kept house for him. Archaeologists trying to estimate the size of a Viking household from the sleeping area of their longhouses have come up with an estimate of twenty-five to thirty people for a large farm. Gunnar Karlsson in his *History of Iceland* (2000), however, notes that the population estimate of 40,000 for twelfth-century Iceland, which is widely quoted by archaeologists and which is based on a census recorded by Ari the Learned in *The Book of the Icelanders,* takes "the large households that are sometimes described in sagas to be either fictional or restricted to a small top layer of society"; it assumes, instead, that "the average household may not have numbered more than eight people: a couple, three children, one elder, and two farm-hands."

page 195—No further expeditions were sent: The Saga of the Greenlanders tells of an expedition led by Leif Eiriksson's bastard half-sister Freydis, whose two ships arrive in Vinland after Gudrid and Karlsefni (with only one ship in this version) have left. An argument arises, and Freydis has one entire ship's crew put to death—she herself beheads the five women. I consider this episode fiction—the saga author's attempt to fill in a gap and explain how a whole shipload of Vinland explorers from Greenland was lost. In this I follow Richard Perkins, who writes, "It seems to me unlikely that Freydis ever existed, let alone ever led an expedition to Vinland. . . . I would suggest that Freydis is an entirely fictional figure, invented to act as a foil to the pious Gudrid." He defends his argument by noting, among other things, that "Freydis's descendants are obscure or nonexistent." Even more telling is the lack of any revenge taken upon Freydis or her men, once they return to Greenland, for the killing of their countrymen.

page 196—half a mark of gold: According to Bruce Gelsinger's *Icelandic Enterprise* (1981), half a mark of gold was equal to at least 1,500 yards of homespun cloth. Yet in *Egil's Saga,* King Aethelstan of England gave Egil two gold arm-rings, each weighing half a mark, and a good cloak in reward for a poem. Olaf the Saint, who reigned from 1014 to 1030, fixed the landing tax at half a mark, or four ounces, of silver; before that, according to Ari the Learned in *The Book of the Icelanders,* it fluctuated between four and five ounces. In the 1200s, a mark of gold was worth eight times as much as a mark of silver.

page 197—the cousin, Arnor Old-Woman's-Nose: Karlsefni had many relatives in Skagafjord who could have provided him with horses. I chose Arnor not only because of his wonderful nickname, but because he lived closest to the harbor at Kolkuos. It is hard to tell if

he was still active in 1010. In one saga, he is called the most important leader in the north in 981; another finds him still feuding in
1030. He does appear to have a close connection to Gudrid's family,
however. His son Asbjorn marries Ingunn, the daughter of Gudrid's
cousin Yngvild of Laugarbrekka. The descendants of Asbjorn and
Ingunn—known as the Asbirnings—are the most powerful family in
Skagafjord in the years 1180 to 1245. During this same time, Gudrid's great-great-grandson Brand Saemundarson was bishop of Holar
(1163 to 1201) and was possibly compiling Gudrid's saga.

page 236—the Vikings' ell: A modern dictionary will give a length of 45
inches for an ell, but the word has been used for various lengths over
the centuries. The original ell, or as the Cleasby-Vigfusson *Icelandic-
English Dictionary* calls it the "primitive ell," was the distance from
the elbow to the tip of the middle finger. This ell, of about 18 inches
or half a yard, was used in Iceland until the 1200s. The Cleasby-
Vigfusson entry for *alin* reads: "About this year, by a law of bishop
Paul, the ell was doubled into a *stika,* a stika being precisely = 2 ells =
an English ell of that time. To prevent the use of bad measure, a just
and lawful stika (yard) was marked on the walls of the churches."

page 240—Gudrid came to Rome: The sagas do not say when Gudrid
took her pilgrimage, only that it was shortly after Snorri married. My
estimate that she left Iceland after 1025 and returned before 1030
is based on Snorri's expected age at marriage and on the political
situation in Europe, particularly in Norway and Rome. Snorri was
born in approximately 1005. Olaf the Saint, who ruled Norway from
1014 to 1030, encouraged pilgrimages; in the period 1025 to 1027 he
was courting the Icelanders and would likely have helped Gudrid sail
from his kingdom to Denmark. Although King Knut of Denmark
and England was trying to overthrow Olaf, not until 1028 did it
become open war. Knut also encouraged pilgrimages, going so far
as to negotiate reduced tolls in central Europe for pilgrims from his
kingdoms. The next interlude of peace in Norway was not until the
reign of Magnus the Good (1035 to 1047), when Gudrid would be
fifty and Snorri thirty. In addition, I would hope that Gudrid saw

Rome during Pope John XIX's reign, from 1024 to 1032. The pope who ruled after him, from 1032 to 1045, was the infamous Benedict IX, considered "a disgrace to the Chair of Peter," who sold the papacy so that he could marry. Between 1045 and 1049, seven popes (one is called an antipope) fought for the chair, as political factions within Europe struggled for control of the Church. If she had seen Rome while it was a battleground, I do not think the experience would have strengthened Gudrid's faith or inspired her to become a nun. Finally, it is logical to assume that huge numbers of well-armed travelers would be taking the various Pilgrim Ways to Rome for the coronation of the Holy Roman Emperor in 1027, making that time the safest for a woman from Iceland to travel.

SOURCES

RECOMMENDED READING

Two scholarly conferences—one in Iceland and one in Newfoundland—and an exhibition at the Smithsonian Institution in Washington, D.C., celebrated the thousand-year anniversary of the discovery of Vinland. The exhibition catalog, which is beautifully illustrated, is the best place to start to learn more about Gudrid and her times; the conference proceedings assume some prior knowledge of the subject matter.

Vikings: The North Atlantic Saga, edited by William Fitzhugh and Elisabeth I. Ward (Washington and London: Smithsonian Institution Press, 2000). See also http://www.mnh.si.edu/vikings/, where you can learn to play *hneftafl.*

Approaches to Vinland: a conference on the written and archaeological sources for the Norse settlements in the North-Atlantic region and exploration of America, edited by Andrew Wawn and Thórunn Sigurðardóttir (Reykjavík: Sigurðar Nordal Institute, 2001).

Vinland Revisited: The Norse World at the Turn of the First Millennium. Selected Papers from the Viking Millennium International Symposium, 15–24 September 2000, Newfoundland and Labrador, edited by Shannon Lewis-Simpson (St. John's, Newfoundland: Historic Sites Association of Newfoundland and Labrador, 2003).

To learn more about the sagas, I recommend Gísli Sigurðsson's *The Medieval Icelandic Saga and Oral Tradition* (Cambridge: Harvard University Press, 2004). Gísli notes that Gudrid acquired the nickname *viðförla*—variously translated as "the Far-Traveler," "the Wide-Traveled," or "the Far-Farer"—long after the Middle Ages. He has not been able to trace the first appearance of her nickname.

MEDIEVAL TEXTS

The Saga of the Greenlanders (Grænlendingasaga) and *The Saga of Eirik the Red (Eiríkssaga rauða)* have been translated many times. The most recent are by Keneva Kunz in *Sagas of Icelanders: a selection* (2000) and Magnus Magnusson and Hermann Pálsson in *The Vinland Sagas* (1965). Excerpts in this book, along with all of the epigraphs and most selections from other medieval texts (except as listed below), are my own translations.

page 21: Wood-Leg's lament from *Grettir's Saga*, trans. Ole Crumlin-Pedersen in "The Sporting Element in Viking Ships and Other Early Boats," *Sailing and Science*, ed. Gisela Sjøgaard (1999)

page 24: sailing directions from *Hauksbók*, trans. Judith Jesch in *A Companion to Old Norse-Icelandic Literature and Culture*, ed. Rory McTurk (2005)

page 28: the wave rune poem from *The Saga of the Volsungs*, trans. Jesse Byock (1990)

pages 58–59: the story of Grettir's Bath from *Grettir's Saga*, trans. Denton Fox and Hermann Pálsson (1974)

pages 83, 86–87, and 197: excerpts from Adam of Bremen's *History of the Archbishops of Hamburg-Bremen*, trans. Francis J. Tschan (1959)

page 83: the destruction of Lindisfarne from *The Anglo-Saxon Chronicle*, trans. Gwyn Jones, *History of the Vikings* (1968)

page 84: the attack on Constantinople from *The Works of Luidprand of Cremona*, trans. F. A. Wright (1930)

page 85: Simeon of Durham's account of the attack at Tynemouth, trans. David M. Wilson, ed., *From Viking to Crusader* (1992)

page 87: Dudo of Normandy (excerpts), trans. Else Roesdahl in *The Vikings* (1991)

page 88: the story of Unn the Deep-Minded from *Landnámabók (The Book of Settlements)*, trans. Hermann Pálsson and Paul Edwards (1972)

pages 121–22: the *hafgerðing* from *The King's Mirror (Konungs Skuggsjá)*, trans. Laurence Marcellus Larson (1917)

page 136: Greenland traveler's verse, "I see death in a dread place," from *The Book of Settlements*, trans. Hermann Pálsson and Paul Edwards (1972) *pages 164–65, 167:* advice to a merchant from *The King's Mirror (Konungs Skuggsjá),* trans. Laurence Marcellus Larson (1917)

page 239: description of the monks from Richer's *Histoire de France,* trans. Richard Erdoes, *A.D. 1000: Living on the Brink of Apocalypse* (1988)

pages 248–49: description of the mass from "The Story of Thorvald the Far-Traveler," trans. Einar Ó. Sveinsson, *Age of the Sturlungs* (1953)

page 249: the blessing of the ale from Snorri Sturluson's *Heimskringla,* trans. Thomas DuBois in *Nordic Religions in the Viking Age* (1999)

pages 251–52: verses from "Words of the High One" *(Hávamál),* trans. W. H. Auden and Paul B. Taylor in *Norse Poems: Edda Sæmundur, selections* (1981)

page 254: Old Norse Homily Book (excerpts), trans. Anders Hultgård in *Old Norse and Finnish Religions and Cultic Place-Names,* ed. Tore Ahlbäck (1990)

The standard dictionary of Old Norse is *The Icelandic-English Dictionary,* Second Edition, by Richard Cleasby, Gudbrand Vigfusson, and Sir William Craigie (1957; rpt. 1969), known as Cleasby-Vigfusson. The translators of *skörungur* are: George Dasent (1861, 1866); W. C. Green (1893); Sir Edmund Head (1866); Eiríkr Magnússon & William Morris (1892–1901); F. York Powell (1896); Muriel Press (1899); W. G. Collingwood & J. Stefánsson (1901); Reeves, Beamish, & Anderson (1901); G. H. Hight (1914); Magnus Magnusson & Hermann Pálsson (1960s); Denton Fox & Hermann Pálsson (1970s); Jenny Jochens (1995); Keneva Kunz (1990s); Anthony Faulkes (2001); Bo Almquist (2001); and Eric V. Youngquist (2002).

ICELANDIC SAGAS AND HISTORY

Uno von Troil, who accompanied Sir Joseph Banks to Iceland in 1772, argued that the sagas were just as trustworthy as Tacitus or Livy. Von Troil wrote in Swedish; I used the Icelandic translation of his letters, *Bréf frá Íslandi,* by Haraldur Sigurðsson (1961). As mentioned above, the best introduction to the sagas is Gísli Sigurðsson's *The Medieval Icelandic Saga and Oral Tradition* (2004).

The recognized expert on the Vinland Sagas is Ólafur Halldórsson. See his "Lost Tales of Gudrídr" in *Sagnaskemmtun: Studies in honour of Hermann Pálsson,* ed. Rudolf Simek, Jónas Kristjánsson, and Hans Bekker-Nielsen (1986); his entry in *Approaches to Vinland;* and, for readers of Icelandic, *Grænland í miðaldaritum* (1978).

Good discussions of women in saga times can be found in:

Carol Clover, "Regardless of Sex," *Speculum* 68 (1993)

Judith Jesch, *Women in the Viking Age* (1991)

Jenny Jochens, *Women in Old Norse Society* (1995)

Preben Meulengracht Sorensen, *The Unmanly Man* (1983)

Other sources in English include:

Rasmus B. Anderson, ed. *The Flatey Book and Recently Discovered Vatican Manuscripts Concerning America as Early as the Tenth Century* (1908)

Lois Bragg, *Oedipus Borealis: The Aberrant Body in Old Icelandic Myth and Saga* (2004)

Thomas Bredsdorff, *Chaos and Love: The Philosophy of the Icelandic Family Saga* (2001)

Jesse L. Byock, *Medieval Iceland* (1988)

———, *Viking Age Iceland* (2001)

W. A. Craigie, *The Icelandic Sagas* (1913)

Paul Durrenberger, *The Dynamics of Medieval Iceland* (1992)

Stefán Einarsson, *A History of Icelandic Literature* (1957)

Bruce Gelsinger, *Icelandic Enterprise* (1981)

Guðrún Ása Grímsdóttir, *The Arnamagnaean Institute Manuscript Exhibition* (1992)

Gunnar Karlsson, *The History of Iceland* (2000)

Magnus Magnusson, *Iceland Saga* (1987)

Rory McTurk, ed. *A Companion to Old Norse-Icelandic Literature and Culture* (2005)

William Ian Miller, *Bloodtaking and Peacemaking* (1990)

Vésteinn Ólason, *Dialogues with the Viking Age* (1998)

Páll Ólafsson, *Iceland the Enchanted* (1995)

William Pencak, *The Conflict of Law and Justice in the Icelandic Sagas* (1995)

Margaret Clunies Ross, ed. *Old Icelandic Literature and Society* (2000)

Jón Viðar Sigurðsson, *Chieftains and Power in the Icelandic Common-wealth* (1999)

M. I. Steblin-Kamenskij, *The Saga Mind* (1973)

Einar Ó. Sveinsson, *Age of the Sturlungs* (1953)

SHIPS AND SAILING

Arne Emil Christensen and Ole Crumlin-Pedersen have long been the recognized experts on Viking-ship technology. In addition to their articles in the collections recommended above, see Christensen's "Viking Age Boatbuilding Tools" and "Viking Age Rigging, A Survey of Sources and Theories" in *The Archaeology of Medieval Ships and Harbours in Northern Europe* (1979); and "Boats and Boatbuilding in Western Norway and the Islands" in *The Northern and Western Isles in the Viking World*, ed. Alexander Fenton and Hermann Pálsson (1984). Ole Crumlin-Pedersen and Olaf Olsen describe the retrieval of the Skuldelev ships in *Acta Archaeologica* 38 (1967). See also "Viking Shipbuilding and Seamanship" in the *Proceedings of the Eighth Viking Congress* (1981) and "The Sporting Element in Viking Ships and Other Early Boats," *Sailing and Science*, ed. Gisela Sjøgaard (1999).

The voyage of the replica Gaia is chronicled by Judy Lomas, *The Viking Voyage* (1992); that of Snorri by Hodding Carter, *A Viking Voyage* (2000).

Other sources on Viking ships, navigation, timekeeping, and sailing in the North Atlantic include:

J. R. L. Anderson, *Vinland Voyage* (1967)

Páll Bergþórsson, *The Wineland Millennium* (2000)

A. W. Brøgger and H. Shetelig, *Viking Ships: Their Ancestry and Evolution* (1951)

Stephen Bruneau, *Icebergs of Newfoundland and Labrador* (2004)

Birthe Clausen, ed. *Viking Voyages to North America* (1993)

Frederica DeLaguna, *Voyage to Greenland* (1977)

John R. Hale, "The Viking Longship," *Scientific American* (February 1998)

Rockwell Kent, *N by E* (1930)

Sean McGrail, ed. *Sources and Techniques in Boat Archaeology* (1977)

Þorsteinn Vilhjálmsson, "Time and Travel in Old Norse Society," *Disputatio* II (1997)

VIKINGS IN THE BRITISH ISLES

The area around Uig, Lewis, is claimed by the MacAulays, or in Gaelic, Clann Amhlaeibh; Amhlaeibh is the Norse name Olaf. Alfred P. Smythe argues that Unn the Deep-Minded's husband, Olaf the White, king of Dublin (853 to 870), was the Olaf Geirstaðaálfr who ruled the Norwegian province of Westfold (871 to ca. 890), making him a good candidate to be the man buried in the Gokstad ship circa 900. See *Scandinavian Kings in the British Isles 850–880* (1977).

Gillian Fellows-Jensen explains the derivation of place-names in "Vikings in the British Isles," *Acta Archaeologica* 71 (2000): the *-by* ending is the Norse *býr* or *bær* (farm or settlement, as in Glaumbær), *-bister* and *-poll* are shortenings of *bólstaðir* (homestead), *-skill* and *-skaill* come from *skáli* (longhouse), Laimiseadar comes from *lambasætr* (lamb shieling), Lacsabhat is from *laxavatn* (salmon lake), *kirk* is Norse for church.

Other important sources for the Vikings in the British Isles are:

James Graham-Campbell and Colleen Batey, *Vikings in Scotland: An Archaeological Survey* (1998; rpt. 2001)

Anna Ritchie, *Viking Scotland* (1993)

For DNA evidence, see:

S. Goodacre, A. Helgason, et al., "Genetic evidence for a family-based Scandinavian settlement of Shetland and Orkney during the Viking periods," *Heredity* (2005)

Agnar Helgason, et al., "mtDNA and the Origin of the Icelanders: Deciphering Signals of Recent Population History," *American Journal of Human Genetics* 66 (2000)

Agnar Helgason, et al., "Estimating Scandinavian and Gaelic Ancestry in the Male Settlers of Iceland," *American Journal of Human Genetics* 67 (2000)

THE VIKINGS IN GENERAL

Although it's a little dated, I prefer Gwyn Jones's *History of the Vikings* (1968; rev. 1984); he's a good storyteller. Other sources I consulted include:

Bertil Almgren, *The Viking* (1966)

Holger Arbman, *The Vikings* (1961; rpt. 1965)

Eric Christiansen, *The Norsemen in the Viking Age* (2002)

Paul du Chaillu, *The Viking Age* (1890)

Peter Foote and David M. Wilson, *The Viking Achievement* (1970)

James Graham-Campbell, ed. *Cultural Atlas of the Viking World* (1994)

James Graham-Campbell and Dafydd Kidd, *The Vikings* (1980)

James E. Knirk, ed. *Proceedings of the Tenth Viking Congress, Larkollen, Norway, 1985* (1987)

Magnus Magnusson, *Vikings!* (1980)

Andras Mortensen and Símun V. Arge, eds. *Viking and Norse in the North Atlantic: Select Papers from the Proceedings of the Fourteenth Viking Congress* (2005)

Rudolf Poertner, *The Viking* (1975)

Frederick J. Pohl, *The Viking Explorers* (1966)

Else Roesdahl, *The Vikings* (1991)

Else Roesdahl and David M. Wilson, eds. *From Viking to Crusader* (1992)

Ross Samson, ed. *Social Approaches to Viking Studies* (1991)

J. M. Wallace-Hadrill, *The Vikings in Francia* (1975)

The St. Brice's Day massacre is mentioned in *The Anglo-Saxon Chronicle*, as well as in the chronicles of William of Jumièges (d. 1090), William of Malmesbury (d. 1143), and Henry of Huntingdon (d. 1155). Michele Wates supplies the full text of the royal charter in "Massacre at St Frideswide's," *Oxford Today*, vol. 15, no. 1 (2002–03), available at www.oxfordtoday.ox.ac.uk.

Sources specific to the Oseberg ship burial are:

Niels Bonde and Arne Emil Christensen, "Dendrochronological dating of the Viking Age ship burials at Oseberg, Gokstad, and Tune, Norway," *Antiquity* 67 (1993)

A. E. Christensen, A. S. Ingstad, and B. Myhre, eds. *Oseberg*

Dronningens Grav (1992); portions are translated on the Web site www.forest.gen.nz/Medieval/ by members of the Society for Creative Anachronism.

Anne-Sofie Gräslund, "Dogs in graves—a question of symbolism?" *PECUS: Man and Animal in Antiquity,* ed. Barbro Santillo Frizell (2004)

Thorleif Sjøvold, *The Oseberg Find and the Other Viking Ship Finds* (1969)

For Viking dress and weaving techniques, the publications (in Icelandic) of Elsa Guðjónsson of the National Museum of Iceland are indispensable; in English see:

Eva Andersson, *The Common Thread: Textile Production during the Late Iron Age and Viking Age.* Ph.D. dissertation, Lund University (1999)

Paul C. Buckland, et al., "An insect's eye-view of the Norse farm," *The Viking Age in Caithness, Orkney, and the North Atlantic,* ed. Colleen E. Batey, Judith Jesch, and Christopher D. Morris (1993)

Richard Hall, *The Viking Dig: The Excavations at York* (1984)

N. B. Harte and K. G. Ponting, *Cloth and Clothing in Medieval Europe: Essays in Memory of Professor E. M. Carus-Wilson* (1982)

Michele Hayeur-Smith, *Draupnir's Sweat and Mardöll's Tears: An Archaeology of Jewellery, Gender, and Identity in Viking Age Iceland* (2004)

Marta Hoffmann, *The Warp-Weighted Loom* (1974)

Else Østergård, *Woven into the Earth: Textiles from Norse Greenland* (2004)

Stefán Aðalsteinsson, "Importance of Sheep in Early Icelandic Agriculture," *Acta Archaeologica* 61 (1990)

ARCHAEOLOGY IN ICELAND

Some GPR results from Glaumbær—along with Dean Goodman's movie of Emperor Trajan's eel pond—are available online at gpr-survey.com/. Results of John Steinberg's research are available at www.fiskecenter.umb.edu/SASS/SASS.htm. Guðný Zoëga's reports on Keldudalur are available online at the Web site of Hólar University College, http://www.holar.is/holarannsoknin/.

Orri Vésteinsson has published his work in English in the collections recommended above. See also Orri Vésteinsson, Thomas H. McGovern, and Christian Keller, "Enduring Impacts: Social and Environmental Aspects of Viking Age Settlement in Iceland and Greenland," *Archaeologia Islandica* 2 (2002); and Thomas McGovern, Orri Vésteinsson, et al., "Landscapes of Settlement in Northern Iceland: Historical Ecology of Human Impact & Climate Fluctuation on the Millennial Scale," *American Anthropologist* (submitted March 2005 and supplied to me in manuscript). "Increasingly comprehensive destruction" comes from Orri's "Icelandic Farmhouse Excavations," *Archaeologia Islandica* 3 (2004). Orri and Thomas McGovern each gave papers on Sveigakot and Hofstaðir at the conference, "Cultural and Environmental History in Nordic Viking Age and Medieval Time," Hólar University, Iceland, August 5, 2005. Thomas H. McGovern and his colleagues presented a summary of their analysis of the animal bones from Sveigakot and Hofstaðir at the 2005 Hólar conference.

Guðmundur Ólafsson writes about Eirik the Red's farmstead in a booklet published by the National Museum of Iceland, *Eiríksstaðir í Haukadal: Fornleifarannsókn á skálarúst,* Rannsóknaskyrslur Fornleifadeildar 11 (1998); there is an English summary. He and Hörður Ágústsson compare Eiríksstaðir to Stöng and other longhouses in *The Reconstructed Medieval Farm in Þjórsárdalur and the development of the Icelandic Turf House,* published by the National Museum of Iceland and Landsvirkjun, the National Power Company (no date). See also Thorsteinn Erlingsson's *Ruins of the Saga Time* (1899; rpt. 1982).

Other sources include:

Colin Amundsen, et al., "Fishing Booths and Fishing Strategies in Medieval Iceland," *Environmental Archaeology* 10.2 (2005)

James H. Barrett, ed. *Contact, Continuity, and Collapse: The Norse Colonization of the North Atlantic* (2003)

P. C. Buckland, et al., "Holt in Eyjafjallasveit, Iceland: A Paleoecological Study of the Impact of Landnám," *Acta Archaeologica* 61 (1990)

Paul Durrenberger and Gísli Pálsson, eds. *The Anthropology of Iceland* (1989)

Bjarni Einarsson, *The Settlement of Iceland, a Critical Approach: Gránastaðir and the Ecological Heritage* (1995)

Grétar Guðbergsson, "Í norðlenskri vist," *Búvisindi: Icelandic Agricultural Sciences* 10 (1996)

Steinunn Kristjánsdóttir, *The Awakening of Christianity in Iceland: Discovery of a Timber Church and Graveyard at Þórarinsstaðir in Seyðisfjörður*, University of Gothenberg Ph.D. dissertation (2004)

Thomas H. McGovern, Gerald Bigelow, Thomas Amorosi, and Daniel Russell, "Northern Islands, Human Error, and Environmental Degradation," *Human Ecology* 16 (1988)

Christopher D. Morris and D. James Rackham, eds. *Norse and Later Settlement and Subsistence in the North Atlantic* (1992)

Kevin P. Smith, "Landnám: the settlement of Iceland in archaeological and historical perspective," *World Archaeology* 26 (1995)

HISTORY OF GREENLAND

Early descriptions of the Viking ruins are found in:

Sigurður Breiðfjörð, *Frá Grænland* (1835; rpt. 1961)

Árni Magnússon, *Ferðasaga Árni Magnússon frá Geitastekk 1753–1797*, ed. Björn K. Þórólfsson (1945)

Other sources include:

Per Danker, *This Is Greenland 2000–2001: The Official Directory* (2000)

Jared Diamond, *Collapse: How Societies Choose to Fail or Succeed* (2004)

Guðmundur J. Guðmundsson, *Á Hjara Veraldar: Saga norræna manna á Grænland* (2005)

Birgitte Jacobsen, Claus Andreasen, and Jette Rygaard, eds. *Cultural and Social Research in Greenland 95/96: Essays in Honour of Robert Petersen* (1996)

Robert McGhee, *The Last Imaginary Place: A Human History of the Arctic World* (2005)

Jens Rosing, *Things and Wonders: The Norsemen in Greenland and America* (2000)

Kirsten Seaver, *The Frozen Echo: Greenland and the Exploration of North America* (1996)

Vilhjalmur Stefansson, *Greenland* (1944)

ARCHAEOLOGY IN GREENLAND

The Farm Beneath the Sand is discussed in the collections recommended above. See also Guðmundur Ólafsson and Svend E. Albrethsen, "Bærinn undir sandinum," *Árbók hins íslenzka fornleifafélags* 98 (2000); Else Østergård, *Woven into the Earth* (2004); and Jette Arneborg's introduction to Inge Bødker Enghoff, "Hunting, fishing and animal husbandry at the Farm Beneath the Sand, Western Greenland," *Meddelelser om Grønland, Man & Society* 28 (2003).

Other sources include:

Svend E. Albrethsen and Christian Keller, "The Use of the *Sæter* in Medieval Norse Farming in Greenland," *Arctic Anthropology* 23 (1986)

Jette Arneborg, *Saga Trails: A Visitors' Guidebook* (2006)

Jette Arneborg, et al., "Change of Diet of the Greenland Vikings Determined from Stable Carbon Isotope Analysis and 14 C Dating of Their Bones," *Radiocarbon* 41.2 (1999)

Colleen E. Batey, Judith Jesch, and Christopher D. Morris, eds. *The Viking Age in Caithness, Orkney, and the North Atlantic: Select Papers from the Proceedings of the Eleventh Viking Congress* (1993)

Vagn Fabritius Buchwald, *Ancient Iron and Slags in Greenland, Meddelelser om Grønland, Man & Society* 26 (2001)

Paul C. Buckland, et al., "Bioarcheological and climatological evidence for the fate of Norse farmers in medieval Greenland," *Antiquity* 70 (1996)

Karen Marie Bojsen Christensen, "Aspects of the Norse Economy in the Western Settlement in Greenland," *Acta Archaeologica* 61 (1990)

Bent Fredskild, "Agriculture in SW Greenland in the Norse period (ca. 982–ca. 1450)," *PACT* 31 (1990)

Bent Fredskild and Lilli Humle, "Plant remains from the Norse farm Sandnes in the Western Settlement, Greenland," *Acta Borealis* 1 (1991)

Ole Guldager, Steffen Stummann Hansen, and Simon Gleie, *Medieval Farmsteads in Greenland: The Brattahlid Region 1999–2000* (2002)

Christian Keller, "Vikings in the West Atlantic," *Acta Archaeologica* 61 (1991)

Knud J. Krogh, *Viking Greenland* (1967)

Thomas H. McGovern, "Bones, Buildings, and Boundaries" in *Norse and Later Settlement and Subsistence in the North Atlantic,* ed. Morris and Rackham (1992)

Thomas McGovern, Paul Buckland, et al., "A Study of the Faunal and Floral Remains from Two Norse Farms in the Western Settlement, Greenland," *Arctic Anthropology* 20 (1983)

Julie Megan Ross, *Paleoethnobotanical Investigation of Garden Under Sandet, a Waterlogged Norse Farm Site, Western Settlement, Greenland (Kaiaallit Nunaata).* Master's thesis in anthropology, University of Alberta (1997)

Aage Roussell, "Sandnes and the neighboring farms," *Meddelelser om Grønland* 88 (1936)

G. Richard Scott, Carrin M. Halffman, and P. O. Pedersen, "Dental conditions of medieval Norsemen in the North Atlantic," *Acta Archaeologica* 62 (1991)

C. L. Vebæk, "Narsaq—a Norse *Landnáma* farm," *Meddelelser om Grønland, Man & Society* 18 (1993)

————, "Hunting on land and at sea and fishing in Medieval Norse Greenland," *Acta Borealis* 1 (1991)

VINLAND

Helge Ingstad's curriculum vitae was drawn from his *New York Times* obituary, printed March 30, 2001; Ingstad lived to be 101. He published *Westward to Vinland* (1969) eight years before the University of Oslo brought out Anne Stine Ingstad's archaeological results in *The Discovery of a Norse Settlement in America: Excavations at L'Anse aux Meadows, Newfoundland, 1961–1968* (1977). The Ingstads collaborated on *The Viking Discovery of America* (2001).

"Leif Eiriksson Slept Here" was the title of a lecture Birgitta Wallace gave at Gros Morne National Park, Newfoundland, on August 23, 2006. She describes her reassessments of the Ingstads' work in the three collections recommended above, as well as in "L'Anse aux Meadows: Gateway to Vinland," *Acta Archaeologica* 61 (1990). Other sources consulted include:

Rasmus B. Anderson, *The Norse Discovery of America* (1906)

Geraldine Barnes, *Viking America: The First Millennium* (2001)

Catherine Carlson, "The (In)Significance of Atlantic Salmon," *Federal Archaeology* (Fall/Winter 1996)

A. M. Davis, J. H. McAndrews, and Birgitta Lindroth Wallace, "Paleoenvironment and the archaeological record at the L'Anse aux Meadows site, Newfoundland," *Geoarchaeology* 3 (1988)

James P. Howley, *The Beothucks or Red Indians: The Aboriginal Inhabitants of Newfoundland* (1914)

Gwyn Jones, *The Norse Atlantic Saga* (1964)

Farley Mowat, *Westviking* (1965)

Richard Perkins, "Medieval Norse Visits to America," *Saga-Book* 28 (2004)

GUDRID'S PILGRIMAGE TO ROME

One scholar who believed Gudrid spoke about Vinland on her pilgrimage was Father Josef Fischer, to whom Kirsten Seaver ascribes the design of the notorious Vinland Map. This map, purchased by Yale University in October 1965, is said by Yale's experts to be an authentic medieval map and by nearly everyone else to be a forgery. Seaver argues that Father Fischer made it for himself while living in Germany under the Nazi regime, not with the intention of fooling anyone else, but as an aid to his own scholarship. She writes in *Vinland Revisited* (2003): "Fischer's convictions came from combining the saga information with modern cartographical knowledge, and from his certainty that there had once been cartographical representations which took into account information reaching Rome directly, beginning with Gudridr Thorbjarnardottir's pilgrimage in the eleventh century." See also Seaver's *Maps, Myths, and Men: The Story of the Vinland Map* (2004). Novelist Margaret Elphinstone provides us with a fictional realization of Gudrid's conversations with a churchman in Rome in *The Sea Road* (2000).

For the history of the popes, I depended on the *Catholic Encyclopedia* (1909), online at http://www.newadvent.org/cathen/index.html. For the pilgrim routes across Europe, see Association Via Francigena (http://www.francigena-international.org/).

Several papers presented at the Thirteenth International Saga Conference, Durham and York, 6–12 August 2006, address this topic and are available as preprints at http://www.dur.ac.uk/medieval .www/. See in particular:

Gísli Pálsson and Astrid Ogilvie, "Weather and Witchcraft in the Sagas of Icelanders"

Tommaso Marani, "The Roman Itinerary of Nikulás of Munkaþverá: Between Reality and Imagination"

Bernadine McCreesh, "Elements of the Pagan Supernatural in the Bishops' Sagas"

Jens Ulff-Møller, "The Gaelic Impact on Churches in Iceland and Greenland"

Other sources consulted include:

Tore Ahlbäck, ed. *Old Norse and Finnish Religions and Cultic Place-Names* (1990)

Jessica A. Browner, "'Viking' Pilgrimage to the Holy Land," *Essays in History* 34 (1992)

Martin Carver, ed. *The Cross Goes North: Processes of Conversion in Northern Europe, AD 300–1300* (2003)

Victoria Clark, *The Far-Farers: A Journey from Viking Iceland to Crusader Jerusalem* (2003)

H. R. Ellis Davidson, *Gods and Myths of Northern Europe* (1964)

Thomas A. DuBois, *Nordic Religions in the Viking Age* (1999)

Eleanor Shipley Duckett, *Death and Life in the Tenth Century* (1971)

Richard Erdoes, *A.D. 1000: Living on the Brink of Apocalypse* (1988)

Henri Focillon, *The Year 1000* (1971)

Joyce Hill, "Pilgrimage and Prestige in the Icelandic Sagas," *Saga-Book* 23 (1993)

Robert Lacey and Danny Danziger, *The Year 1000* (1999)

Katherine Morris, *Sorceress or Witch?* (1991)

James Reston, *The Last Apocalypse* (1998)

Margaret Clunies Ross, *Prolonged Echoes* (1994)

Rudolf Simek and Judith Meurer, eds. *Scandinavia and Christian Europe in the Middle Ages: Papers of the Twelfth International Saga Conference* (2003)

INDEX